MANAGING
PEOPLE AT WORK

MANAGING PEOPLE AT WORK

Peter J. Makin, Cary L. Cooper and Charles J. Cox

Manchester School of Management
University of Manchester
Institute of Science and Technology

Quorum Books
New York . Westport, Connecticut

Published in the United States and Canada by Quorum Books, Westport,
Connecticut

English language edition, except the United States and Canada, published by
The British Psychological Society in association with Routledge Ltd.

First published in 1989

Library of Congress Cataloging-in-Publication Data:

Makin, Peter J.
  Managing people at work.
  Bibliography: p.
  Includes index.
  1. Personnel management. 2. Psychology, Industrial.
I. Cooper, Cary L.   II. Cox, Charles J.   III. Title.
HF5549.M29524 1989   658.3   89-8475
ISBN 0-89930-505-9 (lib. bdg. : alk. paper)

Library of Congress Catalog Card Number: 89-8475

ISBN: 0-89930-505-9

CONTENTS

List of Figures and Tables

INTRODUCTION

It is traditional to start books such as this with a detailed argument as to why the management of an organization's human resources is important. In our experience managers do not need convincing on this point. Their own experiences have led them to conclude that the management of people is an important yet difficult and frustrating factor in their job. Often, the higher up the hierarchy they climb, the more important an aspect of their job people management becomes. Unfortunately, until recently formal training in this area has been neglected. Considerable time and resources have been devoted to training for the technical aspects of the job such as accounting or engineering. But so far as the handling of people is concerned, managers have often been left to fly by the seat of their pants. This situation is now changing. Courses in higher education and those leading to professional qualifications in subjects as diverse as engineering, accountancy and pharmacy now contain elements of people management or human resources management. These developments can only be welcomed if organizations are to improve their efficiency.

If you have bought this book it is probably because you need to know more about managing people at work. This may be because of a desire to improve your own managerial effectiveness or because you are doing a course that requires you to learn more about the subject area. These reasons underlie the dual purpose of *Managing People at Work*. Its aims are:

- To provide a book that managers can read and find of practical value.

- To provide a text that can be used on courses that contain elements of people management and organizational psychology, ranging from courses in business studies and MBAs to those providing professional and technical qualifications.

The reader who is interested in managing people at work is above all concerned with the practicalities of the subject, rather than with a purely theoretical knowledge of who has done what research. However, it is also useful, especially for people on training courses, to be able to support statements with relevant references. When a particular theory is discussed, reference is therefore made to the main, and often original source. The version of the theory presented in this book is the current one, modified and updated by subsequent research. We hope that this ensures the book's accessibility for everyone, while those readers who want to investigate further can consult the list of suggested readings provided for each topic.

The general plan of the book is to move from the micro aspects of managing people to the macro. Thus the first part concentrates upon dealing with individuals by examining such issues as: How do individuals differ in terms of their personalities and how can the manager cope with these differences? How can people be motivated? Are leaders born? What mangement style should be adopted in different situations?

Part two concentrates upon people working in groups and such issues as: How does group decision making differ from individual decision making? What effects does the way a group reaches a decision have on the motivation of group members? When is intergroup competition appropriate? What causes conflicts between groups, and how can the ill-effects of this conflict be minimized?

Organizations, what they are and how they change over time is the subject matter of part three. What problems are caused by the growth of an organization? How can it structure itself so as to be able to respond and adapt quickly in a rapidly changing environment? How can the individual manager seek to influence the organization?

Finally, in the last chapter, we consider an important, yet neglected, aspect of management: how to manage your boss.

Each chapter contains exercises to help managers develop their skills. Some of these are questionnaires that will enable managers to gain more self-knowledge, others are case studies drawn from real life.

Sir John Harvey-Jones, the former Chairman of ICI, recently indicated that he disliked and distrusted books that offered a 'cure all' for managers' problems. 'In one bound, Jack was free' is the category that Sir John suggests for such books – we agree. This book does not provide miracle cures. If such a cure were possible, it would have been universally implemented a long time ago. What we are attempting here is to distil the theory and research in industrial and organizational psychology, to help managers deal with their day-to-day and strategic problems in the workplace. We have worked with some diligence to minimize the psychological jargon, to squeeze out the important aspects of various concepts and research findings in an effort to blend them together into a useful *guide* for managers.

Personality and Individual Differences

As mentioned in the introduction, the main emphasis of this book will be on those aspects of theory that have most relevance to managers. We will not, therefore, spend too much time considering how personalities are formed, or examining the construction and use of personality tests. The former the manager can do nothing about, the latter is more the concern of those psychologists who specialize in selection and recruitment. Having said this, there is one area of personality theory that needs to be included not perhaps because of its immediate usefulness, but because it gives structure to the way we describe personality, both of ourselves and others. The first section of this chapter therefore, deals with theories that view personality in terms of 'types' or 'traits'.

Overall, this chapter will be concerned with attempting to provide some answers to the following questions:

- In what ways do people differ in their behaviour patterns?
- What problems does this cause when they interact with others?
- What can we do to minimize these problems?

To answer the first question we have to examine the ways in which we can describe behaviour.

Before examining the descriptions generated by psychologists, we would like you to try to write down a brief description of your own personality. A series of single words or phrases will suffice. If you are brave enough, you might also ask someone who knows you well to describe you.

When asked to describe a person to others we tend to start with physical characteristics, followed perhaps by such things as their occupation. We are also likely to use shorthand descriptions of the way they tend to behave. Thus, we may describe people as aggressive, happy-go-lucky, lonely, introverted, or many other adjectives that are intended to give an indication of their personality. Each of these adjectives is what psychologists would call a *trait*. The list of such traits is obviously very large. Indeed, as long ago as the 1930s researchers estimated there were over 17,000 such words and the list has no doubt grown since then.

The trait is the basis for many influential theories of personality. Indeed, it has been called the layperson's unit of psychological currency. A trait is a generalization made from observing the way a person habitually behaves in certain classes of situation. It is perhaps best summed up as a predisposition to behave in certain ways in certain situations.

TRAIT AND TYPE THEORIES

Trait theories attempt to reduce the large number of traits in common usage down to a smaller number of more general traits. There are a number of ways of achieving this. It would be possible to take an individual, or panel of individuals, and ask them to group together those traits that they consider to be alike in some respect. There are obviously a number of errors that could occur using such a method. For this reason, modern trait theorists use highly sophisticated statistical techniques to identify the underlying traits. The responses of thousands of individuals are subjected to these procedures, thus reducing the possible errors.

We will examine two of the most influential trait theories, those of Cattell and Eysenck. Both use highly statistical methods, but they differ as to the number of basic traits they consider to be important.

Raymond Cattell was born and educated at university in England before emigrating to the USA in the 1930s. In his highly productive career in psychology he concentrated on trying to collect data on all aspects of human behaviour that constitute what he calls the 'personality sphere'. The sources of this data were various. They included descriptions of an individual's actual behaviour. This was combined with the person's own report of their personality, collected by means of questionnaires. In addition, tests of various skills and abilities were used. From this wealth of data, Cattell's analyses (1965) suggested that sixteen 'source traits' could be reliably identified. In order to provide a reasonably short means of assessing each of these source traits, or *'factors'*, Cattell developed a self-report personality test. This questionnaire is called the *16 Personality Factor*, or 16PF for short. It is most probably his best known contribution to psychology. Many of you may have been administered this test at some time, as it is perhaps the most widely used personality test, especially in the selection of managers. The 16 factors are shown in Figure 1. As you will see, each factor has bipolar descriptions, one at each end of the continuous scale. (Of the 16 factors measured by the questionnaire, twelve were similar to those obtained from descriptions of actual behaviour. The last four are unique to factors obtained from self-report questionnaires. For this reason they are identified by the labels Q1 to Q4, rather than continuing the alphabet from O.)

	LOW SCORE DESCRIPTION											HIGH SCORE DESCRIPTION
A	Reserved, detached, critical, aloof,	1	2	3	4	5	6	7	8	9	10	Outgoing, warm-hearted, easygoing
B	Less intelligent, concrete thinking	1	2	3	4	5	6	7	8	9	10	More intelligent, abstract thinking
C	Affected by feelings, easily upset	1	2	3	4	5	6	7	8	9	10	Emotionally stable, calm, mature
E	Humble, mild, conforming	1	2	3	4	5	6	7	8	9	10	Assertive, competitive
F	Sober, prudent, taciturn	1	2	3	4	5	6	7	8	9	10	Happy-go-lucky, enthusiastic
G	Expedient, disregards rules	1	2	3	4	5	6	7	8	9	10	Conscientious, moralistic
H	Shy, timid	1	2	3	4	5	6	7	8	9	10	Socially bold
I	Tough-minded, realistic	1	2	3	4	5	6	7	8	9	10	Tender-minded, sensitive
L	Trusting, adaptable	1	2	3	4	5	6	7	8	9	10	Suspicious, hard to fool
M	Practical, careful	1	2	3	4	5	6	7	8	9	10	Imaginative, careless
N	Forthright, natural	1	2	3	4	5	6	7	8	9	10	Shrewd, calculating
O	Self-assured, confident	1	2	3	4	5	6	7	8	9	10	Apprehensive, troubled
Q1	Conservative, respects established ideas	1	2	3	4	5	6	7	8	9	10	Experimenting, radical
Q2	Group dependent, good 'follower'	1	2	3	4	5	6	7	8	9	10	Self-sufficient, resourceful
Q3	Undisciplined, self-conflict	1	2	3	4	5	6	7	8	9	10	Controlled, socially precise
Q4	Relaxed, tranquil	1	2	3	4	5	6	7	8	9	10	Tense, frustrated

FIGURE 1. *Cattell's 16 Personality Factor questionnaire (from Cattell et al., 1970)*

Using the test, an individual can be given a score for each of these factors, over the range of 0 to 10. An individual's position on any particular factor is independent of any of the other factors. Thus, a vast number of patterns of trait is theoretically possible. It is common practice (although theoretically suspect, since there is no logical or statistical relationship between adjacent factors) for the individual's score on each scale to be joined, thus producing a *personality profile*. Each individual will, therefore, have his or her own profile. The most common use of the test in industry is in staff selection. By obtaining the profiles of successful people in a particular occupation, it is claimed that a common personality profile may emerge that can be used for the purposes of selecting potential employees.

At this point it might be worth returning to your self-description. How do the words you used compare with those used by Cattell? It may also be useful to repeat the exercise, this time using Cattell's factors. Place yourself on each scale, using the average male or female of your age as your reference group. If you can risk it, ask your partner, or someone else who knows you well to rate you as well. Figure 2 gives the average profile for managing directors (MDs) reported by Charles Cox and Cary Cooper (1988) in their book *High Flyers*.

As with all psychological tests, it is not absolute scores that are important, but how your score compares with those of your peers. (Parents of children at school need to know not just what their child scored in a particular exam, but also how this compares with others in the class.)

Do not worry if your profile does not match those for MDs too closely. There are a number of reasons why this may be. These are the same as the criticisms that may be made of the over-rigid use of such 'profile matching'. First, the fact that present employees show a particular profile does not mean that only those who show that profile could do the job. Second, such profiles are obtained by averaging a large number of profiles. This may disguise wide variations between different individuals, all of whom may be successful. Finally, some of the traits may be more stable than others. For example, people can be trained to be more assertive. All this is not to deny that tests may have their uses in selection, merely to suggest that test results should be considered as pointers that can be followed up at other stages in the selection process, perhaps at an effective interview.

Although we have said that the sixteen traits are independent of each other, they can, according to Cattell, be reduced still further to eight *second order factors*. Only four of these need concern us here. Of the other four, two are not clearly defined and two are very similar to the source traits of intelligence (B) and conscientiousness (G). The main four are described as follows, but without using the precise technical language used by Cattell:

	LOW SCORE DESCRIPTION											HIGH SCORE DESCRIPTION
A	Reserved, detached, critical, aloof,	1	2	3	4	5	6	7	8	9	10	Outgoing, warm-hearted, easygoing
B	Less intelligent, concrete thinking	1	2	3	4	5	6	7	8	9	10	More intelligent, abstract thinking
C	Affected by feelings, easily upset	1	2	3	4	5	6	7	8	9	10	Emotionally stable, calm, mature
E	Humble, mild, conforming	1	2	3	4	5	6	7	8	9	10	Assertive, competitive
F	Sober, prudent, taciturn	1	2	3	4	5	6	7	8	9	10	Happy-go-lucky, enthusiastic
G	Expedient, disregards rules	1	2	3	4	5	6	7	8	9	10	Conscientious, moralistic
H	Shy, timid	1	2	3	4	5	6	7	8	9	10	Socially bold
I	Tough-minded, realistic	1	2	3	4	5	6	7	8	9	10	Tender-minded, sensitive
L	Trusting, adaptable	1	2	3	4	5	6	7	8	9	10	Suspicious, hard to fool
M	Practical, careful	1	2	3	4	5	6	7	8	9	10	Imaginative, careless
N	Forthright, natural	1	2	3	4	5	6	7	8	9	10	Shrewd, calculating
O	Self-assured, confident	1	2	3	4	5	6	7	8	9	10	Apprehensive, troubled
Q1	Conservative, respects established ideas	1	2	3	4	5	6	7	8	9	10	Experimenting, radical
Q2	Group dependent, good 'follower'	1	2	3	4	5	6	7	8	9	10	Self-sufficient, resourceful.
Q3	Undisciplined, self-conflict	1	2	3	4	5	6	7	8	9	10	Controlled, socially precise
Q4	Relaxed, tranquil	1	2	3	4	5	6	7	8	9	10	Tense, frustrated

FIGURE 2. *16 Personality Factor questionnaire showing managing directors' average personality profile (from Cox and Cooper, 1988)*

▶ Extroversion versus introversion
▶ Emotional adjustment versus anxiety
▶ Feeling versus thinking
▶ Dependence versus independence.

In reducing the number of traits, Cattell is in agreement with Eysenck.

Hans Eysenck, until recently, held a chair in the University of London. He was born in Germany, but emigrated to England to avoid Nazi persecution. His original desire was to read physics at university, but his academic background was not acceptable for entry to the course. Looking around for an alternative he came across psychology. Some would say that his reductionist approach to the study of human behaviour reveals the underlying physicist. He is most probably the best known British psychologist (1977).

In his earlier work, Eysenck reduced the number of traits to two: stable–unstable (sometimes called neuroticism) and extroversion–introversion. To these he has recently added a third, psychoticism. The *stable–unstable* dimension is concerned, as might be expected, with emotional stability. Those with high stability tend to be calm and even-tempered, whilst those with low stability are anxious and moody. The trait of *extroversion–introversion* is part of everyday language and widely understood. It is composed of two closely related components, sociability and impulsiveness. People high on the *psychoticism* dimension tend to be uncaring about others and opposed to accepted social norms. As with Cattell, these traits are independent of each other. In other words, knowing a person's score on one trait will tell you nothing about their scores on the others. For simplicity's sake, we will consider the two original traits. The third, psychoticism, is more appropriate to clinical uses.

Using these traits, a two dimensional 'map' of personality emerges, as shown in Figure 3. The adjectives close to the centre of each sector are those used by the ancient Greeks in their description of personality which Eysenck feels are equivalent to his own. The Greeks based their explanation for personality on the balance of the various bodily fluids in the individual. Thus, for instance, the choleric personality is characterized by a preponderance of bile.

Recently Paul Kline (1987) has reanalysed a large amount of data from personality questionnaires and has concluded that Eysenck's three dimensions are correct, but that a further two can be identified. These, he suggests are *sensation seeking* and *obsessionality*. The description of sensation seeking is the same as that in everyday language. Those scoring high on this trait are likely to involve themselves in activities which satisfy their need for sensation, such as driving fast cars or hang-gliding.

The obsessive personality is characterized, as might be expected, by obsessive behaviour but also by an over-rigid adherence to rules. Its most usual manifestation is as an over-emphasis on procedure, often

INTROVERTED

STABLE INTROVERT	UNSTABLE INTROVERT
Passive	Quiet
Careful	Unsociable
Thoughtful	Reserved
Peaceful	Pessimistic
Controlled	Sober
Reliable	Rigid
Even-tempered	Anxious
Calm	Moody
(Phlegmatic)	(Melancholic)

STABLE ——————————————————————————— **UNSTABLE**

(Sanguine)	(Choleric)
STABLE EXTROVERT	UNSTABLE EXTROVERT
Leadership	Touchy
Carefree	Restless
Lively	Aggressive
Easygoing	Excitable
Responsive	Changeable
Talkative	Impulsive
Outgoing	Optimistic
Sociable	Active

EXTROVERTED

FIGURE 3. *Eysenck's typology of personality (adapted from Eysenck, 1975)*

accompanied by extreme tidiness and, sometimes, parsimony with money. Another manifestation is authoritarianism, for those in a position in which they can be autocratic.

Being able to describe someone's personality may have its uses, for example, being able to predict a person's likely behaviour in novel situations, but it has its drawbacks. Trait theorists do not claim that knowing a person's score on a particular trait will enable prediction of their precise behaviour in a particular situation. Rather that this will represent a range of behaviour averaged across a number of similar situations. For this reason, as has been mentioned, the main use of personality tests is in personnel selection and internal placement.

As well as differing in terms of their personalities, people also differ in the extent to which they can process information and the ways in which they prefer to process it. It is to these individual differences that we will now turn, as they may throw light upon some of the so-called personality clashes that often occur in organizations.

INDIVIDUAL DIFFERENCES

The best known difference between individuals concerns their capacity to process information. The name most commonly given to this ability is intelligence. Most intelligence tests measure the ability to process certain kinds of information that are usually verbal, mathematical, or abstract in nature. Some theorists suggest that there are many different types of intelligence, depending upon the nature of the material being processed, and the operations carried out on it.

As well as differing in our capacity to process information, we differ in the way that we prefer to carry out the processing. It has not been shown that any particular method of processing information is superior to others in all situations. The way in which we prefer to work can, however, cause problems if, for example, it differs substantially from those of our colleagues, or indeed the organizational culture. One such difference, suggested by Michael Kirton, is perhaps particularly relevant to behaviour in organizations.

ADAPTORS VERSUS INNOVATORS

The distinction between the two styles of *Adaptor* and *Innovator* was made by Kirton (1984), based on his study of the way management initiatives are taken, how they proceed through the organizational decision-making structure, and why they succeed or fail. As a result of his studies, Kirton suggests that many of his observations can be explained by the cognitive (or thinking) styles of the individuals concerned, especially when dealing with problem solving. Strictly speaking, Adaptors and Innovators do not represent two totally distinct styles. They are, in fact, seen as the opposite ends of a continuous scale. Thus, a particular individual does not necessarily have to be at one end or the other, but may be anywhere between the two extremes. For the purposes of description, however, it is easier to stick with the two 'pure' types who lie at the two extreme ends of the scale.

A shorthand explanation of the difference between the two styles is, that while the Adaptor likes doing things better, the Innovator prefers to do things differently. This difference has considerable implications, especially when the two styles have to work together, as we will see.

In order to do things differently, it is often necessary to consider, and even implement, solutions that lie well outside the current way of doing things. Thus, a major difference between the two styles is the extent to which they stay within the current framework, both for solutions and their implementations. Unlike the Innovator, the Adaptor will try to modify the existing system in order to make it better. Let us look, therefore, at how the two styles differ in the ways they define problems, seek solutions, and implement these solutions. These differences will not only affect how individuals prefer to work, but also how they perceive those who have a contrasting style.

In terms of defining the problem, it could be said that Adaptors wait to be given the problem, whilst Innovators almost seek problems out. However, it is in the type of solution that the main differences occur. Adaptors are concerned to solve problems by modifying the existing systems: this produces greater efficiency, while maintaining the organization's continuity and stability. It is likely that they will feel comfortable in an organization that slowly adapts itself and is not likely to undergo substantial and rapid change. For the Innovator, on the other hand, the challenge consists in finding new, and possibly unexpected, solutions to problems.

Both these types have their strengths and weaknesses. The Adaptor can effectively adapt the present system, but is apparently blinkered in not seeing solutions that lie outside that system. The Innovator, on the other hand, is happier generating new solutions. Unfortunately, such individuals often find difficulty in having their ideas accepted by others within the organization, and become frustrated by what they see as irrational inertia within the organization. Their ways of implementing decisions also differ. The Adaptor prefers work characterized by precision, method, and discipline, and is capable of maintaining high levels of accuracy over long periods of time. The Innovator, on the other hand, appears undisciplined, and incapable of maintaining work of a routine nature for very long. To the rest of the organization, the Adaptor is seen as safe, dependable and conforming, while the Innovator is seen as a maverick, with apparently endless self-confidence who is constantly coming up with lists of ideas, some obviously impractical.

As well as individuals having preferences for the way they work, there is evidence to suggest that organizations can also be classified as predominantly adaptive or innovative. This is not to suggest, of course, that the whole organization is the same. There may be differences between different types of department within the overall structure. Given that each organization, or department, has its particular adaptive or innovative climate, this will influence those who choose to work within it. Adaptors will not find an innovative climate to their liking and vice versa. This will lead them to resolve the resulting discomfort in one of two ways. First, and apparently most commonly, by leaving. Second, by finding a niche within which they can happily isolate themselves from the dominant climate and finally, the majority may actually generate such a niche for a particular individual in order to insulate themselves. This often occurs when the chances of moving that individual are small.

As described, the two styles can obviously complement each other, but the perception of each by the other may be a problem. To the Adaptor, the Innovator is seen as an extrovert, generating lists of new ideas but almost totally insensitive, both to the demands of the system and to the feelings of others. This abrasive personal attitude means that the Adaptor feels uncomfortable when working with such an individual, who constantly questions perceived wisdom. To the Innovator, the Adaptor appears as a conservative, timid conformist, always ready to agree, both with the system and with the boss. It is not that Innovators are deliberately rude and inconsiderate to others, but that they expect everyone else to be filled with the enthusiasm that they feel. Likewise, the Adaptor does not agree with his or her boss through weakness, but rather because the boss is also likely to be an Adaptor, and hence have a similar way of approaching problems.

Kirton found that the clash of these styles could often explain why innovative ideas failed to be implemented in organizations. This, of course, is likely to be the sort of clash that takes place whenever departments with different climates interact. Each will see the other in the same way as differing individuals would do. Kirton has found that Adaptors tend to predominate in the public sector and in organizations such as banking. Both these types of organization are, however, under pressure to react to market forces, either by adapting or innovating. This pressure may result in the creation of new departments, some of which may be given the job of innovating. Such new, innovative departments within organizations may lead to interdepartmental conflict because of the difference in perspectives. Ways in which such intergroup conflict may be minimized will be addressed in Chapter 5.

As has been said before, both styles have their strengths and are appropriate in different circumstances. We are not sure that we would like our bank managers to be 'innovative' with our savings.

If, as is suggested, these styles are relatively permanent, what can managers do to avert or minimize clashes between individuals? Basically, the solution must lie with understanding, together with an acceptance of the other person's position. This may sound like pie in the sky but, as will be seen later, the recognition that another person has a preferred way of working, can often be enough to defuse situations that might otherwise lead to disagreement. Knowing someone else's style enables prediction of what they will, or will not, like, and hence reduces uncertainty. If both parties are familiar with the concepts and the jargon, it may even become a source of amusement when working together.

TYPE As VERSUS TYPE Bs

Before reading this section turn to Appendix 1 and complete the type A/type B questionnaire.

The concept of type A and type B personality was developed by Meyer

Friedman and Ray Rosenman (1974) during a study of patients with coronary heart disease. They found that many of their patients behaved in similar ways. They tended to be extremely competitive, high-achieving, aggressive, hasty, impatient, and restless. They were also characterized by having explosive patterns of speech, tenseness of the facial muscles, and always appeared to be under time pressures. Type As have also been described as being so deeply involved and committed to their work that other aspects of their lives become neglected. The connection between the two types and coronary heart disease has since been confirmed by other studies. It should not be thought, however, that type A personalities are automatically susceptible to heart disease. The danger occurs when type As are subjected to high levels of demand and stress. (Ways of managing type A behaviour are examined later in this chapter.)

The easiest shorthand description for extreme type As is that they suffer from 'hurry sickness'. Everything has to be done at once. In addition, they are normally doing a number of different things at the same time. Waiting in queues is likely to prove highly stressful for type As. All this frantic activity might be quite all right if it were not for the fact that they are unable to relax – when not doing something they feel vaguely guilty. Surely there must be something that they ought to be doing. The frantic activity of 'getting somewhere' also means that they are not able to enjoy the journey. Type Bs are the opposite of type As. They work without agitation and relax without guilt. The same pressures of time urgency do not affect them.

The descriptions so far have been those of extremes of each type. In reality, most people lie somewhere between the two. For the sake of convenience four different types are normally used. If your score on the questionnaire was between 104 and the maximum possible score of 140, then you are an extreme type A1. About ten per cent of the population fall into this category. If your score was between 91 and 103 you are type A2, and between 62 and 90 type B3. About 40 per cent of the population fall into each of these categories. Finally, if your score was between 10 and 64 you are a type B4. In our experience, most managers fall into the type A1 and type A2 categories, but this is not always the case.

Managing type A behaviour. Since many managers are type As, it would perhaps be unfair to leave them without some specific suggestions as to how to 'manage' their behaviour. Since type A/type B is a personality characteristic, there is no point in trying to change it. What can be 'managed', however, is the behaviour that results from it. Type As need to take steps to manage their behaviour style so that they do not set themselves up for a stress-related illness. These steps often include such things as relaxation exercises, but often what is needed is to refrain from those behaviours that characterize type As.

Friedman and Rosenman (1974) recommend a number of 'drills against hurry sickness', which they maintain work for their type A patients.

▸ Stop trying to be the centre of attention by constantly talking. Force yourself to listen to others, and don't keep finishing their sentences for them.

▸ If you do continue talking unnecessarily, ask yourself: a) 'Do I really have anything important to say?' b) 'Does anyone want to hear it?' c) 'Is this the time to say it?' If the answer to any of these is 'no', then keep quiet, even if you have to bite your lip.

▸ Put yourself in positions that force you to slow down, or penalize yourself for hurrying. Friedman and Rosenman suggest that you should frequent restaurants where you know there will be long periods of waiting. They also suggest that, if you find yourself speeding up to get through the traffic lights on amber, you should penalize yourself. You should turn left (or right) at the next corner, go back on yourself, and go through the same lights again. (They do not report the effects of this sudden manoeuvre on the type A driver in the car behind!)

▸ Put your type A behaviour into perspective by asking yourself the following questions: a) 'Will this matter have importance five years from now?' b) 'Must it be done right away, or do I have time to think about the best way to do it?'

▸ Take up some outside activities that require not only attention, but patience, such as reading or the theatre. Beware, however, that you do not turn these into surrogates. We are aware of one individual who deliberately took up golf to manage his type A behaviour, but then became obsessional about winning.

▸ Try not to make unnecessary appointments or deadlines. Remember, the more deadlines you make for yourself, the worse your hurry sickness will become.

▸ Learn to say 'no' and protect your time. If you don't protect it, no one else will!

▸ Take stress-free breathing spaces during the course of the day. They need not be long, but should be frequent. Research has shown that, as well as reducing stress, they can also increase efficiency. Many managers work in stretches that mean their performance declines. We advise students who are revising for exams to study for 50 minutes and break for ten. Such breaks give our mental processes time to recover, and also allow the brain to 'sort out' the information it has absorbed.

▶ Try to create opportunities during the day or night when you can totally relax. Do not try to work and relax in the same situation. While you try to relax all the reminders of work will be there. Have a room, or even just a chair, that is for relaxation only.

It is also important for type As to realize the effects they have on other people. One of the characteristics of type As is that they are perceived by others as being overly 'hostile'. Type As should continually remind themselves of this fact. One way of countering this is to try to reward people for their efforts – not taking them for granted. Time spent in relaxed social interchange is, for many type As, so much 'wasted time'. They should realize that time spent this way is, in fact, time well spent.

Type As are extrapunitive; they place the blame for their own disappointments and failures on others. As Friedman and Rosenman have commented, 'Over and over again we have listened to type As rationalize their hostility as stemming from disappointment over the lack of ideals in their friends.' The search for 'idealists' is a waste of time because type As are only looking for excuses to be disappointed and hence hostile towards others.

As with Adaptors and Innovators, both type As and type Bs can be effective. It could even be argued that both are needed. All that can be done is to reach a mutual understanding by recognizing the other person's way of operating and making allowances for it. We will return to this mutual acceptance at the end of the chapter.

Some of the ways in which psychologists suggest that people differ in their personalities have now been considered, but how do we, as ordinary people, assess someone else's personality? We do not usually have the results of personality tests in front of us when we first meet someone yet, within a very short time, we will have formed an impression of their personality. As managers we may often have to form this impression within the brief time of a selection interview. The consequences of an incorrect assessment at this stage may be costly.

'SUBJECTIVE' IMPRESSIONS OF PERSONALITY

What dimensions do we judge other people on, and what factors are important in reaching conclusions?

There is considerable evidence that we each have an *implicit personality theory*. Much as the trait theorists discussed above seek to group traits together in order to make a more manageable number of higher order traits, so each of us has an implicit theory about which traits go with which, and their relative importance. On this last point, people tend to rate others on those dimensions that they personally consider important. On the former point, concerning which traits go together, there appears to be some similarity between people, although individual differences do occur.

Consider the and/but generator shown below. You have to describe an imaginary person using *two* of the adjectives in the lists. Your description will, therefore, have one of the following patterns.

a) X is _____ and _____

b) X is _____ but _____

First of all choose two words from column 1 of Figure 4. Then choose two words from column 2. Finally choose two more words, one from each column. Now decide whether each of these pairs should be linked together either using 'and', as in a), or 'but', as in b). Notice that there is

Column 1	*Column 2*
generous	ungenerous
wise	shrewd
happy	unhappy
good natured	irritable
humorous	humorless
sociable	unsociable
popular	unpopular
reliable	unreliable
important	insignificant
humane	ruthless
good-looking	unattractive
persistent	unstable
serious	frivolous
restrained	talkative
altruistic	self-centred
imaginative	hard-headed
strong	weak
honest	dishonest

FIGURE 4. *The and/but generator (adapted from Brown, 1986)*

no logical or grammatical reason why either 'and' or 'but' should be preferred. Despite this most people use 'and' when the words both come from the same column, whether it be column 1 or column 2. On the other hand, most people use 'but' when the words come from different columns. You will most probably have noticed that those adjectives in column 1 are 'desirable', whilst those in column 2 are less so.

The use of 'and' as a conjunction implies that the two adjectives naturally go together. Using 'but' however, carries the implication that they are rather strange bedfellows. This highlights a common phenomenon when considering personalities. Put simply, 'good goes with good' and 'bad goes with bad'. There is evidence that this even applies to physical characteristics; 'beautiful is good'.

This is further evidenced in the way that people are surprised when they discover that people they considered 'good' have faults. Field Marshal Montgomery, for example, was much admired by many in the immediate post-war years but, according to his biographers, he was inadequate in his personal life. To repeat, there is no logical reason to assume that one particular characteristic must go with others. We do, it appears, have a preference to reach a unified and global judgement about those with whom we interact, often in a way that does not do justice to their 'real' personality. The extreme case of this is, of course, the stereotype, in which a whole range of characteristics are attributed to an individual on the basis of one prominent characteristic such as race, sex or accent.

Having discovered the tendency to rate things as either 'good' or 'bad', are there common dimensions upon which many would agree? Again it would appear that there are. There appear to be two major dimensions upon which we judge individuals. These two dimensions are nearly, but not quite, independent of each other. The first is that of intellectual ability, the second that of sociability. (In psychologists' terms these are 'cognitive' skills and 'interpersonal' skills respectively.) Any manager who has read, or indeed written, a reference for an individual will most probably recognize the format. First comment on intellectual or technical skills, then add something about how he or she gets on with people.

There are two other aspects of impression formation, both related to the amount of information that an individual receives about the other person. The first of these is that of *primacy*. When we first meet someone else, the first pieces of information we receive about them will obviously be perceived as important because previously we had none. The evidence suggests that we do, in fact, place great weight on this information. First impressions do count! The second aspect is that some adjectives, or traits, carry more information and are more influential than others. For this reason they are often referred to as *central traits*.

In general therefore, our impression of someone's personality is influenced by the first important piece of information we receive about the two dimensions, intellectual and social. Evidence also suggests that, once we have formed such an impression, we are loathe to modify it. We seek information that confirms, rather than conflicts with, our initial view. Evidence from research shows that in a selection interview the selectors make their judgements within the first four minutes and rarely change them thereafter.

In summary, people make judgements about other people's personalities based upon first impressions of two major factors. A global judgement, either positive or negative, is the normal outcome. This initial judgement is usually quick and unchanging. Over the long term, with more constant contact with the person concerned, our judgements become more refined. We begin to see the person as they 'really are'. Why then the apparent need for the first, inaccurate, judgement?

The reason would appear to lie in our discomfort with uncertainty. 'Not knowing' produces tension. The first impressions lead to reduction in this tension, even if they are wrong. We feel happier with our illusions. They can, when all's said and done, be corrected later. Perhaps, however, we should acknowledge our potential inaccuracy and be prepared to modify our initial judgements more readily in that light.

ATTRIBUTION THEORY

So far we have been discussing the concept of personality as a 'cause' of people's behaviour. This assumption, that the main, if not the sole, influence on the way people behave is their 'internal' personality traits, is widely accepted. But is it true?

As well as being influenced by our internal drives, we also have to take into account the nature of the situation in which we find ourselves. Our behaviour is likely to be influenced by both factors – our own personality and the constraints and opportunities of the particular situation. Indeed, some psychologists argue that the situation is more influential than personality. Take for example, the situation in which a member of the public obviously requires help, perhaps he or she is having an epileptic seizure. How likely are people to help? If 'tendency to help', or any other name you might like to give it, is a personality trait, then the bigger the crowd that assembles, the more likely it should be that there will be someone in the crowd who will help. Not so! Experiments in real life in such situations show that, the more people gather, the *less* likely anyone is to help. This must mean that the situation is exerting an important influence over people's behaviour.

The problem remains, of course, as to which is the more important? In case you think that this is idle, academic speculation, let us use some more examples from real life to illustrate how important the difference is between whether we attribute behaviour to *internal* factors (e.g. personality) or *external* (e.g. situational) factors.

Take a situation where something has gone wrong. What went wrong is not in doubt, nor are the actions of the individuals involved. The question that has to be answered is where does the blame fall?

One example from recent years was the case of Mrs Cherry Gross who was shot, by an armed policeman, during a raid on her house. The object of the raid was to arrest her son who, it happened, was not in the house at the time. As a result of the shooting a policeman was charged with an offence concerning the wounding. In this case, of course, the matter came before a jury whose duty it was to decide where the blame, if any, for the incident lay. The facts of the case were not in dispute between the prosecution and the defence; what each tried to do however, was to attribute blame to different factors. The prosecution attempted to show that the policeman involved was to blame, that his lack of foresight and consideration for the safety of others were to blame. In short, that he was negligent, hence was personally responsible and should be punished. The defence, on the other hand, took the approach of trying to place the blame on the situation. In that situation, they argued, any policeman, no matter how well trained and conscientious, would have behaved in the same way. If anybody, placed in that situation, would have behaved in the same way, how can one particular individual be said to be responsible? The prosecution attempted to lay the responsibility for the individual's behaviour on his personal characteristics, while the defence attempted to lay it on the nature of the situation. In this case, the defence succeeded in convincing the jury that the situation was the main cause.

As another example, consider the *Herald of Free Enterprise*, the cross-channel ferry which capsized with the loss of many lives when its bow doors were left open. The assistant bosun admitted being asleep in his cabin when he should have been closing the bow doors. Did he fall asleep and neglect his duties because he was negligent or, given the hours the system required him to work, could anyone be forgiven for falling asleep?

In everyday life, including at work, we are constantly making such attributions. Not all attributions, of course, are concerned with blame; we also have to decide where responsibility lies when things are successful. Did an individual do well because of his or her own effort and skills, or were they lucky? Pay, promotion, transfer, the sack, and many other important decisions may hang on whether attribution of responsibility is made to the person or the situation.

Three questions arise therefore:

- When do we attribute causes?
- What factors influence us as to whether the causes are internal or external?
- Are there any systematic faults that we make in attribution?

Despite what has been said, we do not spend our time looking for attributions for all actions (e.g. why did he go for lunch when he did?). We tend to look for attributions or causes under a number of circumstances. First, and most obviously, when we have to – when somebody wants to know 'why?'. Second, when the events are unexpected.

For example, when a previously reliable worker behaves in an irresponsible manner. The other two circumstances are similar, in that they are related to our personal relationships with the other person. When we are likely to depend on someone else, we like to know why they behave the way they do. Is your fellow manager helpful to you because you are friends, or because the system requires him or her, for whatever reason, to be helpful? The answer will obviously influence your feelings and behaviour towards your colleague. Finally, we seek causes when we are trying to empathize with someone else, that is, put ourselves in their position.

Factors influencing attribution. It is worth bearing in mind the examples listed above when considering the factors that influence our attributions. For example, what information would have convinced you, as a juror, that the policeman was innocent or guilty of wounding Cherry Gross?

When the factors are laid out they appear obvious, but psychologists have refined our common sense into what they call a 'causal calculus'. Three factors enter the equation of this calculus: *consensus*, *distinctiveness* and *stability*. The first concerns the characteristics of the situation, the second those of the person, and the third the stability of both.

CONSENSUS – Does only Fred upset a particular customer, or do all sales personnel generate the same reaction with that customer?
(Note that the situation can be other people, in this case the customer.)

DISTINCTIVENESS – Does Fred upset other customers, or does his behaviour with this particular customer stand out as distinct from his behaviour with others? If only Fred upsets this particular customer, and he upsets other customers, who is at fault? On the other hand, if this customer gets upset with all sales personnel, and this is the only customer who Fred upsets, where then does the fault lie?

It would appear that, if consensus is high (i.e. most people would do the same in that situation), and distinctiveness is high (i.e. Fred does not behave the same way in similar situations), then the 'blame' lies with the situation. If consensus is low, (i.e. most others do not behave that way in that situation), and distinctiveness is low (i.e. Fred behaves that way in all similar situations), then Fred is at fault.

STABILITY – The third factor to be taken into account is the stability of the cause over time. The attribution can be either internal (the person) or external (the situation), and each of these can be either stable or unstable. Thus, Fred does this all the time (internal, stable), or Fred was unlucky this time (internal, unstable). Likewise for the situation.

Biases influencing attribution. Having outlined the factors that influence attribution, are we susceptible to any systematic biases? It would appear so. One with which we are all familiar, if we care to admit it, is the self-serving bias. When things go right, it's because of *my* personal qualities. When things go wrong, on the other hand, the fault lies elsewhere. As one author's former colleague used to say: 'If I break a plate whilst washing up, and my wife is upstairs cleaning, it can sometimes take me as long as 30 seconds to work out why it's her fault'. Most people see success as being due to internal, stable causes, while failure is often seen as due to unstable, external causes, such as luck. This is especially so in areas in which we claim expertise, and helps protect our self-esteem against potentially damaging failures. There is a group of people, however, for whom this attribution is reversed. For a depressive, when things go right it is luck (unstable, external), and when wrong it is always 'my' fault (stable, internal). Attempts to convince them otherwise are usually doomed to failure.

Another bias, which is certainly less obvious, is called the fundamental attribution error. Basically, when we judge the behaviour of others, we *underestimate* the power of the situation in determining behaviour. Again, let us take an example. Those who have ever taken part in role-playing interviews, where they were given feedback on their interpersonal skills, will most probably recognize the following situation. At the end of the role-play interview, if the interviewer is asked, for example, why he did most of the talking, he will probably reply with explanations such as 'well the other person wouldn't talk, so I had to'. The observers, however, will normally give an explanation along the lines of 'you're an overbearing so-and-so'. The former is, of course, an explanation in terms of the situation, the latter in terms of personality. Who is right? Experiments across a range of situations suggest that the fundamental attribution error description is correct – we underestimate the effects of the situation. This also helps explain why first impressions can be wrong. It may be that you first saw the person at a time when situational pressures were particularly strong.

There is a possible explanation for this bias. We tend to attribute causality to where our attention is drawn. For example, the effects in the role-playing interview can be reversed. If the observers are asked to direct their attention to the interviewee, they adopt a situational explanation. And, after watching a video tape of their performance, the interviewer will adopt a personality explanation – 'I am an overbearing so-and-so, aren't I?'

What, then, is the lesson to be learned from attribution theory? We should be aware of our tendency to underestimate the effects of situational factors on people's behaviour. As another example, consider the job applicants at interview. Their performance is taken as a clear indication of their personality, but consider the situational factors. Interviews are situations where there are considerable pressures to behave in certain ways: it is expected that you will not argue or answer back. Most people will conform to these situational pressures, therefore, telling you very little about how they will behave in other situations.

We will return, briefly, to attribution theory when examining staff appraisal in Chapter 3 on leadership.

So far, our consideration of the implications of personality for managers has been limited to understanding some of the reasons why people behave differently, and understanding some of our own biases in our perception of other people. We will now move to a theory of personality, and of personal interaction, that suggests ways in which we can interact more effectively.

TRANSACTIONAL ANALYSIS

Transactional analysis (TA) is a theory which covers both the structure of personality and interaction between people. It was developed by the American psychiatrist Eric Berne (1972), but it soon became apparent that it had applications outside the consulting room. Despite its clinical pedigree however, many psychologists do not regard it as much as other, more traditional, personality theories. Part of the reason for this may be the terminology the theory uses which, to some, seems rather 'frivolous'. In our experience a large number of managers do find the theory useful as it relates to understanding organizational behaviour.

First we will deal with the part of the theory that concerns itself with the structure of personality, before moving on to consider the analysis of transactions.

(Before continuing, read the case study in Appendix 2, draft a reply to each of the memos, and write down your impressions of the personality of Bob Jeffries. Then consider how you felt when reading the memos.)

THE STRUCTURE OF PERSONALITY

Berne suggests that the personality consists of three major parts, or *ego states*: Parent, Adult and Child. We will start with a brief description of each, together with some consideration as to their origins. Before doing so a word of warning is required. The terms Parent, Adult and Child do not mean the same in TA terminology as they do in everyday speech. Child does not, for example, mean the same as childish.

According to Berne, as human beings we are all initially totally dependent upon our parents, or surrogate parents. Thus, virtually all our experiences in the first few years of life are determined by our interactions with our parents. These experiences, it is argued, are never forgotten. We develop what he likened to a tape, or video, recording of these early experiences, together with our own learnt responses. Thus, the memory contains all the taught behaviour of the parents, as observed by the infant. These range from experiences of loving, experiences involving the imposition of rules and demands, and those concerned with the setting of standards.

As well as our memories about the actual experiences, we also remember our reactions to the parental behaviour. Most commonly, this is in terms of the feelings associated with them. This collection of childhood experiences and our feelings about them constitute the Child ego state. Such feelings may be those of guilt, joy, rebellion and so on.

Finally, at about the age of ten months, the infant starts to become independent and to explore and test the world around it. To the 'taught' Parent and 'felt' Child, is added the information-processing function of the Adult.

This then is the basic structure of personality and is usually presented diagramatically as three adjacent circles, as shown in Figure 5. As can

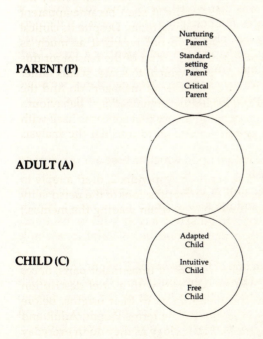

FIGURE 5. *The transactional analysis approach to the structure of personality*

be seen the Parent and Child are subdivided. These subdivisions represent the different ways in which the Parent can control, or the Child may feel.

In the Parent, the subdivisions are those of *Critical Parent*, *Standard-setting Parent* and *Nurturing Parent*. In the Child they are *Free* (or *Spontaneous*) *Child*, *Intuitive Child* (referred to by Berne as the 'Little Professor') and *Adapted Child*. This last category, of Adapted Child, is further subdivided into Compliant Child, and Rebellious Child. Both sorts of Child, as we will see, are often found within organizations. (The Adult may also be subdivided, but this is not particularly relevant for our purposes.)

The balance between these three ego states will vary from individual to individual. For example, some individuals may have a particularly strong Critical Parent. Such an individual will often be seen as authoritarian and inconsiderate of the feelings of others. In our experience, it is likely that many of you will have described Bob Jeffries in words associated with Critical Parent. Other individuals may have a strong Adult, perhaps with very little Child. Such an individual is very logical and rational, but lacks the sense of humour associated with the Free Child.

What Berne also noticed was that whilst we all have, to a greater or lesser extent, all three ego states, our behaviour at any particular moment is controlled predominantly by only one of them. Thus, a person may behave at different times as perhaps a Critical Parent or a Free Child, but not both at the same time. From this, it is perhaps apparent that TA suggests that, although we may have preferred ego states, we move between all three, often dependent upon what we are responding to.

ANALYSING TRANSACTIONS

We now have the basic information upon which to base our description of transactional analysis itself.

The *transaction* is the basic unit of behaviour. It involves you saying or doing something to me, and me responding (or vice versa). For the sake of simplicity, we will concern ourselves largely with verbal transactions, although there are others that are more behavioural, for example shaking a fist.

A transaction originates in one of the ego states. The one from which it originates can be identified by both the content and the way in which it is said. In addition, every transaction is 'targeted' at a particular ego state in the other person. The sender hopes that the receiver will respond from the targeted ego state. This, as we will see, does not always happen.

Consider the memo from Bob Jeffries (see Appendix 2), which was written from the Critical Parent. Before considering your memo in reply, let us consider how you would feel if, in real life, you received such a memo. Critical Parent transactions are targeted at the Adapted Child, in particular the Compliant Child. In the jargon of TA, the Critical Parent tries to 'hook' the Compliant Child. In our experience, especially with managers, this rarely happens. What is a more common initial reaction is that of Rebellious Child – 'Who the hell does he think he is?'. (This often happens, we suspect, after a very brief period of 'What have I done wrong?' – Compliant Child.)

What now would have happened if you had written the memo back in terms associated with Rebellious Child? The subsequent reply might have been 'Sorry, I realize I was somewhat heavy-handed', but we suspect not. The reply is more likely to have involved more, and heavier, Critical Parent, resulting in a sequence of transactions known as *Uproar*, for fairly obvious reasons.

We more commonly find that the content of the replies is not wholly Rebellious Child, although it is often hinted at in a disguised fashion. (A common veiled Rebellious Child utterance is 'with respect . . . !') More commonly still, the response is from the Adult, stating what has been, or is planned to be, done in order to ensure that the same mistake is not repeated in the future.

PARALLEL AND CROSSED TRANSACTIONS

These two alternatives demonstrate a further aspect of TA, the *parallel* versus the *crossed* transaction. These are shown, diagrammatically, in Figure 6. In a parallel transaction the initial statement succeeds in hooking the appropriate ego state, and elicits a response from it. In a crossed transaction it does not hook the appropriate ego state. In general, a parellel transaction will continue, while a crossed transaction will cease. The only way in which a crossed transaction can continue is if one of the individuals moves to the appropriate ego state. Thus, any reply from Jeffries to a memo from your Adult will either have to be in Adult, or be another attempt to force you to move to Compliant Child. If either of you refuse to move, memos will soon cease.

Obviously, there are a large number of possible transactions, but we will consider some of the more common patterns. We have, of course, already considered Critical Parent to Adapted Child.

Adapted Child to Nurturing Parent. This is in some ways a mirror image of the example of Bob Jeffries. Rather than the Parent criticizing the Child, the Child appeals to the Nurturing Parent for help. Taken to extreme, this may be seen as 'crawling', especialy if it is the boss to whom the appeal is made. Used correctly, it can be a highly effective way of resolving some problems. For example, trying to get faulty goods exchanged, is often done from the Critical Parent. The result is often

PARALLEL TRANSACTIONS

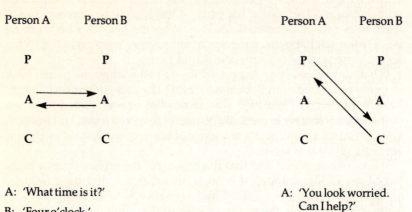

A: 'What time is it?'

B: 'Four o'clock.'

A: 'You look worried. Can I help?'

B: 'Yes please. I don't know how to do this.'

CROSSED TRANSACTIONS

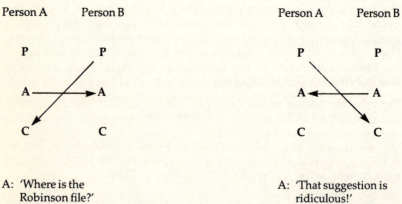

A: 'Where is the Robinson file?'

B: 'How come you never know where anything is?'

A: 'That suggestion is ridiculous!'

B: 'Could you give me the evidence that leads you to that conclusion?'

FIGURE 6. *Types of transaction*

Uproar. Asking for help to resolve your problem is often a more effective approach as it hooks the Nurturing Parent. The memo from Steve Holland requesting help is an example of an appeal from the Child, and that from Mary Holland is an offer of help from the Nurturing Parent.

Critical Parent to Critical Parent is a transaction which often occurs on training courses, or over a drink. The name often given to this pattern is 'Ain't it awful'. For example:

'This organization never takes any notice of me.'

'I know, my boss never even talks to me.'

Whilst it may be nice to get things off your chest, this does not get things done.

Child to Child. Free Child to Free Child is 'Let's have fun'. This fun may, in its pure form, be harmless. If, however, the Rebellious Child is involved, the motivation, rather than harmless fun, is that of doing mischief, for example as in the handwritten memo from Steve Holland: 'let's get our own back on Jeffries'.

Free Child is often given its head in so-called 'brain-storming' sessions. in such sessions, ideas are produced but neither criticized (Parent), nor evaluated (Adult). Evaluation takes place later.

Adult to Adult. Whilst it may be beneficial to have a good moan, or to have fun occasionally, it is only when operating from Adult that things get done. Adult to Adult is concerned with information exchange, evaluation, and rational decision making. Both memos from Bill Owen are written predominantly from the Adult.

IMPROVING INTERACTIONS

Now that the various transactions have been described, it is worth examining how TA can be employed to improve interactions. Recognizing the ego state that is the source of a transaction is the first step in gaining greater control over it. Secondly, you need to be aware of the ego state it is intended to hook, especially if it is the Child, for this is the source of feelings. Finally, decide if you want the transaction to continue between the two ego states. If you do not, then cross the transaction. The other person will either have to follow you (normally to Adult), or give up.

The source of a transaction is indicated in a number of ways. Verbally, both the words and the tone of voice used can indicate the ego state involved, as can the general manner of the person. Nonverbally, gestures and expressions also indicate the ego state involved. Table 1 lists the most common managerial ego states and some of their characteristic words, tones, gestures and attitudes.

TABLE 1. *Verbal and nonverbal characteristics of ego states*

	Critical Parent	Nurturing Parent	Adult	Free Child	Adapted Child Compliant (C) Rebellious (R)
WORDS:	Never Should Ought Do/don't	Let me Don't worry Be careful Well done	Correct Where? Why? What?	Hi Fun Wow Great	Sorry (C) Please (C) Won't (R) No! (R)
VOICE:	Critical Condescending	Sympathetic Encouraging	Confident Inquiring	Excited Free	Apologetic (C) Defiant (R)
EXPRESSIONS:	Frowning Pointing	Accepting Smiling	Thoughtful Interested	Spontaneous Uninhibited	Helpless (C) Sullen (R)
ATTITUDE:	Judgemental Authoritarian	Understanding Caring	Open Evaluative	Curious Changeable	Agreeing (C) Rebellious (R)

Finally two points that, whilst not strictly analyses of transactions, may be of some interest. As well as dealing with reality, the Adult also has the job of ensuring that the experiences and feelings of childhood, recorded in Parent and Child respectively, are still appropriate. For example the internal Parent may still be dictating 'leave a clean plate' at meal times. Modern nutritionalists however question this dictum. Logically there is no longer any nutritional reason why we should have to eat everything placed before us. Nevertheless, the Child may experience feelings of guilt when these are inappropriate. It is the Adult's job to question the rationality, both of the judgement from the Parent and the corresponding feeling of the Child.

Although the three ego states have been shown as totally separate, sometimes the Adult can become 'contaminated'. When contaminated by Parent, untested judgements are presented as real. For example, 'all trade union leaders are communists'. The common name for this is prejudice. If, on the other hand, the Child contaminates the Adult, the result is illusion i.e. wishful thinking presented as reality.

From the above discussion, it may have become apparent that transactions need not always be between two people. There can be an internal dialogue. The Parent chiding the Child when things go wrong, patting it on the back when things go well. Again, it is the Adult's job to ensure that both judgement and feeling are still valid in the changing world, and not just the automatic replay of childhood experiences.

EXISTENTIAL POSITIONS

There is one more piece of theory from TA which we have found of considerable value for managers. It concentrates on the *existential position* from which people operate. It will be easier to explain the meaning of this phrase once the essential concept involved has been covered. This concept is concerned with whether a person is 'OK' or 'Not OK'. Unlike the concepts of Parent, Adult, and Child, the term OK means very much the same in TA as it does in everyday language. If someone is seen as 'OK' then they have value as a person and their views and opinions have to be considered seriously. They are competent, and are generally in control of their life. Someone who is seen as 'Not OK', on the other hand, is perceived as the opposite of this. They do not appear to be in control, and their views and opinions can be dismissed without consideration. They have little or no value as a human being.

The concept of being 'OK' or 'Not OK' can be applied both to oneself and to others. Thus I can be 'OK' or 'Not OK', likewise You can be 'OK' or 'Not OK'. Putting these two factors, 'OKness' and I/You, together produces four possible combinations, as shown in Figure 7. For obvious reasons it is often referred to as the 'OK Corral'. Let us consider each of the positions in turn and consider their implications for our interactions

I'M OK YOU'RE NOT OK	I'M OK YOU'RE OK
I'M NOT OK YOU'RE NOT OK	I'M NOT OK YOU'RE OK

FIGURE 7. *Existential positions (adapted from Ernst, 1971)*

with other people. The diagram was originally devised by Franklin Ernst (1971) for use in psychotherapy. For this reason we will give some clinical, as well as managerial, examples.

I'm OK, You're Not OK. If I'm OK then I have value as a person and my ideas and views also have value. You, on the other hand, have little or no value. The logical conclusion is that if you don't count, then I am justified in getting rid of you. In its extreme clinical form this is the position of homicidal psychopaths. It is also the position adopted by some extreme religious groups. In managerial terms it is the 'hire and fire' culture.

I'm Not OK, You're OK. In many ways this is the reverse of the first box. Everyone else but me appears to be in control, and to have value as a person. In this situation, the logical conclusion is to get rid of myself. In extreme clinical cases, the ultimate solution is suicide. Indeed, an analysis by Berne of suicide notes revealed that this was a very common position. In organizational terms, the result is often resignation. 'It's my fault again, I'll have to go.' (The memo from Jim Slater in Appendix 2 is an example of a response from this position.) A milder, and more common version is to keep a low profile. It is a common feeling during the first weeks or months of a new job.

I'm Not OK, You're Not OK. In this situation no one knows what is going on, and no one is in control. In clinical terms, the outcome is to go insane. 'You may think I'm strange, but you should see my psychiatrist.' It often expresses itself in a very mild organizational form in the type of office stickers that read 'you don't have to be mad to work here, but it helps.'

I'm OK, You're OK. In this position, both parties have value and are in control. There may be disagreements, but they do not mean that either party dismisses the value or ideas of the other. In this situation, the motto is not to 'get rid of' but to 'get on with'. It is the only position from which people can interact effectively. The theory suggests that people exist in, and operate from, one of these four positions, hence the term 'existential position'. Which position a person is operating from will change, depending upon their own preferred existential position and that of the person with whom they are interacting. In everyday life we suspect that most people spend most of their time in 'I'm OK, You're OK'. We also suspect that most people have a preferred fall-back position, which becomes apparent when things go wrong. For most managers, we suspect that the common fall-back is 'I'm OK, You're Not OK' – when things go wrong it's someone else's fault. The effect of responding from this position is to push the other person to their fall-back, which is also likely to be 'I'm OK, You're Not OK'. The result is likely to be Uproar. Judged from their behaviour, we suspect that some drivers operate from 'I'm OK, You're Not OK'. Their behaviour has the effect of pushing other, normally 'I'm OK, You're OK', drivers into the same position.

The next most common fall-back is most probably 'I'm Not OK, You're OK'. This position is, however, very uncomfortable. For this reason we suspect that those who fall back to this position often quickly convert to 'I'm OK, You're Not OK'. (At this point you may have noticed the links between the 'OK' states and the ego states mentioned earlier. 'Not OK' comments always originate in either Rebellious Child or Critical Parent.)

We find that the OK Corral is a very useful aid to managers in their interactions with others. First, it helps them understand when they, or others, are slipping into 'Not OK' positions. Second, it points out that the only way to interact effectively with others is to stay 'OK', both about yourself and those with whom you are interacting. Finally, the position you occupy at any particular time is a voluntary choice. As Eleanor Roosevelt once said, 'no one can make you feel inferior without your consent'. Staying 'OK' may make you feel better and be more effective.

We have now considered the ways in which personality can be described, the reasons for some 'personality clashes', and how interpersonal communications may be improved. It is impossible for managers to change the personalities of those around them, but an understanding of the ways in which people differ can help managers avoid or defuse potential trouble. In addition, an ability to analyse transactions and construct appropriate responses is an important tool in effective people management.

2

Motivation

An independent consulting firm in the USA recently carried out a survey of employees' attitudes. While most workers were generally satisfied with their pay and benefits, less than half thought that their boss was doing a good job of motivating them. This applied to all levels, from the shop floor to the boardroom. Similar results have been found in the UK.

Before looking at various theories of motivation, and their implications for management, we have found that it often helps to look at what it is that motivates ourselves. It is worth spending about ten minutes jotting down answers to the following questions:

- Why do I work?
- Why do I work for my present company?
- Why do I work hard (or otherwise)?

Having done this, it is often interesting to answer the questions above (especially the first one), on behalf of a group of which you are not a member. If you are a manager, try the exercise for blue-collar workers, and vice versa.

What normally results from such an exercise are lists of *needs*, which have a degree of similarity, but which also reveal some individual differences. This is not surprising, as it is likely that some reasons for working apply to everybody. Other reasons have particular importance for particular individuals. The list of all our needs is, however, very long. What we require is some form of theoretical structure that will help organize the large number of needs, or potential motivators, into smaller, more manageable, categories. Such a theoretical structure will help us when we have to consider what it is that motivates particular employees, or groups of employees. Later we will consider how people are motivated.

Since the early part of the century, theorists have considered what such a structure might be like and it is interesting, therefore, to look at the history of need theories of the motivation to work. Each of the theories has been shown to be lacking as a full explanation of motivation at work, but each has left its influence on subsequent theories.

NEED THEORIES OF WORK

TAYLOR'S SCIENTIFIC MANAGEMENT

The first modern systematic commentator on motivation at work was most probably Frederick Taylor (1911). In the first decades of this century he described what he called *scientific management*. Note that we call Taylor a commentator, rather than a theorist. His 'theory' was stated as a set of 'principles', rather than in the form of a comprehensive theory. Basically, Taylor's principles advocated strict division of labour, based on systematic job analysis, high levels of control, and the use of money as a motivator linked to various objectives. There is no doubt that money is indeed an important motivator, because of its universal ability to be exchanged for other, more practical, motivators. If it did not appear on your list of why you work one might be suspicious. What Taylor overlooked however, is that people also work for reasons other than money. A survey reported in the early 1980s (Warr, 1982) asked a large sample of British men and women if they would continue to work if it were not financially necessary for them to do so. Nearly 70 per cent of men and 65 per cent of women said they would continue. Interestingly, while there was some difference between professional and unskilled manual workers, it was not as large as might have been expected. Nearly 60 per cent of male unskilled manual workers said they would continue working. (These results have to be treated with a certain amount of caution. What people say they will do and what they actually do may not be the same.) If they would continue working despite not needing the money, then what other needs must be being met at work?

HAWTHORNE STUDIES

The next major revision of need theory came from some work done in the USA in the 1920s and 30s at the Hawthorne works of the Western Electric company. The name most commonly associated with the Hawthorne studies is that of Elton Mayo. Although he used much of the data to support his own theories, Mayo himself was never directly involved in them.

Initially, the researchers were trying to establish the relationship between various physical conditions, such as temperature and lighting, and productivity. What they found was that there were no consistent relationships. Productivity increased, both in the experimental group and in a control group. The level of lighting remained constant for the control group, but was varied in the experimental group. At one point, the level of lighting for the latter was equivalent to that of moonlight. Despite this, productivity did not drop. The researchers eventually concluded that psychological, rather than physical, factors were at work.

In order to test this hypothesis they conducted various small group experiments. From the results of these, they concluded that motivation was best explained in terms of 'social relationships'. The productivity had risen in the control and experimental groups because the members felt that the researchers were taking an interest in them. Indeed, the 'Hawthorne effect' has entered sociological and psychological vocabularies; that is, that just observing people will have an effect upon them.

Although the studies took place over 50 years ago the results of these studies are still a matter of discusion and controversy. Most researchers now accept that the studies were poorly constructed and controlled. For this reason, the results can be explained by factors other than just social ones. Nevertheless, they have left their mark by drawing attention to psychological needs in motivation.

MASLOW'S HIERARCHY OF NEEDS

The first comprehensive attempt to classify needs was undertaken by Abraham Maslow in the 1940s. Maslow's theory (1971) essentially consists of two parts. The first concerns the classification of needs, the second concerns how these classifications are related to each other. He suggested that needs can be classified into a hierarchy. This hierarchy is normally presented in the form of a pyramid, as shown in Figure 8, with each level consisting of a particular class of needs. The relationship between the needs is related to the pyramid structure. Maslow argues that the lower down the needs lie, the more basic they are. Thus, the most basic needs are those concerned with physical survival. These needs have to be satisfied, at least to some minimum level, before the next level of needs becomes important. Once each level is adequately satisfied, the needs at this level become less important. The only exception to this is the top level of self-actualization. Self-actualization is the need to become the kind of person you ideally envisage yourself to be. As such it can never be totally satisfied. According to Maslow, individuals work their way up the hierarchy, but each level of needs remains dependent on the levels below. Thus, if you are motivated at work by the opportunity to 'self-actualize' and suddenly you are made redundant, the whole system collapses, as the need to feed and provide for yourself and your dependants again becomes the predominant need.

The theory, especially when the redundancy example is used, has considerable appeal to managers. Its message is clear: find out which level each individual is operating at and pitch their rewards accordingly. Unfortunately, the theory is weak in many respects. Some levels of the classification appear not to exist for some individuals, while some rewards appear to fit into more than one classification. Take money, which can be used to purchase the essentials of life, but which can also be seen as a status symbol, or an indicator of personal worth. As to the

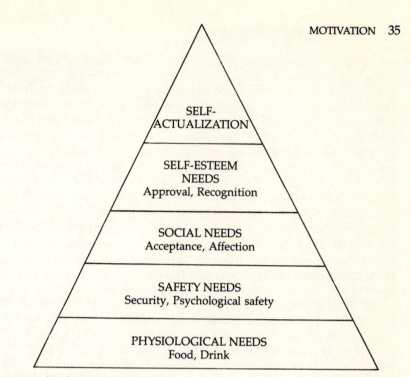

SELF-
ACTUALIZATION

SELF-ESTEEM
NEEDS
Approval, Recognition

SOCIAL NEEDS
Acceptance, Affection

SAFETY NEEDS
Security, Psychological safety

PHYSIOLOGICAL NEEDS
Food, Drink

FIGURE 8. *Maslow's hierarchy of needs*

relationship between the different levels, there appear to be considerable individual differences as to what constitutes 'adequate satisfaction' at any particular level.

Empirical research, therefore, has failed to support the theory, and most psychologists would rate its accuracy, on a scale of 1 to 10, somewhere about 2 or 3. Despite this, it is still taught on many management courses without its faults being highlighted. This is not to suggest that the theory is without value. The classification of needs is useful as a guide to ensure that all possible types of need are considered. In addition, it is likely that people's needs are organized in a hierarchical manner. What has to be recognized is that the nature of this hierarchy will vary from one person to another.

HERZBERG'S TWO-FACTOR THEORY

The next significant theory was that of Frederick Herzberg (1966), which did not look at motivation directly, but at the causes of job satisfaction and dissatisfaction. Herzberg did this using a technique known as *critical incidents* analysis. He asked a group of professional engineers and accountants to describe incidents in their jobs in the recent past that had given them strong feelings of either satisfaction or dissatisfaction. He then asked them to describe the causes in each case. Based on an analysis of their descriptions of what happened and why, Herzberg suggested a two-factor theory of job satisfaction/dissatisfaction ('two-factor' because the causes of one were distinct from the causes of the other). Job satisfaction is the result of what Herzberg called *motivators*. These were such things as 'a sense of achievement', 'an opportunity for personal growth', 'the sense of having done a job well' etc. Dissatisfaction, on the other hand, appeared to be caused by *hygiene* factors. These included such things as 'money', 'working conditions', and 'company policy'. According to the theory, these two factors, motivators and hygiene, are qualitatively different, and have different effects. If you want to remove dissatisfaction, improve the hygiene factors. Improving them beyond the level at which dissatisfaction disappears will not, however, lead to an increase in satisfaction. The only way satisfaction will be increased is by giving more of the motivators. The converse also applies. Giving more of the motivators will not by itself remove dissatisfaction.

On initial examination the theory has some merit. Think of the annual pay rise, or an improvement in working conditions. They may have an initial effect on satisfaction, but they are soon taken for granted. But experimental examination of the theory has not been so kind. The results can only be replicated using the same sorts of people (i.e. professionals), and the same technique (i.e. getting the people themselves to describe the causes of their feelings). If you can recall attribution theory (see pages 18–22), you will remember that we have a tendency to blame things 'out there' when things go wrong, but 'things in me' when they go right. This would appear to be the explanation for Herzberg's findings. As with Maslow, Herzberg's work is initially appealing, but on further examination turns out to be conceptually flawed. As with Maslow's theory, however, it continues to be taught uncritically.

Herzberg has, however, left his mark. His classification of motivators and hygiene factors is disputed, but the distinction itself may still be seen in the concept of 'intrinsic' versus 'extrinsic' sources of motivation. Intrinsic motivators are those within the job itself (such as feelings of accomplishment). External motivators, on the other hand, are outside the job (such as money). As will be seen, the former are more effective, and cheaper!

In addition, in the area of job and work design, Herzberg's concepts of job enlargement and job enrichment are still in use in the area of job and work design. It is to this area that we will now turn.

JOB DESIGN

Job design is concerned with the characteristics of jobs and how these affect people's behaviour. Many managers consider that job or work design has little to do with them. This may be so, but in a workplace that is rapidly changing, we think it unlikely. For example, the introduction of word processors in place of typewriters may, on the surface, appear simply to involve swapping an out-of-date typewriter for a more sophisticated one. But the implications often go further, as those who have undertaken such a change will tell you. Even such a simple move as changing the office in which someone works may have effects on such things as job performance and absenteeism. In addition, it may also influence the levels of job satisfaction, anxiety, and depression of those concerned.

Changes in job design have the potential for both degrading and improving jobs. At the worst, they can lead to the 'de-skilling' of previously skilled jobs. They have also the potential to enhance and supplement those skills. Which impact they have is not solely dependent upon technology. For example, the introduction of word processors has the potential for both de-skilling and enhancement, depending upon *how* it is used. If the operators are used just to type in the initial material which is then modified and edited by others using their own terminals, the job will be de-skilled. The operators will become no more than copy typists. If, on the other hand, the operators are given the opportunity to use their own initiative, the job can be enhanced. For example, operators could be given the job of seeking out the information required to update routine documents, or producing the agenda for regular meetings.

What the effects of job redesign will be, and their magnitude, will depend upon many factors. The practising manager therefore needs some form of checklist in order to adequately diagnose and understand this process. This will at least help ensure that when contemplating changing the way people work due consideration is given to the major factors. Most importantly, the manager should realize that job design does not apply only to massive changes, such as automated factories, because even apparently minor changes, such as reorganizing office layout, can have an impact on a worker's attitudes and/or behaviour.

In considering the major aspects of job design we will group the relevant factors as follows: first, factors associated with the job itself; second, those associated with the context of the job, both social and organizational; finally, we will consider the differences in effects due to differences in the individuals involved.

THE JOB ITSELF

Job factors may themselves be subdivided into two broad, and overlapping, classes: *quantitative* and *qualitative* factors. Put briefly, quantitative refers to the amount of work involved in the job, while qualitative refers to the perceived quality of that work.

Quantitive changes concern the demands made upon the physical and mental capacities of those involved. When job changes are planned, physical demands are usually taken into consideration because they are most obvious. The extra walking, or the extra muscle power required is something that becomes immediately apparent.

Mental demands are less often considered. In considering mental demands, it is perhaps easiest to draw an analogy between workers and computers. Both, in particular aspects of the job, are information processors. Both can be either overloaded or underloaded. The difference is that computers, unlike people, don't get anxious or bored. Continuing the analogy, information processing consists of three broad stages, at each of which demands may be made:

▶ *Demands on attention* – i.e. recognizing and imputting the information.
▶ *Demands on memory* – i.e. storing the information.
▶ *Demands on decision making* – i.e. processing the information.

The major influences on these factors are, of course, the volume of information and the time-scales involved. Under normal circumstances, these demands are usually well within the processing capacities of the individuals concerned. Problems often arise, however, when demands suddenly increase. To give a tragic example, in July 1988, the American destroyer *Vincennes* shot down an Iranian airliner with nearly 300 people on board. At the time, the destroyer, said to be the most sophisticated anti-aircraft warship afloat, was engaging Iranian warships. According to one of the officers aboard, the highly complex radar systems aboard the ship had to be 'tuned down', because the information being supplied by the computers was too much for the operators to cope with. It is unlikely that managers will be faced with a job design task with such potentially disastrous consequences, but how can they recognize when overload is occurring?

It is easy to spot overload in computers. They make mistakes or stop working. Humans, on the other hand, do not usually fail catastrophically, rather they go into a gradual decline. The ways in which they cope are by limiting either the input, or the processing. Limitation of input can be accomplished either by stopping it altogether (go sick or strike) or by reducing it (form queues). Limitation of processing, on the other hand, means that approximations are made, which are sometimes correct because of past experience, but which are often wrong in some detail. These wrong decisions, if detected by others and referred back, then join the ever-growing queue. Unfortunately, many workers will use such techniques to cover up the overload for fear of disclosing what they perceive as their inability to cope. It is easy for hard-pressed managers to ignore such indicators but, if they do, in the long run both the job and the worker will suffer. Managers should be prepared to probe past the offered explanations of 'it will be all right soon', 'it's only temporary', and not wait for the inevitable, and possibly disastrous error.

Qualitative changes are best summarized by the job characteristics model (JCM), which was developed by Richard Hackman and Greg Oldham (1976) and is shown in Figure 9. According to Hackman and Oldham, certain central, or 'core', features of the job will influence certain important, or 'critical' psychological states in individuals. These states will themselves then determine people's attitudes and behaviours towards the job. The model suggests therefore that the *core job dimensions*, on the left, will influence the *critical psychological states*, which will influence the *personal and work outcomes* on the right. The strength of this relationship will, however, be different for different individuals. It will be influenced by the particular individual's *growth need strength*, which is discussed further on pages 42–43 in the section on individual differences.

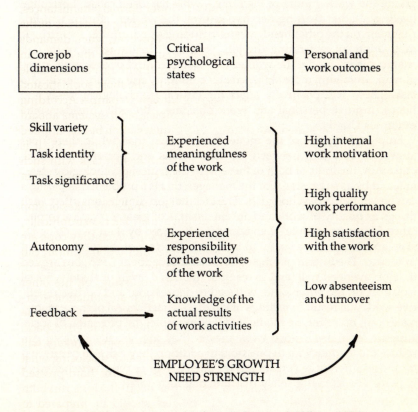

FIGURE 9. *The job characteristics model (from Hackman and Oldham, 1976)*

Whilst the descriptions given in the figure for critical psychological states, and personal and work outcomes are easily understood, we perhaps need to describe the core job dimensions in a little more detail. They comprise:

▶ *Skill variety* – The extent to which the tasks require different skills.
▶ *Task identity* – The extent to which the worker can complete a 'whole' piece of work, as opposed to a small part of it.
▶ *Task significance* – The extent to which the work is perceived as influencing the lives of others.
▶ *Autonomy* – The extent to which the worker has freedom within the job to decide how it should be done.
▶ *Feedback* – The extent to which there is correct and precise information about how effectively the worker is performing.

The model is, in many ways, a synthesis of previous theories and the legacy of Herzberg can be detected. Herzberg differentiated between job enlargement and job enrichment. The former consisted of really just giving the worker more of the same – what has been called 'horizontal loading'. Rather than tighten five screws, the worker tightens ten! Enrichment, on the other hand, means including opportunities for intrinsic motivation by expanding the job 'vertically'. In the terms of the job characteristics model the worker thus gains control over a larger piece of work, involving more skills, greater autonomy and a more meaningful task. These will positively affect the critical psychological states and hence improve personal and work outcomes. We will consider some examples shortly.

Empirical studies of the model have shown that, while there does appear to be a link between job dimensions and personal and work outcomes, the links of both of these with the critical psychological states may not be as suggested. For the manager, this is a problem that perhaps can be left to the psychologists. The fact that job dimensions affect such things as quality of work and absenteeism is of greater practical importance. However, people's behaviour *is* influenced by their psychological state and it would be useful to know what factors of the job have what influence. The British psychologist Donald Broadbent (1985) has argued that job overload will tend to result in increased levels of anxiety. Social isolation, on the other hand, will lead to depression; and boring, repetitive work will result in feelings of job dissatisfaction. All of these mental states can, however, be moderated. For example, the provision of social support for those whose work means they are socially isolated can reduce the tendency for depression. In addition they will also be affected by those differences considered on page 33 concerning whether work is perceived as being solely instrumental in nature.

THE CONTEXT

As well as factors concerning the job itself, there are those concerning the context within which a change is planned, that can have an influence on workers' attitudes and behaviour. The most prominent of these are those concerned with the social aspects of the job, and the 'climate' of the organization.

Since the Hawthorne studies, the importance of social contact and support in the workplace has been recognized. Indeed, many companies encourage social, as well as work-related, contact between their staff. Because of its importance, individuals will find ways of increasing their level of social contact if it is low. For example in one factory studied by the authors, mechanics had collected what they considered to be evidence of sabotage by machine operatives, of whom there were five to a machine. While the machine was being repaired considerable social activity took place between the operatives. When the machines were running, such interaction was not possible because of the noise and locations of the operatives. Another telling example is that of people who occasionally work at home. Anyone who has done this will tell you that, because of the lack of interruptions, you can get a lot of work done. However, it is something that can only be tolerated, by most people, for a limited period. The lack of social contact is felt after a few days. This factor has yet to be taken fully into account by those organizations who are considering 'electronic offices', which would allow some staff to work at home almost permanently.

Given that, for most people, social contact is not only desirable but necessary, how should it affect job design?

The most common way in which it has been used is in autonomous working groups. In this system, a group is made responsible for a particular task. For example, in well-reported cases, Volvo and Saab in the 1970s and General Motors in the 1980s, established factories based on such working teams. By combining people together in groups a number of benefits can be obtained. First, because tasks are being combined, there is the possibility for more skill variety, task identity, and task significance. There is also the potential for greater autonomy. All of this is in addition to the satisfaction of social needs. For example, a group may be made responsible for the fabrication of the engine. How they arrange their work is entirely up to them, with the proviso that they maintain a 'buffer' supply of completed engines so that the next group on the production line is not held up. Another limited example is that of Quality Circles (QCs), where staff working in a particular area are encouraged to meet together during work time to discuss methods of improving product quality and work practices. The results are generally encouraging. In our experience, where QCs fail they do so because of lack of support from top management.

The introduction of such changes is also dependent upon the organizational 'climate', that is, the array of norms and traditions that have built up about 'how things get done around here'. For example, many job redesigns involve the devolution of greater responsibility to staff, on the assumption that this will be accepted. This may not be the case. For reasons that will be considered in Chapter 3 on leadership and management style, the sudden change from highly controlled work practices to a more participative approach may be met with apathy or, in some cases, even outright rebellion. Large changes in working practice that go against the organizational climate are likely to have one of two effects. First, if the change is persisted with, a period of considerable difficulty will have to be tolerated. Alternatively, and we suspect more commonly, the change is abandoned and the status quo re-established, but with additional ill-feeling caused by the abortive change.

THE INDIVIDUAL

So far it has been tacitly assumed that all people faced with the same job characteristics in the same context will behave and feel the same way. This is obviously not true. As individuals we differ.

One of these differences has already been referred to in the job characteristics model, that of growth need strength (GNS). A person high in GNS will react more strongly when his or her core job dimensions are improved. A crude but easy way of defining GNS is by means of Maslow's hierarchy of needs (see page 34). Someone with needs near the top would have a high GNS score, someone near the bottom a low score. Thus, those with high GNS are characterized by having high needs for autonomy and personal growth, perhaps coupled with a high level of self-esteem and a tolerance of high levels of ambiguity. If work is to be delegated to an autonomous work group, then those with a low need for social contact might not be appropriate members. At the other end of the hierarchy are those individuals who view work in purely instrumental terms – 'I'm here for the money and nothing else'. Such individuals may, from a management view, appear to have a rather negative attitude to work. There are many in this category who derive their major satisfactions from outside activities. These may be leisure related or may involve public service such as council work. As long as they 'pull their weight' at work, do we have a right to expect everyone to be enthusiastic? If they do not pull their weight, then it is management's job, perhaps using some of the techniques to be described later in this chapter, to ensure that they do.

We are not aware of any research that has studied the relative importance of individual differences and organizational climate, but believe that the effects of the former are smaller than those of the latter. How people respond to greater autonomy and responsibility is largely dependent upon how they have been treated in the past and the expectations that this engenders. It may be characterized in the often heard expression 'I'm not paid to make decisions'.

Continuing the consideration of individual differences in motivation, the work of David McClelland on 'need for achievement' is one of the most significant.

McCLELLAND'S MANAGERIAL NEEDS

David McClelland (1961) is a prolific researcher and writer, and his theories have been the stimulus for hundreds of studies. The popularity of the theory diminished somewhat in the 1970s, but recently it has been enjoying a revival.

McClelland's basic assumption is that people learn in early childhood that certain behaviour leads to gratification, and hence they develop a need based on this behaviour. There are, he argues, three basic needs: achievement, affiliation, and power. These are usually referred to by the abbreviations *n-Ach*, *n-Aff* and *n-Power* respectively. Originally, McClelland considered n-Ach to be the most important, but in later work the focus has switched to n-Power.

Need for achievement is, according to McClelland, one of the keys to a country's economic growth. Those who have high n-Ach become active entrepreneurs and businessmen and women, whose joint efforts lead to an increase in economic prosperity.

Such individuals want to take personal responsibility, like to take calculated risks, and like immediate feedback on their performance. However, managers high in n-Ach tend to hold fewer meetings than other managers, preferring to work on their own. They also tend to be unresponsive to those around them. The reason is that those high in n-Ach are playing the game single-handed. Goals and standards are internally set, and they are not dependent on another person for approval.

McClelland suggests that when people think in n-Ach terms 'things begin to move fast'. Because needs are learnt in childhood, he and his colleagues have examined the n-Ach content in children's and popular literature from many countries and over many years. This literature should give a good indication of the values that society considers desirable. His results suggested a strong relationship between their n-Ach content and macro-economic performance. For example, in terms of n-Ach content, Britain in 1925 ranked fifth amongst 25 countries. By 1950 it had dropped to 27th out of 39.

McClelland suggests that n-Ach is encouraged by parents who set moderately high achievement goals for their children, but who are warm, encouraging, and non-authoritarian in helping them achieve these goals. He also claims that it can be encouraged in adults through appropriate training courses.

Need for affiliation. In the course of his early work, McClelland found that some of the major figures in industry did not, as he had first expected, score highly on n-Ach. He reasoned that, at this level within large organizations, goals are achieved by co-ordinating the activities of others rather than by individual effort alone. What appears to be the major requirement in these circumstances is the ability to *relate* to other people. Those who have this need are said to be high in n-Aff. Managers with high n-Aff strive for approval, both from their subordinates and their superiors. High n-Affs are sensitive to the needs of others.

Latterly, however, it has been suggested that there are two forms of n-Aff, one more managerially effective than the other. The two forms are *affiliative assurance* and *affiliative interest*. Affiliative assurance is a striving for close relationships, basically because of the security that they bring. Such an individual tends to look for approval and is anxious about possible rejection. An interest in close relationships because of the support they offer means that energy is concentrated on maintaining relationships. This expenditure will be at the expense of getting the job done. In addition, the manager high in affiliative assurance would rather hang on to team members than see them promoted. For these reasons, those high in affiliative assurance may not be suited to some managerial jobs.

Affiliative interest, on the other hand, is expressed as an interest in the feelings of others, but not at the expense of getting the job done. It is a 'concern' for the legitimate needs and feelings of others. This, it is argued, is the type of n-Aff which will lead to greater organizational effectiveness.

While the combination of n-Ach and n-Aff explains the low n-Ach of some major figures in industry and commerce, there were still circumstances that it could not explain. For example, McClelland found that n-Ach and n-Aff did not explain why people became leaders, rather than managers.

Need for power. Those with high n-Ach and high n-Aff still had problems of leadership, power, and social influence with which they could not cope. What was needed was something to get people to work together. This he termed the power motive. McClelland recognized that a need for power was often seen as socially undesirable, but why? There appears to be a 'love–hate' reaction to power. This, he suggests, is because power has two faces, one positive, the other negative. Negatively, it is an unsocialized concern for personal dominance at the expense of others.

More positively, it shows itself as an interest in persuasion and interpersonal influence.

Once again, this need is learnt during childhood socialization. The original source of power is physical; the older child has power over others because of his or her greater strength. This exercise of power often leads to positive outcomes, which also leads to positive feelings of accomplishment in the child. As socialization of the child continues, such physical dominance is normally discouraged and the need becomes channelled into more socially acceptable routes of social influence. The extent of this re-direction will vary from child to child. Some parents may not inhibit expressions of personal dominance in their children; others may. According to McClelland, the level of such activity inhibition will determine which of the two types of need for power predominates. Those high in activity inhibition will satisfy their need for power in socially acceptable ways, for example through interpersonal influencing skills.

Research suggests that people high in n-Power hold more offices, and seek occupations of influence. If they are low in activity inhibition they tend to have more arguments, and may be impulsively aggressive. Interestingly, it is often thought that great leaders dominate their followers. Research by McClelland, who played tape recordings of speeches by leaders, such as Churchill and Kennedy, to students suggests that this is incorrect. Rather than dominate, these leaders increase their followers' feelings of power. They lead by making others feel that they too have power.

Although this chapter is concerned with motivation, rather than leadership, the two overlap at some points. N-Ach theory is such a point, and it is perhaps worth briefly mentioning the *leadership pattern* of need motivation.

Leadership motivation pattern. Research suggests that successful leaders are high in n-Power, low in n-Aff, but high in activity inhibition. They are high, therefore, on interpersonal influence rather than dominance.

In one large American corporation measures of this leadership pattern were taken for a large number of managers. Follow-up studies some eight and sixteen years later found that managers with this pattern advanced more rapidly than others. The same was also true in a study conducted in the US navy. These findings, however, only applied to non-technical managers. For those in specialist technical jobs, this pattern is not likely to be a predictor of success. Power in these areas seems likely to depend more on knowledge than interpersonal influence.

So far this chapter has been largely concerned with 'what' motivates people. In the theories that follow, we will switch our attention from 'what' motivates, to 'how' they can be motivated, (that is, the process of motivation rather than the content).

EQUITY THEORY

The value of equity theory is that it gives an insight into why people sometimes feel that the organization is not properly rewarding their efforts. It is based on a particular approach to the analysis of human interaction, both within and outside the world of work – that of *social exchange theory*.

Social exchange theory works on two very basic and fundamental premises. First, that individuals will tend to engage in those actions that promise to be most profitable for them in terms of social rewards. On the surface, this would appear to be a very selfish reason for undertaking social interaction and, indeed, it would be, if there were not a second premise – that of reciprocity. It would appear that there is almost a universal norm, common amongst people in all sorts of societies, that interactions have to be approximately equivalent for both parties over a period of time. If they are not, one of the parties will terminate the relationship.

This theory is, perhaps surprisingly, applicable to a wide range of situations – even marriage and friendship. There is considerable evidence to support the premise that, unless each partner gets roughly equivalent rewards (as defined by the person concerned) from the relationship, then it will end, in spirit if not in law. You may wonder what the rewards could possibly be in some partnerships of your acquaintance but, if they are stable, then they will be there. Another influence determining whether the partnership continues will also be the availability of other partnerships offering greater rewards. The balance is, however, complicated by the time spans over which reciprocity has to be established. Long-standing and close relationships can tolerate considerable periods where one partner is continually giving, while the other is only receiving. (In fact, one way to tell when a relationship is under stress is when the time scale over which the 'balance sheet' is balanced shortens. In such situations the participants begin to expect almost immediate repayment of favours done: 'I cut the lawn for you, the least you could do for me is . . . '.)

It will most probably not have escaped your attention that social exchange is very similar to economic exchange. They differ in some respects, but not in what might be thought to be the obvious way – the presence or absence of money. These differences are, in fact, the extent to which they are specific and formal. Economic exchanges, for example, are usually extremely formal and specific. Costs and benefits can be quantified, and equated one to the other. In addition they can be openly discussed and indeed may be made legally enforceable through formal procedures. Social exchanges, on the other hand, are far more complex and diffuse, and are generally not enforceable by law. This is not to say, however, that a form of contract does not informally emerge. There is often an implied 'psychological contract', which may be just as difficult to break.

These two types of exchange are often confused, sometimes deliberately, more often unconsciously. Sales staff, for example, often try to establish social obligations through such techniques as using first names and taking an interest in personal aspects that are unconnected with the sale. This establishes, it is hoped, a feeling that the attention and interest has to be reciprocated, which will, the sales staff hope, make it more difficult for the potential customer to withdraw from the economic part of the exchange. The unconscious confusion of social and economic exchanges often occurs in work situations. As has been pointed out, we go to work for both economic and social reasons; usually the two can be kept separate, but the confusion becomes apparent when difficulties arise. It is often difficult, for example, for managers to discipline those with whom they have a strong personal relationship. The same can sometimes occur when we mix business and pleasure. Doing work on a commercial basis for a friend, or employing a friend, may again bring the two into conflict.

Social exchange theory is a useful way of viewing interactions, but it has its limitations. *Equity theory* is an extension of social exchange theory that is made more general by the addition of two extra concepts. These are *equity ratios* and *investments*.

The main limitation of social exchange theory is the assumption that each party has to gain approximately equal 'absolute' benefits from the exchange. In equity theory, this is modified to state that the benefits of a situation are equitable when their ratio of inputs (e.g. effort) to outputs (e.g. pay) is approximately equal to others in a similar position. To use a rather simple example, someone who works a standard working week does not expect their pay packet to be the same as a fellow worker who also works overtime. If the ratio of inputs to outputs balances, then all is well. If they do not balance, then the individual will experience tension. Tension is uncomfortable, leading the individual to take steps to reduce it. Again using pay as an example, let us see how tension can be reduced. Consider a situation where a person, or group of people, feel underpaid compared to those with whom they compare themselves. In such a situation, there are two obvious, and one not so obvious, ways of restoring the balance. First and most obvious, is to get a pay rise large enough to restore the balance.

Second, if a pay rise is not possible, or is not large enough to restore the balance totally, then another alternative is to reduce the level of effort. The form this reduction will take will depend upon the payment scheme in operation. If the rewards are based upon the number of units produced (i.e. piecework), then it would obviously be counterproductive for the workers to produce fewer. In this case, something will suffer that does not affect wage levels, perhaps quality. If payment is by a time rate (i.e. hourly, weekly, monthly, or an annual salary), then output levels may suffer, or quality, or both. The same applies when the individual or group, rather than feeling underrewarded, feel overrewarded. This, in our experience, is rare! The reason for this can most probably be explained by the third method of restoring balance.

We have said that people compare their ratio of inputs to outputs with other individuals or groups. This begs the question, of course, of which particular individual or group is chosen for comparative purposes, and there are many alternatives. You might, for example, compare yourself with others inside your organization or, alternatively, with those outside the organization in similar jobs. You may also judge yourself against your own work history – 'I've done well compared with where I started'. This choice of individuals or groups against whom we compare ourselves is important, as it will affect our feelings of equity. If we compare our general life situation with the jet set (choose your own example here), we may feel somewhat dejected. If, on the other hand, we compare ourselves with most of the population of the Third World, or, indeed, disadvantaged groups in our own society, different feelings will be evoked about our own position. (Notice we do not say what the particular feelings will be, as these will vary from person to person.) By changing the group to which we refer, that is our *reference group*, we can move ourselves into or out of balance. The third way of restoring balance, therefore, is to change the reference group to one that produces a balance. This may often be overtly used in pay negotiations – 'Ah, but look how well you are doing compared with . . . ', which the other side often counters by choosing a less favourable example.

Research into which reference groups people choose suggests that the most important ones are those in the same, or similar, occupations in the 'market' as a whole. The ability of the employing organization to pay, and the individual's productive contribution to that organization, appear to play a negligible role in determining the perceived equity of rates of pay. This perhaps explains why workers in loss-making companies make wage claims that appear, to outsiders, not to be justified by the relevant performance indicators. There are, however, some exceptions to individuals' choice of reference groups. In particular, those who are, in general, 'satisfied' with their organization, tend to compare themselves with others in the organization, rather than with those in the same occupation in different companies.

We have talked a lot about equity, but, if equity is based purely on a comparison between 'effort put in' and 'benefits taken out', there are situations where we all appear to accept apparent inequities. Most shop-floor workers, for example, do not see the difference between what they get paid for a week's work and what a professional gets paid for a week's work as necessarily inequitable. Why? The answer lies in the second addition to exchange theory, that of *investments*.

Investments has a very similar meaning in equity theory to that in economics in which an investment is something that has a value, and hence a return on that value is expected. Investments in equity theory are not as easy to quantify however, in that they can be anything that people think is an investment. Some of these are almost universally accepted, about others there is much disagreement. Let us take one example of each.

A widely accepted investment is qualifications and skills. The fact that someone has invested time and effort in obtaining them, means that they have investment value. Indeed, to obtain most qualifications, people have to forego immediate financial rewards for rewards in the future.

Consider, on the other hand, the position of someone who has been 'passed over' for promotion. Such an individual may claim as investments things that those responsible for the decision may not accept. For example, an investment that is often claimed is that of long service – 'I've given my life to this company, and this is how they repay me!'. Many arguments concerning perceived inequity revolve around agreement as to what counts as an investment, and how great its value is.

What implications does equity theory have for managers? Because feelings of overreward are relatively uncommon, equity theory is most useful for demotivation situations. In such situations, its value is as a diagnostic aid, identifying the ratios and investments concerned. Recent research by Miriam Dornstein into reference groups gives some insight into why some groups of worker make wage demands that the organization obviously cannnot afford. Rather than comparing themselves with people in different jobs in the same organization, it appears that most of those in Dornstein's study compared themselves with those in similar jobs in different organizations, and with wage rates in the 'market' in general. Wage demands are based, therefore, on general market conditions and what is happening to wages in similar jobs elsewhere rather than the organization's profitability.

Equity theory is useful in understanding possible dissatisfaction, but what positive steps can be taken to increase motivation? There are two possible approaches: goal setting and management by objectives.

GOAL SETTING AND MANAGEMENT BY OBJECTIVES

These two theories are similar in some respects, though management by objectives (MBO) is most probably better known to managers. We will deal with goal setting first as it could be said to form part of MBO.

Goal-setting theory is at present one of the most influential theories of motivation, at least for academics, yet it is based upon fundamentally simple assumptions. The name most commonly associated with it is that of Ed Locke. According to Locke (Locke and Latham, 1984), the widespread assumption that in order to improve job performance you need to improve job satisfaction, is the wrong way round. Satisfaction comes from achieving specific goals. In addition, the harder these goals are, the greater the effort and subsequent satisfaction. There is considerable evidence to support these contentions, but first, how does goal setting work?

First, it has the effect of directing people's attention towards the task involved. This also, of course, has the effect of removing uncertainty as to what precisely is expected of them. Second, having had their attention directed, they then have to seek appropriate methods to get the task done. When the task is clear and precise it is possible to rule out a large number of alternative strategies and concentrate on those most directly relevant. Finally, goal setting mobilizes and maintains effort. According to Locke, this is how goal setting has its effect. The fundamental, and basically simple, assumption behind the theory is, that people will do what they say they will do, and then they will strive hard to do it!

Goal setting appears to many managers to be little more than applied common sense, but let us look a little closer. Within the description of why goal setting works, lies another suggestion about the effectiveness of goal setting that is borne out by a mass of evidence. That is, the more specifically the goal is stated, the more positive the effects. Goals along the lines of 'do your best' cannot be, and are not, effective in directing attention and choosing appropriate strategies. The more specific the goal, the better.

But what of the perceived difficulty of the task? The theory would seem to suggest that the more difficult the task, the higher the effort invested in trying to achieve it. But are there no bounds to this? Research shows that the only limits are that the goal has to be accepted by the person concerned. The way in which such commitment to the goal is achieved is still under active investigation, but there are some pointers.

Participation in goal setting. It is not unusual for goals, especially at managerial level, to be set in conjunction with the person concerned. Most studies show, somewhat surprisingly, that the person's commitment is generally unaffected by this participation. Participation is, however, a rather wide term. What precisely does it involve? A chat where the subordinate's views are politely listened to, or a genuine sharing of the decision making?

Studies appear to show that two considerations are in the subordinate's mind concerning the goal which determine whether he or she will accept it: what are their subjective expectancies of success, and what is the value of that success, either in material or psychological terms? Participation may generate commitment in two ways – by convincing the person that they can do the task and that it is worth doing. For these reasons, it has been found that goals that are merely assigned, without any discussion, are still better than no goals at all. It is likely that, in these cases, the individuals concerned already believe that they can succeed, and that the pay-offs are obvious. Money is an obvious and tangible example of a pay-off, but it is not the money itself that leads to increased effort. It is the achievement of the goal that is the crucial factor. Money has an effect, in that it may lead to hard goals being accepted and/or higher levels of commitment.

Feedback. So far nothing has been said about letting people know how close they are to achieving their goal – in other words *feedback*. It has been shown that feedback by itself can lead to higher levels of performance, as does goal setting by itself. The two together are more powerful still. Feedback allows people to plot their own performances. However it does not have a significant effect on those who are 'on target', rather it leads to increased efforts by those who are falling short.

This, in summary is *goal-setting theory*. Its message is simple. Set specific, hard goals that people believe they can achieve and that will provide them with a benefit, either tangible or psychological. In addition, provide feedback as to how they are progressing. As we have said before, it sounds simple, but in our experience it is rarely implemented. This is supported by the reported experiences of many hundreds of managers on courses we have run. With few exceptions, managers at all levels claim that their goals are not clear, and that their boss never tells them how they are doing. And if this feeling is as universal as our experiences suggest, their subordinates would say exactly the same about them!

Many managers will have noticed the similarity between Locke's goal setting and Peter Drucker's management by objectives (1954). As some commentators have said, MBO is as desirable as 'the flag, motherhood and apple pie'. but the evidence for its long-term effectiveness is largely anecdotal. Many schemes have been implemented, but few have a long life. The reasons for this are not entirely clear. Our suspicion is that one reason why the schemes fail has to do with the specificity of the 'objectives'. Too often objectives are set that, whilst apparently specific, are not actually so. They are too broad, such as 'increase profit margins by X per cent'. The problem with such an objective is that the many ways of achieving it mean that effort is dispersed. In addition, factors may influence the goal that are not under the control of the person involved, hence responsibility is diffused. The result is that the system becomes discredited and gradually falls into disuse. Perhaps the initial emphasis in any goal-setting or MBO system is to get goals that are *specific* – 'develop a scheme to reduce the processing time of routine orders in your department from five days to three days!'.

The next theory to be considered developed separately from goal setting, and has different explanations for behaviour. Nevertheless, in recent years links have developed between the two that make them a powerful combination.

ORGANIZATIONAL BEHAVIOUR MODIFICATION

Before going further, you should turn to Appendix 3 and read the case study on absenteeism.

The basic postulate of organizational behaviour modifcation (OBMod) can be stated very simply – so simply that some may say it is just applied common sense. It is that behaviour is determined by its consequences. In other words, people learn to behave in ways that produce rewards, and avoid behaving in ways that either produce no rewards or even punishment. Inevitably managers will already be using some of the techniques that will be discussed, but without understanding their theoretical background. By providing a theoretical structure, we will enable managers to make more effective use of the techniques.

OBMod is based on the work of psychologists who studied learning or, to use the technical term, *conditioning*. In particular, the names most frequently associated with the theory are those of Thorndike and, perhaps most commonly, Skinner. Skinner takes the approach that since we cannot observe such mental states as attitudes and personality traits, we should concern ourselves only with observable behaviour. If we extend this to the work situation, what managers should be concerned with is not employees' attitudes, but how they behave (i.e. what they *do*). It is often difficult to get managers to talk only of behaviour. They often, quite understandably, slip into talking about personalities and attitudes. But employees' attitudes are not our concern, as long as they are behaving correctly. Organizations do not pay people for the attitudes they hold, but for their behaviour. As such we are perfectly justified in asking someone to behave differently. We are not justified in trying to change their personality or attitudes, even if we could! As with goal setting, however, the behaviour must be described as precisely as possible.

We have said that behaviour is determined by its consequences. How can these be classified? The possible range is shown below:

▶ We receive something nice.
▶ Something nasty is taken away.
▶ Something nice is taken away.
▶ Something nasty is given.

The first two consequences will lead to an increase in the behaviour that preceded them. To use the correct technical term, they are *reinforcers*, because they reinforce the behaviour concerned. The first, giving something nice, is called positive reinforcement. The second is called negative reinforcement, because something nasty is taken away. The last two are different forms of punishment. They will tend to suppress the behaviour that occurs before them.

All of these may be neatly summarized in a diagram, as shown in Figure 10. There is one outcome, however, that will not fit into the diagram, that is, if the behaviour is neither rewarded nor punished. This will lead to the behaviour is neither rewarded nor punished. This will lead to the behaviour not being repeated.

Most managers, we find, are fairly happy with positive reinforcement, but negative reinforcement is not as clear. Let us take an example from parenthood. We find it unpleasant when a baby cries. If, by picking the

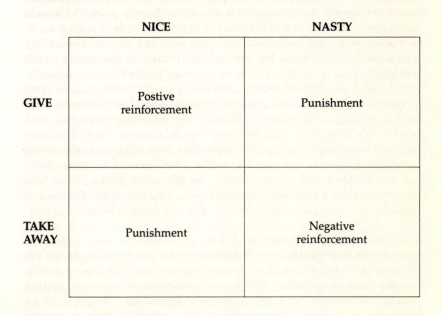

	NICE	**NASTY**
GIVE	Postive reinforcement	Punishment
TAKE AWAY	Punishment	Negative reinforcement

FIGURE 10. *Typology of reinforcers*

baby up, we stop it crying, we will pick it up again next time it cries. Stopping the cries negatively reinforces our action of picking the baby up, as it stops the nastiness. Note that, from the baby's point of view, being picked up is nice and hence the crying is positively reinforced. Next time the baby wants to be picked up, it will cry.

Now that the range of possible consequences has been described, let us consider how effective each one can be at influencing behaviour. This is where, in some respects, common sense and psychology part company. But we think you will agree, after considering what we have to say, that psychology is the more accurate of the two.

The effectiveness of each of the consequences is largely determined by how frequently it follows, or does not follow, each occurrence of the behaviour. These patterns of how frequently behaviour is rewarded or punished are called *schedules*.

How to maintain new behaviour. If we are trying to get someone to learn a new behaviour then it is appropriate to reinforce their successful attempts every time they occur; but what about maintaining behaviour that has already been learnt? Consider a schedule that has already been learnt, where, behaviour is rewarded, let us say, every 20 times it occurs. For example, pulling a lever to obtain a reward. If this mechanism were switched off, how quickly would you realize there was no point in pulling the lever any more? Probably after about 20 further pulls. Now consider a situation where the reward occurs *on average* after every twenty pulls. The reward could be on the next pull of the lever or many hundreds of pulls later. To determine when this mechanism had been switched off would take a very long time indeed. This is the principle, of course, of one-armed bandit machines. This is also why you keep being trapped by the company 'bore'. You have only to produce a reward by paying attention once every so often and he or she will continue to pester you. This is called *variable ratio reinforcement*, and is far more effective in maintaining behaviour, even undesirable behaviour, than reinforcement that occurs every time (fixed ratio reinforcement). The person knows that their behaviour will pay off some time so they keep trying. (As well as fixed and variable ratios, there can also be fixed and variable times. The effects are similar; fixed time reinforcement is a relatively ineffective way of maintaining behaviour. It remains, of course, the most common way of paying salaries.)

How to stop undesirable behaviour. What are the options open to us if we now try to stop undesirable behaviour? The strategies available are those of punishment and non-reward. Notice here that non-reward is not the same as ignoring. Non-reward means that the person gets no benefit whatsoever as a result of their behaviour. Which of these strategies, non-reward or punishment, do you think is likely to be more effective in changing behaviour?

All the evidence suggests that non-reward leads to behaviour being 'extinguished'; punishment merely suppresses it. This is not to say that punishment is never effective. Punishment, by itself, can be effective under certain conditions. (When reading further it might be interesting to think of the ways that society tries to suppress crime.) The conditions under which punishment is effective are when:

- The behaviour is punished immediately after it occurs.

- The behaviour is punished every time it occurs.

Contrast these stringent requirements with the variable ratio reinforcement schedule that is keeping the undesirable behaviour going.

Assuming that it were possible to punish behaviour very soon after it occurred, and every time, how strong should the punishment be? When used by itself, the evidence suggests that it should be moderately harsh. Both mild and harsh punishment have their drawbacks. Very harsh punishment raises anxiety levels so high that it interferes with the process of learning the alternative, desirable, behaviour. On the other hand, if the punishment is mild, people get used to it.

As an example of how organizations attempt to use punishment, take the example of an individual's persistent lateness. One method commonly used is the memo, as when a memo pointing out the requirements for strict time-keeping is sent to everyone, including the culprit. This may affect the culprit's behaviour for a short time, but he or she will then start re-offending. The other effect it will have is on those who are innocent, who may arrive late on occasions but do not abuse the system, and compensate by working into their lunch break. These individuals will rebel, often by working strictly to the clock.

The other common method is when each incidence of bad time-keeping is not commented on, but is left until an unacceptable number have accumulated. The punishment then escalates very gradually, from verbal to written warnings and then to formal dismissal procedures. Under these circumstances, punishment is unlikely to be effective. For it to be so, the individual needs to be made aware that each and every incidence will be questioned as soon as it occurs, and that moderate sanctions will be applied. (Very harsh sanctions would most probably lead to avoidance through absenteeism.)

So far, we have been considering the effects of punishment alone. Most effective, however, is when punishment for the undesirable behaviour is coupled with reinforcement of the desired behaviour. Under such circumstances, the punishment does not have to fulfil the requirements above; even mild and infrequent punishment will be effective. Just raised eyebrows from a boss who uses reinforcement effectively will be enough to discourage unwanted behaviour.

Before leaving punishment, here are a couple of further examples where it is ineffective. Hangovers rarely teach people a lesson once their ill-effects have subsided. This is because the punishment is delayed too long for the inebriated brain to realize its inevitability. In the light of this theory, we believe that an advertising campaign stressing the dangers of contracting AIDS through casual sex is not likely to be as effective as it could be. It warns of punishment some years hence, to be considered at a time when reason is not at its strongest! It might be better to find some way of showing that the use of condoms is sexy – the reinforcers in this situation are apparent.

Now that we have dealt with the basic concepts of organizational behaviour modification, it is worth mentioning some of its possible applications. One nice example of the difference between fixed ratio and variable ratio reinforcement is one that will be immediately applicable – if you want to improve the productivity of beaver trappers! A group of beaver trappers working in Canadian forests were given $1 bonus for every beaver skin. Another, similar group were given the chance to roll dice each time they brought in a skin. If they rolled two successive odd numbers they got $4. The cost of each of the schemes was the same. Productivity in the first group rose by 50 per cent, in the latter group by 108 per cent.

Another area in which OBMod has been used is in dealing with absenteeism and lateness. At this point you should turn to your suggestions for solving the problem at Chestnut hospital (Appendix 3). We suspect that you will have adopted a *medical* model (no pun intended) in trying to solve the problem. Such a model sees absenteeism as a symptom of some underlying problem. The assumption is that absenteeism is a symptom of dissatisfaction with some aspect, or aspects, of the job. The solution, therefore, is to improve job satisfaction. This may, indeed, have some impact, but there is often a limit to what can be done in improving satisfaction. Shift work still needs to be worked, and many other 'dirty', and undesirable, jobs need to be done. In addition, the rewards for staying away from work are powerful, and rarely capable of being influenced by management.

OBMod, on the other hand, looks not at the *influences* that are thought to underlie absenteeism, but rather at the *consequences* to the employee of attendance or non-attendance. It adopts a *direct action* model. Let us consider some possibilities.

Some schemes have used reinforcement as an alternative. One such example was reported from a factory in Liverpool. The factory was to be closed and the production lines transferred to another part of the country. The workers were under notice of redundancy, but it was essential that production be maintained until the new factory was in production. Unfortunately, the factory was suffering absenteeism levels of 30 per cent and above, due to a 'mystery virus' that appeared to strike mainly on Mondays and Fridays. Because of the law relating to redundancy, pay could not be stopped for these absences. In order to improve attendance, management instituted a weekly prize draw of £500. Participation in the draw was by means of tickets. Employees received a draw ticket whenever they arrived at work on time. Absenteeism dropped to very low levels and the management reported that workers were even turning up on their days off in order to collect tickets. Other schemes have used a cash bonus, paid to every employee who had attended on a number of randomly selected days during a set period – the random choice of days provided the variable ratio.

These further examples demonstrate one of the conditions under which such reinforcement works best. This is the expenditure of a little additional investment on the part of the individual, together with the potential for a large payout – for example, football pools and premium bonds. Indeed, the use of prize draws is widely used as a marketing technique.

Some managers object to such schemes on the basis that you are paying people extra to do what they are already being paid to do. This is a perfectly legitimate position to take. If, however, you have tried everything else, what do you do? Your principles may also have a cost – continued high levels of absenteeism.

REINFORCERS

So far, we have a major assumption about the nature of reinforcers – that everybody's reinforcers are the same. Some reinforcers are, indeed, almost universal. Money is a good example. It is universal, because it can be exchanged for other things that people want. If, however, the pay-off were a night at the opera, how would you feel? Different people will have different reactions. Some reinforcers are difficult for others to understand. For example, adolescent daughters often get reinforcement from 'winding up' their mothers. The parents find this difficult to understand, as they feel that by shouting at their children and sending them to their room they are punishing them. It may also pay off because, when such arguments occur, real issues can be avoided. (This is Uproar in TA terms – see page 25.)

To take an example from contemporary British society, what are the reinforcers for football hooligans? The only method of accurately determining this is to remove potential reinforcers. When the behaviour stops, you have found the key. We can, however, speculate as to what they might be. It is quite likely that group approval is involved. As we will see later, social rewards are amongst the strongest reinforcers known. The disapproval of society may also be a potential reinforcer. For some, appearing in court or in the papers is reinforcing – much as the adolescent and parent situation described above. Given that these are some of the potential reinforcers, what can society do about it? As we have seen, punishment, especially when it fulfils the conditions of immediacy and consistency described earlier, is most probably impossible. We may be able to remove some of the reinforcers, for example, press coverage. In recent disturbances in Germany involving British supporters, the 'riots' received more coverage in the British media than in the German. Another method is to change the hooligans' perception of what is reinforcing. We will return to this shortly.

A nice example of the removal of reinforcers was recently reported by Merseyside police. They used to concentrate upon catching those who were stealing car stereo equipment, with little effect. Then they switched their strategy to that of identifying those cars whose owners might have purchased stolen stereos. They examined parked cars, looking for incongruities, for example, an old car with a highly priced modern stereo, and then contacted the owners for an explanation. As soon as it became known that this was happening, the market for stolen stereos declined sharply.

It is very common, in fact, to find organizations actually rewarding the very behaviour they say they wish to discourage. Some, for example, give annual budgets to departments. If the money is not all spent then it is reclaimed by the centre and next year's budget is cut. As the manager of such a department what do you logically do in these circumstances – you spend up to your budget limit!

There are also however, organizations which use positive reinforcement effectively, perhaps without knowing the terminology involved. One of them employs tanker drivers to deliver hazardous liquids and gasses, which are transferred through complicated valves and pipes from their tankers to the customers' tanks. Drivers who phone for advice receive a bonus each time they do so. It might be thought that this would encourage them to phone for trivial reasons and, indeed, the system may be open to some abuse. Consider however, the situation that may often occur where workers are discouraged from asking, usually because they fear some form of punishment, even if only ridicule. Which costs would the company rather bear – some trivial requests for advice, or a tanker exploding in a city street?

Two other examples are from organizations which most probably are aware of the theoretical background of their policy. Both are large American companies – Xerox and American Airlines. At Xerox, 'X' certificates, redeemable for $25, were introduced into the personnel department. Every member of the department, not just managers, can give Xs to others. They may be given for any work-related behaviour, for example excellent attendance or co-operation. They may also be given to people in other departments. At American Airlines, passengers are given coupons that they may give to staff who they feel deserve some recognition.

A final example concerns the problems associated with routine maintenance procedures. All the employees' rewards and punishments are geared to encourage shortcuts: if a part is not checked, it will most probably be all right anyway, and the mechanic saves time right now. In addition, they have no reinforcer to encourage them to carry out the checks as specified. If something does eventually go wrong, then what evidence is there to refute the claim that 'it seemed all right when checked'? The evidence of successive reports by the consumer magazine *Which?* on the quality of car servicing by garages lends strong support to our analysis.

SOCIAL LEARNING THEORY

Before reading further, complete the career questionnaire in Appendix 4.

In recent years some theorists, in particular Albert Bandura (1977) and Walter Mischel (1986), have extended learning theory to take account of some behaviours that could not previously be explained. For example, when joining a new company we do not attempt to find out what the norms are about timekeeping by arriving five minutes later each day until someone in authority objects. Rather, we observe what behaviour in others is rewarded or punished. In other words, we learn vicariously, by watching other people. We assume that if we follow their examples, we will reap the same rewards, and avoid punishment. In Bandura's terms, we model our behaviour on theirs. Under these conditions, our behaviour is influenced not by the immediate consequences, but by our *expectancies* of the consequences. These expectancies mean that we are not merely pawns waiting for the rewards or punishments associated with behaviour, rather that we can influence the situation as well as the situation influencing us. For example, the way punishment is most commonly used is not by direct application, but by the use of threats. These threats can be either avoided, or escaped from. It is our expectancies of punishment that are influencing our behaviour, rather than the punishment itself.

Modelling, we suspect, not only applies to behaviour itself but also to what people will value as reinforcers. For example, peer approval is a very powerful reinforcer. It someone with whom a person can identify is seen achieving rewards through a particular behaviour, not only will the behaviour be copied but the associated consequences will also acquire value. Advertisers are very aware of this fact. This is why they use 'personalities' to endorse their products. Another way of influencing the behaviour of football hooligans, therefore, may be to change the perceived value of their current reinforcers, using 'opinion leaders'. Everyone's reinforcers change over time – think of how you used to behave as an adolescent (if it's not too painful). Setting an example, especially if the example is reinforced, can often be an effective way of changing behaviour.

The other concept that Bandura has introduced is the concept of self-regulation. We have already said that people are influenced by vicarious, as well as direct, consequences, but there is another source of consequences which may be overlooked. These are self-administered consequences. We all set standards, by which we judge our own behaviour. Thus, we can either reward or punish ourselves for our actions. The way in which we acquire such standards is also learnt through modelling. Children from families where high standards are set will tend to adopt such standards themselves. It is not unusual for people, when offered a reward for what others consider to be a good performance, to turn it down, or delay it until they reach the standard that they themselves have set. These different sources may be best illustrated if we deal with punishment. Unpleasantness is the result of direct punishment. Vicarious punishment leads to fear, while self-administered punishment leads to feelings of guilt.

More recently, Bandura has introduced another self-regulatory concept into the theory, that of *self-efficacy*. Self-efficacy is the individual's belief as to their ability to achieve the results they desire. We have mentioned before the effects of expectancies, in particular the expectancies associated with the consequences of behaviour (i.e. whether it will be rewarded or punished). Self-efficacy, on the other hand, is an expectancy associated with the ability and skills necessary to perform that behaviour. A lot of Bandura's work in this area was in clinical settings (Bandura, 1982). He found, for example, that there was a strong relationship between a person's recovery from the effects of a heart attack, and their own belief in their ability to recover.

This concept most probably has its roots in the work of Julian Rotter (1966) on the locus of control of reinforcement. Rotter suggested that people differed in the extent to which they believed they had control of the reinforcers in their lives. In particular, they could be either *internals* or *externals*. The former believe that their reinforcers lie largely within their own control, the latter that, no matter what they do, the control of reinforcers lies externally and is due to such influences as chance or the influence of powerful other people.

At this point you should work out your final score for the career questionnaire (Appendix 4) and compare it with those of other managers, details of which are provided on page 197.

The questionnaire was developed by one of the authors in order to measure locus of control in a specific area – career development. A more general questionnaire was developed by Rotter, and a large number of studies have been carried out using it. In general, the findings are that internals are more successful than externals. In one well-known study (Anderson, 1977), a group of small businessmen in America, whose businesses had been destroyed by a hurricane, were followed over a period of years. The internals recovered from this disaster far better than the externals.

If you think back to attribution theory (see pages 18–22), you will recall the effect that attribution of causality has on our perception of other people. In some respects self-efficacy and locus of control are concerned with how we attribute causality for ourselves. It is apparent that our own beliefs about our abilities, together with our expectations about their consequences, have a considerable influence on our performance.

IMPLEMENTING THE THEORIES

It may have occurred to you that some of the concepts of goal-setting theory, behaviour modification theory, and social learning theory (SLT) have common elements. Goal setting, in SLT terms, is the generation of expectancies. Indeed, self-efficacy has recently been incorporated into goal-setting theory by Locke (Locke *et al.*, 1984), who sees it as an important addition. Reinforcers also appear in all three, although they differ as to the reasons for their beneficial effects.

What then are the implications of these two influential theories? To reiterate from goal-setting theory, managers should:

☐ Set specific goals.
☐ Set hard goals.
☐ Set goals that the person believes they can achieve.
☐ Provide feedback.

To this we can now add that they should also:

☐ Ensure that desired behaviours are reinforced.
☐ Ensure that undesired behaviours are punished or not rewarded.
☐ Use variable ratio reinforcement to maintain desired behaviours.

Reinforcers. The problem remains, of course, as to what we, as managers, can use as reinforcers.

Before reading further, try making a list of what reinforcers you have under your control that you can use. Look back to your list of what motivated you for some suggestions. Remember that this has to be a tentative list. As we mentioned before, what is a reward for one individual will not be for another. Some people like attending courses. The fun of spending time away from home at company expense tends, in our experience, to fade with familiarity. In psychological jargon, they 'satiate'.

Your list of possible reinforcers will obviously be unique to you. Some managers have control over merit awards and promotion. Most, especially in large organizations, have a more limited influence. However, there will be two that should appear on most managers' lists that are very powerful.

The most powerful reinforcers are *social*. Our own self-image can only be sustained, in the long term, if it is accepted by others. Thus, it is to others that we turn for our rewards. This applies to even those individuals who appear impervious to the praise or punishment of others. For them, the individual or group from whom they obtain their rewards are not the current ones. As you will recall from SLT, we can reward or punish ourselves internally, but this will not last forever. The internal rewards need confirmation every so often from real people.

Within the work situation *praise* is used far less effectively than it might be. Variable ratio reinforcement suggests that praise should not be used on every occasion; indeed, if over-used it will eventually lose some of its value. This being said, the evidence is that it is hardly used at all. Why is this? A survey amongst managers suggested a number of reasons. Some took the view that it was inappropriate – their employees were already being well paid for what they did. For the majority, however, it was the embarrassment of giving praise. It is somehow 'not macho'. Many, however, thought that they already did give praise. Over 80 per cent of managers in one organization claimed they praised their employees for work well done. The researchers then asked those employees about the praise. Only 14 per cent said their manager actually gave praise. Another reason for not giving praise is that we tend to 'manage by exception'. We shout and complain when things go wrong (the exception), but do we praise when things are going routinely well? Compare the number of times you have complained, for example in shops, to the council, or to other managers, with the number of times you have written complimenting them when they have been particularly helpful.

Praise is a very powerful reinforcer, especially when used on a variable schedule. This schedule should not be random, (i.e. the occasional praise for 'work in general'). It should be specific, and very clear to the person which part of their behaviour is being praised. Many organizations, Xerox and NCR to name but two, are now recognizing that training managers in the appropriate use of praise and recognition has considerable value.

The other reinforcer is less obvious. An American student, who was working her way through college, made some timings of the average length of time various tasks took in the store where she worked. These timings were averaged across a number of people. Table 2 shows two columns of figures indicating the length of time taken to do various tasks under two different situations. As you will see, it took 50 per cent longer to complete the tasks in situation B than in situation A. What reinforcers do you think might have been used to obtain the increase in productivity indicated by the shorter times? Neither praise, money, nor any other tangible inducements were involved.

TABLE 2. *Job timings under two different situations (from O'Brien, Dickinson and Rosow, 1982)*

Task	Timings in minutes	
	A	B
Stock sweet shelves	20	35
Stock cigarette shelves	5	15
Vacuum floor	5	15
Dump rubbish	5	10
Clean store	45	90
Check in orders	30	60
Help pharmacist	50	60
Deliver orders	50	60
Totals	210	345

Many of your suggestions might have produced the desired effect, we cannot be sure. It is unlikely that many of you will have found the actual cause. The only difference was that in column A, a nice job was known to be following a nasty job, while in column B a nasty job was known to follow the nice one. To modify Parkinson's law, work expands so as to fill the time available for its completion, but only when the work that follows is worse!

This phenomenon is known as the Premack principle, after David Premack who first observed it in animals. Put generally, more likeable jobs can be used to reinforce less likeable ones. Unfortunately, most of us work the other way round. We put off doing those jobs we dislike, finding another job to do in their place. *Work scheduling*, therefore, has considerable potentialities as a reinforcer. In addition it shows what we hope has been implicit all along, that these techniques can be used to change our own behaviour, as well as that of others.

Finally, some of these techniques may be seen as manipulative. We believe they should be used openly. As was stressed earlier, we are buying and selling behaviour. In doing so, we can be open with the contract – this is what I want you to do, how do you want to be rewarded?

Let us finish with a fairly light-hearted example. Some time ago the *Guardian* newspaper picked up a report of the use of BMod in a clinical setting. A wife had developed an aversion such that she could not bear her husband even to touch her, even though she still loved him. She was also, it transpired, extremely fond of Polo mints. The psychologists involved developed a reinforcement schedule which involved the husband using the mints, over a period of time, to reinforce more and more intimate behaviour. Full conjugal relations were finally restored. The *Guardian*, true to form, speculated as to whether the situation could be reversed, in order to get someone who disliked Polos to like them!

3

Leadership and Management Style

(Before reading further you should turn to Appendix 5 and complete the questionnaire on your leadership style.)

BORN TO LEAD?

When considering leadership, many people begin by recalling those individuals who are, or were, what they thought of as a great leader. Many names come to mind, such as Churchill, Mahatma Gandi, or Martin Luther King. (We have chosen dead leaders so as not to be considered guilty of sins of either omission or commission in our choice of contemporary leaders.) All appear to be charismatic, to have something about them that makes them stand out from others, to be 'great men'. But does this mean that all good leaders have to be charismatic?

Some would argue that Attlee was an extremely effective post-war leader, yet Churchill once described him as 'a modest man with much to be modest about'. To redress the balance, let us allow Attlee to speak through the words of his own poem.

Few thought he was even a starter,
there were many who thought themselves smarter,
but he ended PM, CH, and OM,
an Earl and a Knight of the Garter.

If leaders are what we would call great men or women, are there any particular traits that can be identified as being associated with effective leadership?

Many traits have been examined, but few show any relationship to successful leadership. One possible exception is intelligence. According to researchers there is some relationship, although it would appear to be a curvilinear, rather than a straight line relationship. In other words, while leadership ability increases with increasing intelligence, it does so only up to a certain point, beyond which higher levels of intelligence lead to decreased leadership ability. Alistair Cooke has, for example, suggested that Jimmy Carter was probably the most intelligent post-war president of the USA. He was not the most effective, according to Cooke, because instead of seeing both sides of any situation, he saw 23 sides!

Some have suggested that great leaders have a need to dominate but, as was seen in the previous chapter, great leaders have their effect by increasing their followers' feelings of power, not by subjugating them. Many other traits have been examined, but the evidence is mixed, often because the traits measured are themselves woolly and ill-defined (for example that of 'initiative').

Why are the traits associated with leadership so hard to find? Perhaps some of the reasons lie in the old saying 'some leaders are born, some are made, and some have leadership thrust upon them'. In the latter category might be placed Rajiv Gandi. Gandi was perfectly happy to pursue his career as an airline pilot until the death of his elder brother. At this point he was propelled, by all accounts reluctantly, into the forefront of Indian politics.

Rather than seek the secrets of leadership through the traits that people possess, researchers shifted their studies to what leaders, in particular managers *do*, that is, what are the behaviours associated with leadership?

BEHAVIOURAL APPROACHES

Two major studies into behaviour have made their impact upon leadership theory. Both were undertaken at American universities, and both by teams of researchers, rather than by individuals. (For this reason they are usually referred to by the names of the universities, Ohio and Michigan, although the name of Rensis Likert is often linked with the latter.)

The Ohio study took a large number of possible descriptions of the behaviour of leaders and grouped them into twelve broad categories (e.g. communication). These were then reduced to 130 single descriptions of behaviours that were put into questionnaire format. By administering the questionnaire to a large number of people, they were able to subject their results to *factor analysis*, the same statistical technique used by Cattell to identify source traits. The results of this analysis suggested that all the behaviours fell into four distinct factors or dimensions. The two most useful dimensions have been given many different, though related, names over the intervening period. The correct titles are *consideration* and *initiating structure*, but the more common names are 'people orientation' and 'task orientation'. These descriptions will be used interchangeably. The two dimensions are independent, hence an individual may be high or low on either or both. Although people may change their behaviour, the theory suggests that individuals have a preferred style, with which they feel comfortable.

Someone who is high on the consideration dimension behaves in ways which foster the establishment and maintenance of good interpersonal relations. There is usually rapport between the leader and group members, together with mutual feelings of warmth and trust. Someone high on initiating structure is more concerned with getting the job done than interpersonal warmth. Such a leader behaves in ways which lead to well-defined communication channels and co-ordination.

As we have said, these two dimensions are independent and hence by combining the two, one can produce a diagram upon which various leadership styles can be plotted. Figure 11 shows the diagram, together with some brief descriptions of the various preferred styles. Research suggests that those who are high on task (initiating structure) are perceived as effective, while those high on person (consideration) are seen as providing a pleasant and satisfying work environment. These dimensions have been used as the basis for many managerial applications, perhaps best known of which is the Managerial Grid, developed by Robert Blake and Jane Mouton (1964).

What effect does each of the dimensions have on morale? Studies by Ed Fleishman (Fleishman and Harris, 1962) suggest that employee turnover and grievance levels go up as task orientation increases, but down

High

| Country Club Management | | Team Management |

Dampened Management
(firm but fair)

| Impoverished Management | | Task Management |

Low   High

TASK ORIENTATION

FIGURE 11. *Leadership dimensions (from Blake and Mouton, 1964)*

as person orientation increases. There appears to be a trade-off between the two, so far as morale is concerned. This trade-off is, however, only one way. High person orientation can compensate for high task orientation, but not vice versa.

In real life the requirement to get jobs done means that a high degree of task orientation is required, often at times of crisis or deadlines. In these circumstances, the possible decrease in morale can be offset by higher levels of person-oriented behaviour.

For a leader low in person-oriented behaviour, the situation is not as promising. It might be thought that morale could be increased by reducing task-oriented behaviour. This is not the case. It appears that a moderate level of person orientation is required, irrespective of the degree of task orientation, if morale is to be maintained.

These two facets of leader behaviour need to be met, but not necessarily by the same person. There are many cases where an effective leadership 'team' may emerge with one individual who is task oriented and one who is people oriented. Usually the leader is mainly task oriented, while the second in command soothes the feathers ruffled by his or her boss.

Since its original statement there have been criticisms of the Ohio theory and extensions of the number of dimensions, but the two original dimensions appear to be fairly universal. The main criticism, which as we will see also applies to the Michigan studies, is that it does not take into account that different styles may be needed in different situations.

The Michigan studies differed from those of Ohio in two respects. First, they used only one dimension. At one end were managers who were *production centred*, at the other those who were *employee centred*. This assumes that a person cannot, therefore, be both.

Second, instead of looking at 'satisfaction' with various leadership styles, they looked at levels of productivity associated with differing styles. Three main themes emerged. First, that in the more productive groups, the supervisor spent less time doing the same jobs as his or her subordinates, concentrating instead on co-ordinating and planning activities. Second that, on the whole, general supervision was more effective than close supervision. Finally, that employee-centred supervision was more effective than production-centred supervision.

Despite considerable differences between the two sets of studies, the main themes from the two have had a considerable impact. These themes cover people versus task orientation, together with the emphasis upon general (that is, participative) supervision. If they are to be effective, managers have to realize that both task and people dimensions have an impact upon subordinates' attitudes. In general, the people-oriented manager is likely to have a more satisfied workforce and can afford to increase the level of task orientation when it is required without loss of morale. Managers also need to recognize that performance will be affected by the closeness, or otherwise, of supervision. General supervision, it is argued, is likely, on the whole, to be more effective than close supervision. Whilst all these factors need to be considered, the problem with these suggestions is that they are very general and do not give advice as to which approach should be adopted in specific situations.

FIEDLER'S CONTINGENCY THEORY

As mentioned earlier, one of the main criticisms of the behavioural theories is that they fail to take into account the demands of the situation. Situations change, and with these changes come different leadership demands. To be fair, the later Michigan studies included one situational factor – that of organizational climate. The inclusion of situational factors is a feature of what is perhaps the most influential current theory of leadership – that of Fred Fiedler.

Fiedler's theory (Fiedler and Chelmers, 1984) takes into account the preferred leadership style of an individual as well as various situational factors. According to the theory, the most appropriate style is dependent or, in other words, contingent upon these other factors. For this reason the theory is known as *Fiedler's contingency theory*.

Let us deal first with preferred leadership style. The concept that Fiedler uses to describe leadership style is that of the 'least preferred co-worker' or LPC. Through his early work with psychotherapists, Fielder detected differences between 'good' and 'bad' therapists. These different groups of therapist appeared to differ in the way that they looked on their patients, as compared with themselves. 'Good' therapists saw the patients as essentially similar to themselves, but with particular problems that were troubling them. 'Bad' therapists, on the other hand, saw themselves and the patients as quite dissimilar. From these observations Fiedler developed not only the concept of LPC, but also a scale by which to measure it, also called LPC. The level of LPC is determined by how favourably, or otherwise, the person describes their least preferred co-worker. Those with high LPC scores describe even their least favourite co-worker in relatively favourable terms.

You may recognize that this is the subject of the questionnaire that you completed at the start of this chapter. Scores of 57 or lower would suggest that you are a potentially low LPC leader. Note that, for managers, this does not mean that you are a 'good' or 'bad' leader. (It would suggest, however, that you would not make a very good psychotherapist!)

Those scoring high on the LPC tend to seek self-esteem through interpersonal relations, while those scoring low tend to seek it through task performance. These two orientations appear, on the surface, to be very similar to the two dimensions from the Ohio studies. Fiedler claims, however, that this is not so. Rather he sees them as more of a particular hierarchy of goals, along the lines of Maslow. Different scores on the LPC represent different hierarchies. The nature of these differences is not entirely clear and there has been considerable discussion concerning both the concept and the measurement of LPC. Despite the lack of clarity, many consider that a rough shorthand for high and low LPC are 'relationship' and 'task' motivated, respectively.

The effectiveness of a group, however, is not dependent solely upon the leadership style of its leader, but also upon the extent to which the situation enables the leader to exert influence. According to Fiedler, there are three main factors that have to be considered when assessing the situational characteristics. In decreasing importance these are: leader–member relations, task structure and position power. Each of these can be favourable to a greater or lesser extent. For simplicity's sake, however, the theory considers only two possibilities for each.

Leader–member relations means exactly what it says. Are the relations between the leader and the group members good or poor?

The definition of *task structure* is not so easy and itself is subdivided into four factors. 'Decision verifiability' is the degree to which the solution can be verified as being correct – 'how right was the answer we got?' 'Goal clarity' is the degree to which the task goals can be clearly stated and known by the group members. 'Goal path multiplicity' refers to the number of ways in which the problem can be solved – 'how many ways are there to skin a cat?'. Finally, 'solution specificity' refers to the number of solutions that would be considered correct. Combining these four produces a good or poor rating for the task structure.

The final, and least important dimension is *position power*. This has also been called 'fate control'. Essentially, it is the capacity of the leader to determine, and dispense, rewards and punishments to group members.

These then are the major elements of the situation, but how do they interact with the leader's preferred style? In essence, as a result of a large number of empirical studies, Fiedler suggests that low LPC (task-motivated) leaders will be most effective when the situation is either very favourable or very unfavourable. High LPC (relationship-oriented) leaders will be most effective when the situation is moderately favourable. This relationship is shown diagrammatically in Figure 12, which illustrates leadership style and situation, together with the way they interact. What implications are there for improving group effectiveness?

To a large extent the situational variables are not susceptible to change.

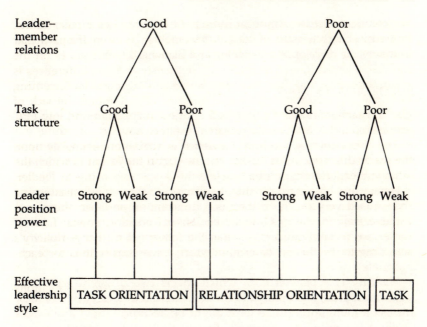

FIGURE 12. *Diagrammatic representation of Fiedler's theory (from Bryman, 1986)*

It might be possible to improve leader–member relations, and give the leader more control over rewards, but the other factors are largely determined by the nature of the task. What then of LPC? According to the theory, our LPC is very stable and similar to a personality trait. As such it is difficult to change. What Fiedler suggests, therefore, is what he calls 'leader match'. Rather than change the situation, select a leader whose preferred style is most appropriate. This may appear a rather drastic solution. It is, however, what is often done, especially when things are going wrong. In these situations, a task-motivated manager will be moved in, often to replace the relationship-motivated manager for whom the situational factors have now 'gone sour'. Those who have seen the film *Twelve O'Clock High*, which used to be shown quite often on management courses, will recognize the situation.

Fiedler's theory is still the subject of much debate and argument. We have already mentioned the controversy over the nature of the LPC scale, but other researchers have questioned elements of Fiedler's research methodology. The debate surrounding the methodology is perhaps too complicated to be dealt with here but you should be aware that the theory is far from being universally accepted.

Although Fiedler's theory takes into account what he considers to be the most important situational factors, there are obviously others that he does not consider. Amongst these are two that relate directly to the individual characteristics of the group members. These are incorporated in the model developed by Hersey and Blanchard (1982).

SUBORDINATES' MATURITY

Like transactional analysis, this model has not found favour in standard textbooks, and there is little research to either support, or refute, the theory. Nevertheless, we find it a useful way of approaching perhaps the major dilemma of leadership – 'how participative can I be', versus 'how authoritarian must I be?'

Hersey and Blanchard consider two factors in their theory: leadership style, based very much on the Ohio dimensions, and one situational variable, *maturity*. As the Ohio dimensions of leadership were discussed earlier, we will now turn to consider the concept of maturity. This will, according to the theory, determine which leadership style is most appropriate.

Maturity is a blanket term which covers two different aspects of behaviour. First, it is applied to the skills required to carry out the task (in fact a more appropriate term might be 'technical capability'). Secondly it is applied to a person's motivational level, or 'psychological' maturity. These, combined together, will decide whether the 'delegating', 'participating', 'selling', or 'telling' leadership style is most appropriate. (Descriptions of each of these styles will be given later in this chapter.) The theory is again best summarized diagrammatically, in Figure 13. In order to determine the level of maturity, Hersey and Blanchard developed scales by which the manager can rate a subordinate's maturity, and the subordinate can rate him or herself. The results of these two ratings then form the basis for negotiations between manager and subordinate, so as to identify the appropriate style.

The emphasis in this theory, rather than accepting leadership style as a trait, is to stress leaders' style flexibility. 'Different strokes for different folks' might be a fair way of summarizing it.

Hersey and Blanchard provide a mechanism whereby the motivational maturity of individual employees can be assessed. More often than not, however, we make assumptions about the reasons why people work, and how they work, that have a considerable influence upon management styles. We will now consider the nature of our assumptions.

ASSUMPTIONS ABOUT PEOPLE AT WORK

It might be thought that a consideration of our basic assumptions about other people at work should have come at the beginning of this chapter

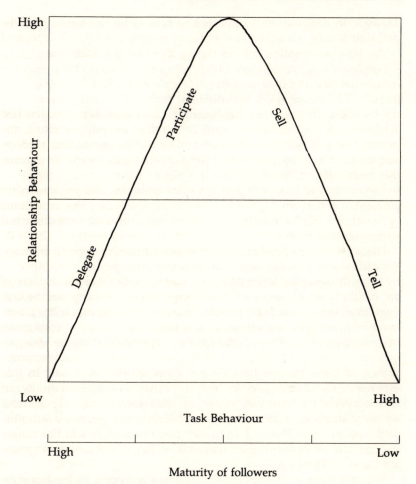

FIGURE 13. *Hersey and Blanchard's theory of leadership*

– and so it could have. We feel however that some knowledge of current theories of leadership is desirable in order to appreciate the power of assumptions. Assumptions are, in effect, our own theories – in this case about why people behave as they do at work. As such they have an important influence on our behaviour towards other people. Unfortunately, unlike scientific theories, they are rarely, if ever, tested against reality.

Douglas McGregor's (1960) work on the nature of managerial assumptions is now rather old. For us, it nevertheless retains its power to illuminate those assumptions. McGregor coined the terms *Theory X* and

Theory Y to describe what appeared to him to be two fundamentally different sets of assumptions about why people work.

The basic assumption behind Theory X can be stated fairly succinctly – 'people are lazy'. Acceptance of this assumption leads to the inevitable conclusion that the only way to get people to work is by using strict *control*. This control takes two different forms. The obvious way is to use coercion, the threat of punishment if rules are broken or targets not achieved. The problem with threats is that they are only effective if the person being threatened believes that they will be carried out. Modern employment laws, coupled with company-wide agreements, have made this route rather difficult for many managers. For this reason, the alternative method of control is perhaps more common, and perhaps more efficient. It is the carrot approach, what some have called the 'seduction' approach. People have to be seduced by promises into producing the performance required.

Theory Y, on the other hand, is rather more difficult to explain. Perhaps the easiest way is to say that it assumes that most people are motivated by those things at the top of Maslow's hierarchy. In other words, people are naturally active, and seek commitment, responsibility, and enjoyment from their work. Most people, given the opportunity, will actively involve themselves in their work, and have the abilities to contribute in a constructive way towards the solution of problems that may arise.

Which of these assumptions do *you* think is most accurate? In our experience many managers say that their own assumptions are closer to Theory Y than Theory X. When, on management training courses, we use a more accurate method of measuring their attitudes we often find they are more Theory X than they care to admit. In addition many suggest that, while they themselves are like Theory Y, their subordinates are closer to Theory X.

The vast majority of organizations behave according to the assumptions of Theory X, especially where non-managers are concerned. The emphasis is on control and the use of money to goad workers into the correct behaviour. If Theory Y is correct, however, then organizations could be more productive by relinquishing control and turning responsibility over to the workers. Why does this not happen?

The reason there are so few organizations that work from Theory Y is two-fold. First, Theory X is, by its very nature, a self-fulfilling prophesy. This is because people develop expectations about how they will be treated. For example, if, as a result of being converted to Theory Y, a manager attempts to implement it, what is likely to happen? The sudden switch from being told what to do, to a situation in which they have to make decisions, is likely, in the short term, to lead to a period of considerable confusion and a resulting drop in levels of performance. The effect of this is to convince managers that their particular workers do not want and, indeed, cannot cope with the new responsibility. The managers' reaction, therefore, is to reintroduce the former controls. Their initial belief in Theory X is strengthened even further – 'I tried it and it failed'. Hence the self-fulfilling prophesy; the initial reaction to the change suggests that Theory X is indeed needed!

DEPENDENCY

To understand why this reaction occurs, we will briefly describe a model with its roots in child and adolescent development. The central idea of this model (see Figure 14) is that of *dependency*. Dependency is just what it says: one individual is dependent on another. In childhood we

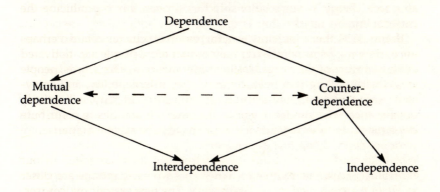

FIGURE 14. *Development of dependency relationships*

are dependent upon our parents for everything. At work, under a Theory X regime, we are dependent upon management telling us what to do. This dependent relationship may be accepted for some time, but at a certain stage of childhood the amount of control exercised by the parent becomes to be resented as the child develops the need to control his or her own life. In the work situation, this dependency is accepted as long as the rewards are big enough and/or the control does not impinge on those areas we feel to be personal (for example British Coal's attempt to take disciplinary action against employees for incidents that were not work-related).

Counterdependence. When the level of control is felt to be unacceptable, people are driven to what is called *counterdependence*, that is, to rebel against authority. There is, however, another way in which counter-dependence can be induced. Perhaps surprisingly, it can be induced by releasing controls too quickly. We often see examples of this at university. Students who have been used to a fairly high level of control, both at home and at school, move in the space of a few weeks to a situation of almost no controls. Nobody tells them when to come in, or when to work. Lecturers are certainly not going to act *in loco parentis* to those who are legally adults. For all students it is a useful experience but, for some, the release is too abrupt and they fall into counterdependence. Some go 'punk'; others join extreme groups, to the dismay of their parents. In this example, Theory X is replaced by almost *laissez-faire* management (i.e. very little, or no, control). The reactions are, however, much the same as those that occur at work when Theory X type practices are suddenly replaced by Theory Y type practices.

Interdependence. How then can we move from the dependent relationship to a Theory Y type relationship based upon interdependence? An interdependent relationship is one in which both parties are capable of doing each other's job; however, for reasons of efficiency and convenience, they may specialize. You may remember that we said that there were two reasons why organizations use Theory X. The first is because it is a self-fulfilling prophesy, because of counterdependence. The second reason is associated with another form of dependence, mutual dependence. The model suggests that there is no direct route from dependence to interdependence. There have to be stages of either counterdependence or mutual dependence.

Mutual dependence is a situation where both parties mutually agree to regulate their interaction in certain ways. The best example of this from everyday life is marriage. 'I will be responsible for cooking and cleaning, if you accept responsibility for doing the gardening and household maintenance.' Such a relationship is very strong, as long as both parties are present. Unfortunately, when one party is no longer present, those activities for which he or she had responsibility do not get done. We suspect a lot of managers and their subordinates are in this kind of relationship. The way to tell is to look at what happens when you are away on holiday. If, in your absence, nothing would get done unless someone takes over your position, then the relationship is likely to be that of total dependence. If, as is more likely, there is a situation of mutual dependence, then what awaits your return will be different. Everyone will have carried on doing their own job, without any need for close supervision. The things that you, and only you, do, will not however have been done without outside assistance. In a totally interdependent relationship, it will be as if you had not been away. All the jobs will have been done, without the need for any extra outside help or direction. Your colleagues will simply have worked a little harder in order to cover for your absence.

The route from dependence to mutual dependence is by negotiation.

'You can stay out late as long as you phone and let me know'. At work, in return for accepting more responsibility, you will be allowed to do some more of the work that you particularly like. The two routes shown in Figure 14, or a mix of both, are the only ways to move from dependence to interdependence, from X to Y. Each has its advantages and drawbacks. Mutual dependence is cosy. It is more comfortable than interdependence which, contrary to what you may think, can be difficult. It is more difficult because disagreements, rather than being solved by orders, have to be genuinely resolved to the satisfaction of all. This is highly effective, but the *process* may be painful. The temptation, therefore, is to stay in mutual dependence. The counterdependence route, on the other hand, is obviously uncomfortable. However, because it is so uncomfortable the transition through it may be quicker. There is, however, another danger associated with counterdependence. If it proves too painful the dependent party may choose complete independence. The adolescent leaves home and is not heard from again; the employee resigns.

You may now think that dependence has its attractions, but it also has disadvantages. It can be nice, especially when a situation is seen as difficult and hard to control. A strong leader, or system of leadership, that promises total support is often seen as desirable. We can hand all our responsibilities to someone else. We have seen how control that is perceived as too pervasive eventually invites rebellion, or counterdependency. Even before this, however, there are disadvantages associated with dependence, which culminate in rebellion. Put simply, dependence breeds passivity. This passivity shows itself in a number of different ways. First, as *inactivity*. If all control rests with others there is no point in doing anything until you are told. This of course may have undesirable consequences, such as the sack! Because of this, a more common type of passive behaviour is *over-adaptation*, or extreme compliance. Orders are carried out, but strictly by the book. Finally, a period of 'agitation' may follow before pent-up feelings are channelled into counterdependence. The trigger for the commencement of open hostilities (such as a strike), may appear trivial to outsiders, and even to some more remote managers. Benevolent autocrats and overindulgent parents are often totally confused by the sudden turn of events. It is not the benefits that they provide that are at fault; rather, it is the fact that they do not allow those in their charge any control or responsibility for their own work or destiny.

The styles considered so far might be said to be 'macro' in their approach. We have been concerned with describing leadership and management styles, and discussing when each may be appropriate. What none of the theories suggest is *how* you can become participative, or task centred, or democratic. In order to do this, we have to take a more 'micro' approach and look at the interactions between managers and those for whom they have responsibility. In particular, we will consider interactions between managers and their subordinates, where the purpose is to influence the subordinates' behaviour. All such interactions, we will argue, are in fact mini-appraisals, and they will therefore be dealt with under this broad heading.

STAFF APPRAISAL

(In much of what follows we are indebted to Gerry Randell, Peter Wright, and David Taylor of Bradford Management Centre.)

In its broadest terms staff appraisal involves the collection of information about people so that decisions can be made about them. Obviously, the type of information that is collected, and how it is collected will depend upon the type of decision that is being made. Staff appraisal systems are intended to fulfil a number of different, yet related, functions. According to Gerry Randell, P. Packard and J. Slater (1984), these are:

i) The allocation and distribution of the 'fruits' of the organization's activities, for example pay, power and status.

ii) Improving and developing the present job performance of each individual member of staff.

iii) Predicting the level and type of work that an individual is likely to achieve in the future, together with an estimate of how long it will take them to achieve it.

Although these functions overlap to a certain extent they should, according to Randell and his colleagues, be kept separate in practice as the techniques, procedures, and information required for each differ. The distribution of rewards should be the subject of a *reward review*, the improvement of performance that of a *performance review*, and the prediction of future level that of a *potential review*. It is not possible, it is suggested, for these different approaches to be integrated into the same interview. For example, the role of the manager in the reward review is akin to that of a judge. In the other reviews, on the other hand, the manager's role may be more often that of a counsellor. There is another good reason why performance and reward reviews should be separated. The inclusion of any discussion of salary often colours the whole of the rest of the review, especially if expectations are not met. Yet it is the below-average performer who is not getting an increase in salary, who is the very person who needs development.

As well as the different reviews being kept separate, Randell and his colleagues suggest that responsibility for each should also be separated.

The level of reward, it is suggested, is the responsibility of the organization as a whole. The determination of levels of reward should be the responsibility of centrally determined procedures that are subject to continuous monitoring and updating. The exception to this concerns small merit rises, the responsibility for which should lie with the manager. These merit rises, whilst relatively small, can have considerable symbolic value to their recipients.

Like the reward review, the potential review should also be a central responsibility, perhaps that of a management development manager. Future potential is notoriously difficult to predict even for experts, and it is unfair to expect managers who are not experts in the field to undertake this task.

Note that we are not suggesting that managers should have no involvement in the reward and potential reviews. Obviously managers have an important role as a source of information about the individuals concerned. What they should not have is the overall responsibility for these reviews. Performance reviews, on the other hand, are very much the responsibility of the individual manager. It is clearly the manager's job to develop their subordinates and improve their current levels of performance.

The different types of interview have different reporting requirements. It is here that the difficult issue of how performance is assessed arises. Many organizations use rating scales, which have the advantage that they can be aggregated and manipulated in various ways. Thus, if it has been decided that the top X per cent of managers will receive a salary increase of Y per cent, this can be calculated from the ratings given by their bosses. Alternatively, if evidence is required for not renewing someone's contract, the relevant poor ratings can be produced in evidence. (All of this assumes that ratings are accurate and that those of manager x can be directly compared with those of manager y. This is far from being the case.)

If the object of assessment is to improve performance, ratings are *not* required. Lest this appear strange, let us take an example. Many rating forms have a number of dimensions upon which a rating is required. These are often 'created' by the personnel department, without any reference to job incumbents. Common amongst them are 'initiative', 'leadership', 'technical competence', and others. Let us now assume that these are marked on a scale from 1 (unacceptable) to 5 (outstanding). You have been given a '3' by your boss. What do you have to do to get a '4'? The rating gives you no guidance whatsoever. What you have to do is discuss specific incidents, covering what did, or did not happen, and how it could be done better in the future. Ratings are for administrative purposes, not for developing the individual's job performance. As we will see shortly, this difference between administrative needs and developmental needs may be one reason behind the inefficiency of many appraisal schemes.

INTRODUCTION OF APPRAISAL SCHEMES

Appraisal schemes are being introduced into many organizations. Even universities are now moving towards formal appraisal of teaching. Many individuals and unions, however, view this introduction with suspicion. In other organizations, schemes that have already been introduced have not lived up to their initial expectations. Why is this? It appears that there are often 'gaps' in three key issues: training, objectives and culture.

The training gap. Schemes are often introduced on the basic assumption that managers already possess the basic skills needed to interview staff, and that all that is required, therefore, is an introduction to how the relevant scheme is to be administered. But we do not expect people to learn to drive by watching a video. They have to practise under the guidance of a tutor. The same is true of appraisal interviewing.

The objectives gap. Management often try to 'sell' the idea of appraisal on the basis of staff development. If we accept Theory Y (see page 74), we must accept that most people want to improve their performance. What most organizations start with, however, is the development of a rating system. Although the employees are not aware of the terminology, what they realize is that rating scales are required for administrative purposes, such as disciplinary procedures. Rating scales are not required for development. Professor Chris Argyris of Harvard Business School (1962) has been studying organizations for several decades, and has come to one unequivocal conclusion: how organizations *say* they work and how they *actually* work are never the same. In his words, their 'epoused' theories are never the same as their 'theories in practice'. In other words, what they say, and what they do, differ. Why organizations say they want to introduce appraisal, and why they actually want appraisal may also be judged in the light of Argyris's comments. This is sometimes reinforced by the fact that the scheme applies to everyone, except the Board of Directors.

The culture gap. Any appraisal scheme has to fit within the organizational culture involved. To attempt to introduce a developmental scheme within a traditionally 'Theory X' structure, would have its dangers. So would the imposition of an administrative scheme on an organization, or department, that was traditionally more 'Theory Y'. This latter case often occurs when such schemes are tried for highly specialist professional staff.

APPRAISAL INTERVIEWS

There is one thing that can be said for all but the best appraisal schemes, which is that managers do not like doing appraisal interviews, will avoid them where possible and do them only with reluctance. Why?

Appraisal interviews can be stressful. It may be relatively easy to deal with a high flyer, perhaps by channelling his or her enthusiasm in the right direction. It may also be fairly straightforward, if painful, to deal with those who are performing well below standard. The vast majority of individuals are somewhere in the middle. They do a reasonable job, but are unlikely to rise much higher. Some may be content to stay where they are, others may be unrealistically ambitious. How do you motivate the former, and let down the latter? In addition to acting as information exchanges, appraisal interviews also have the potential to become very emotional, especially if pay reviews are involved. Social and economic exchanges are often completely intertwined.

The other main reason why managers are reluctant to carry out appraisals is that they are often seen as peripheral activity, imposed over their heads, apparently for some administrative purpose. Carrying them out and returning the forms appears to have no influence on subsequent events. Little apparently happens except perhaps, when someone is summoned away to a training course, often at a few days notice. Not carrying them out results in various reminders from the personnel department. In many organizations the reward review is seen as *the* annual appraisal. This should not be the case. The principal aim of any staff appraisal scheme should be the development of staff and the improvement of their current levels of job performance.

Most managers, we suspect, will think of appraisal interviewing as something that is done, formally, once a year. We would argue that managers are actually doing appraisals all the time, the purpose of which is to influence current and future performance. The only difference is that they are generally informal and the official forms are absent.

It is not by accident that this section on appraisal occurs at the end of a chapter on leadership and management style, which itself follows chapters on personality and motivation. The appraisal interview, as we have defined it, is where all the elements come together as theory and practice meet.

The first part of a manager's job entails reaching decisions about what happened, why, and how this can be improved upon in the future. In doing so he or she will attribute *causality* – who, or what, was responsible? Let us take an example where something has gone wrong. Remember three phenomena of attribution theory discussed on pages 18–22: actor–observer divergence, the self-serving bias and the fundamental attribution error. The first of these, actor–observer divergence, suggests that your subordinate, as the actor, will attribute causality to the situation, an explanation that also fulfils the self-serving bias. You, however, as an observer, will tend to attribute causality to the subordinate. But you may be influenced by his or her past performance. If the person normally performs well, then the tendency to blame the actor may be reduced.

However the general tendency will still be to blame the subordinate. The fundamental attribution error suggests that you will underestimate the influence of the situation. But who is right? The only way to decide is by collecting information.

One of the main functions of the interview, therefore, is the collection of information. This information collection *has to be done without evaluation*. If it is not, the effects may be counterproductive. Bad appraisal interviews, of whatever type, can be worse than none at all. Having gathered all the relevant information about the problem, it has to be decided which style of leadership (ranging from totally authoritarian to totally democratic), is appropriate? The answer to this will be dependent on many of the factors discussed in the leadership theories. In particular, does the person have the maturity, both in the skills required, and the motivation required to initiate the change themselves? Once again, the only way to answer these questions is to gather information.

HOW TO GATHER INFORMATION

The basic building blocks of any information-gathering exercise are questions. One of the quickest ways of increasing effectiveness in any interview is to be able to choose the correct type of question. First, however, we have to be able to recognize the different types and be aware of their uses.

Questions and their uses. Below are listed the different types of question. As an exercise, first familiarize yourself with them, and then analyse some real-life interviews. Any such interviews will do, but we find that the following are often useful in highlighting certain questioning techniques. Compare any chat-show host with more searching interviewers. Some of the best techniques can be found in cross-examinations of politicians by political correspondents. Each of the question types listed in Table 3 has its particular uses but they are, not surprisingly, usually found in combination. Some ways of combining the different types of question into sequences are, however, more effective than others. One sequencing of questions that is particularly appropriate for information gathering has been referred to as the funnel technique. This is used to refine initial, often rather vague, information so that the hard facts can be assessed. It is called the funnel technique because the information becomes more and more precise as the sequence progresses.

Using this technique the discussion about the events in question starts with an open question. This helps the interviewer get an overall view of what happened, for example 'the production line was stopped this morning, what happened?'. Although the open question often elicits a large amount of information covering a wide area, it is often lacking in depth. In order to elicit more detailed information probing questions

TABLE 3. *Question types and their uses (adapted from Randell et al., 1984)*

Question/Statement type	Useful for:	Not useful for:
OPEN 'Tell me what happened when....'	Most openings. Exploring and gathering information on a broad basis.	Very talkative interviewee.
CLOSED 'How many widgets did you produce?'	Getting specific, factual answers.	Getting broadly based information.
PROBING 'What precisely happened next?'	Establishing and checking details of events already known, or arising from open question answers.	Exploring emotionally charged areas.
HYPOTHETICAL 'What would you do if...?'	Getting interviewee to think in broader terms, or about a new area.	If situation is outside the interviewee's range.
MULTIPLE A string of questions or statements.	Never useful.	Never useful.
COMPARISON 'Would you prefer a weekly or a monthly meeting?'	Exploration of needs and values.	Where pairs of alternatives are unrealistic.
SUMMARIES 'What we seem to have decided so far is....'	Ensuring agreement about main points raised. Gaining commitment.	If used prematurely.

are used, for example 'who did you consult about stopping the production line?'. The answer to this question will be more detailed but may omit specific relevant information. If this is so it may be necessary to follow the probe with a closed question in order to produce answers on these specific points, for example 'did you get authority from the Production Manager to stop the line?' Finally it is often useful to use a summary to check that your information is correct. As appraisal interviews often cover a number of job related events it is not unusual to find that this cycle of open, probing and closed questions, together with summaries to check the information, is repeated as the different events are discussed.

The initial use of an open question also has some other advantages. First, it allows subordinates to put their side of the story. In doing so, it may become apparent how much they feel they were responsible. In addition, they may also indicate the extent to which they have already learnt from the events. It may be that they are already taking the necessary corrective action. Second, the use of an open question indicates that the manager has an open mind and is keen to seek all the information. This avoids defensive behaviour on the part of the subordinate. The immediate reaction to attack, in the form a prejudgement of 'guilt' on the part of the manager, is defence. Under these conditions the subordinate will not admit to any fault on his or her part, for fear that the admission will be used to press the attack even further. The tactic becomes one of defending the outer lines, only falling back when absolutely necessary. Such interactions are not likely to be very productive. (In TA terms this is likely to end in Uproar, as the best form of defence is attack.)

Before moving on to look at ways of influencing behaviour, perhaps we should say something about the question types used by chat-show hosts and political interviewers. Political interviewers use probing questions or, with particularly evasive interviewees, leading questions. For example, 'it is the government's intention to . . . isn't it?' A statement is made into a question by adding 'isn't it' at the end. This is the most pointed why of asking for confirmation or disconfirmation. Nevertheless, skilled politicians will often respond with the answer to an entirely different question! It is a technique widely used by barristers when cross-examining hostile witnesses. Chat-show hosts, on the other hand, are normally interviewing people who want to talk. The most appropriate question types are, therefore, open with the occasional probe. Some successful hosts, however, use closed and multiple questions. Fortunately for them most of their guests are from show business, and treat these as open questions. When 'naive' guests, especially young children, are on the show they are likely to treat the closed questions as such, and give one-word answers. The embarrassment of the host on these occasions is obvious.

Dealing with emotions. Thus far, we have been dealing with the rational and logical process of gathering information. This is part of decision-making skills and, as such, an obvious part of a manager's role. There is another aspect of the role with which many managers feel uncomfortable. Human beings have emotions and often express these emotions. While managers are trained to deal with information, they are often not trained to deal with emotions.

There is one cardinal rule for dealing with emotions. They do not mix with reasoned argument! If your partner, in a highly emotional state, complains that you never wash the dishes, we would not recommend that you argue that such a complaint is incorrect because you did wash the dishes last Christmas Day! There are only two ways to deal with emotion. If you have aroused the emotion because of something you did which you now accept as wrong, then an early apology will defuse the situation. On many occasions, however, this may not be appropriate, and the only solution is to let the emotion run its course. This can be encouraged in two ways. Attentive, but silent, listening, and the occasional use of *reflective* questions. Silence can be difficult to maintain as there is a strong temptation to jump in and correct factual inaccuracies. Reflective questions do what their name suggests: they use a summary of what the person has just said and reflect it back, without evaluation. For example, 'you feel you've been undervalued by the firm – is that it?' The effect is to allow the emotion to run its course. High levels of emotion are difficult to maintain without support from others, either in the form of agreement or argument. With no evaluation, the emotional level tends to steadily decrease. In doing so, the course of the outburst often follows a spiral. The same ground is gone over again and again, but with the emotional level declining all the time. When it is over, the time is right for logical discussion.

INFLUENCING BEHAVIOUR

There are many ways of influencing behaviour, but one dimension that should always be borne in mind is that of commitment versus compliance. When people are committed to a course of action they adopt it as their own and will make efforts to ensure that they succeed, without the necessity for continual monitoring by others. When they are being compliant they are only undertaking the action because they fear the consequences of non-compliance. In this latter case they will take advantage of any loophole or excuse that presents itself in order to avoid doing what is required. In general, people are most committed to their own ideas, and least committed to those that are imposed by others.

Potentially the most successful condition for behaviour change is when no influence at all is required. This is the situation when the person has already worked out what they need to change, and has started the process – all the manager needs to do is check that they agree with the proposed course of action, and monitor it to ensure that it is carried out. Otherwise, there is a danger that managers will actually reduce effectiveness. To be told by someone else what you should be doing, when you have already reached the same conclusion, can be very demotivating. Once again, the way for managers to avoid this situation is by the use of open questions.

On the other hand, there are bound to be occasions where commitment is of secondary importance, and where the psychological maturity or skill of staff is such that a directive approach is required. Let us consider the range of options open to a manager to influence other people's behaviour. It includes:

Orders
Requests
Advice and suggestions
Promises
Threats
Explanations
Praise
Criticism
Leading questions

The first three options have certain aspects in common, as they all let subordinates know what you think they should be doing. They differ in the extent to which they give reasons.

Orders leave the least room for any kind of initiative by the subordinate. In the extreme, no questions are allowed. Requests may vary somewhat. The difference between an order and a request is that, in theory at least, a request may be turned down. The latitude to turn down the request will obviously vary. Advice and suggestions offer the greatest opportunity for rejection. The message behind an order is 'because I say so', and that behind a request 'because I would like you to'. The message behind advice and suggestions is 'because it is in your own best interests to'.

All the other methods of influence work on variations on coercion and seduction. Promises and threats you will recognize from the section on OBMod (see page 52). As discussed there, these may be highly effective, but both require a knowledge of the individual to whom they are to be applied. The major pitfall for managers is that of *projection*. We all have a tendency to project our own needs, aspirations, and values onto others. To assume that what we find rewarding or punishing will also be rewarding or punishing for others is a mistake, as is assuming that their aspirations are the same as ours.

The other pitfall, common to both managers and parents, is to threaten punishments that will not be enforced. The reasons may be that you cannot impose them or that you do not want to impose them. The effect is the same, future threats lose their credibility.

Praise and criticism are particular forms of reward and punishment. Both carry information, but the rewards and punishments involved are social rather than tangible.

Leading questions can be used as a method of giving instructions – 'you won't do that again, will you?'. Phrased as a question, the implications are clear, as is the response expected. The tone will suggest whether it is an order, a request, or advice.

TYPES OF INTERACTION

Now we have the building blocks: question types for gathering information and different methods of influencing behaviour. How are these combined in the appraisal to produce the leadership style required?

Wright and Taylor (1986) have suggested that there are six main styles of interaction between managers and staff:

- Tell
- Tell and Sell
- Tell and Listen
- Ask and Tell
- Problem Solving
- Ask and Listen

These styles lie along a scale ranging from total control by the manager, to control by the subordinate. As such they differ in the extent to which they allow subordinate initiative. As we have suggested, there is often a relationship between the degree to which a person has control over decisions that affect them and the extent to which they feel committed to those decisions. Because of this the different styles will differ in the degree of commitment that they are likely to engender in the subordinate. The styles also differ as to whether they emphasize gathering information or giving orders. At one end of the scale there is a lot of order giving but no information gathering – 'Tell'. At the other there is a lot of information gathering, but no ordering – 'Ask and listen'. Let us now consider each of these types. What influencing techniques do they use? What do they rely on for their effectiveness? What are their advantages and disadvantages?

TELL

Uses:	Orders, requests and strong suggestions.
Relies upon:	The manager being right and the subordinate's willingness to accept this.
Advantages:	Saves time and effort.
Disadvantages:	It overlooks the fact that the subordinate may have useful information and may, in addition, create resentment.

TELL AND SELL

Uses:	Orders, requests, advice, suggestions together with explanations, threats and punishments in order to tell the subordinate what to do while also 'selling' the solution to them so that it is accepted.
Relies upon:	The manager being right.
Advantages:	Quick and effective plus, one hopes, some commitment.

Disadvantages: If the selling doesn't work, possible disaster.

TELL AND LISTEN

Uses:	Orders, requests, advice and suggestions, together with praise and criticism.
Relies upon:	The manager being right together with some participation leading to commitment.
Advantages:	More commitment because the person has been listened to.
Disadvantages:	Possibility of an inconclusive outcome because the effects of 'telling' have been dissipated during the listening phase.

ASK AND TELL

Uses:	Information gathering, followed by orders, suggestions, advice and requests.
Advantages:	As more accurate information has been collected better decisions are likely, together with higher commitment.
Disadvantages:	The decision may still not be accepted, especially if strongly held views have been overruled.

PROBLEM SOLVING

Uses:	Information gathering followed by advice, suggestions, promises, praise and explanations.
Advantages:	Potentially high quality decisions together with high commitment.
Disadvantages:	It is not appropriate when the subordinate has low skill or motivational maturity. Nor when there is little genuine room for manoeuvre.

ASK AND LISTEN

Uses:	Information gathering only.
Advantages:	Only appropriate when views are being sought well in advance of any decision. Its other use is when dealing with emotional problems to which the manager has no solution, in other words being a 'shoulder to cry on'.

These are the techniques that any manager can use in his or her everyday interactions with subordinates. Managers, who are paid to make decisions and take the responsibility, have a tendency, in our experience, to be at the 'Tell' or Theory X end of the scale. This is often compounded by the pressures when things go wrong. As a very simple exercise, next time things go wrong, either at work or at home, before 'telling', just 'ask'.

Try a simple open question – 'what happened?'. You may be surprised how much more information you receive, and hence how much better are the decisions you subsequently take.

Both 'macro' and 'micro' theories of leadership have now been covered. The main point that perhaps needs restating concerns the difference between 'espoused' Theory Y, and Theory X 'in practice'. We believe that managers find Theory X, task oriented, traditional, and hence comfortable. Indeed, as we have seen, it is entirely appropriate in some circumstances. There are, however, situations where more participative management is likely to be more effective. It is in the recognition and adaptation of styles in these situations that we believe that training is required.

As discussed on pages 76–77, the position of interdependence is difficult. It is difficult for a number of reasons. It appears, on the surface, that the manager is relinquishing his or her control. When, in role-playing interviews, managers use 'tell' inappropriately, their excuse is often that allowing the subordinate to make decisions means that they, as managers, have 'lost control'. The role of the manager has traditionally been seen as that of the decision maker. If subordinates are allowed to make decisions, there is a feeling that managers may not be doing their job.

Another reason is that interdependence means that each party needs to state their needs openly. This may arouse emotions, on both sides. Management has traditionally been seen as rational, not emotional. We all realize, however, that it is impossible to totally separate the two, in the workplace as well as elsewhere. As Sir John Harvey-Jones recognizes, you cannot communicate effectively unless you are prepared to show emotion.

These two reasons which, like the low use of praise, are largely cultural in origin, are powerful inhibitors of more interdependent management. There is one very simple step that managers can take. It has been stated before, but bears restating because of its importance. Before telling, ask and listen! As managers your raw data is information. Asking helps to provide that information.

4

Group Dynamics
at Work

Working with other people in groups is something that is part of every manager's job. Indeed it often appears as if most of the time at work is spent in meetings of one sort or another. These meetings may be formal, or they may be just an informal gathering of two or three people to solve a particular problem. In general, the higher people go in their managerial careers, the more time they seem to spend in meetings. The question that has to be asked is, of course, why? Why does so much of what happens in organizations, especially at managerial levels, take place in groups?

Perhaps the obvious answer is that many organizational goals cannot be achieved by individuals acting independently. Many of them involve tasks which are extremely complicated. There are two ways in which this complexity may show itself. First, the problem may be *technically* complex, requiring the combined skills of professionals, perhaps from a range of disciplines. Second, the problem may be *administratively* complex. This complexity is one requiring liaison and co-ordination. Some problems may, of course, be both technically and administratively complex.

In order to solve these problems, 'formal' groups are established, whose stated functions are to accomplish certain tasks. Such formal groups may be either permanent, such as standing committees, or temporary, such as working parties, depending on whether the tasks involved are recurrent or 'one-offs'.

Organizations, as we know, do not consist solely of formal groups. Friendship and other informal groupings develop. Again, why should this happen? The reason is that such informal groups satisfy 'psychological' needs. According to Edgar Schein (1980), these may be classified as follows:

a) The satisfaction of the need for affiliation – the simple need to be with other people.
b) The establishment and maintenance of self-identity and self-esteem. Who we are, and our relative status is determined by our membership

of various groups. This will also influence our perception of our own personal value and hence self-esteem. As we will see later, personal advancement is usually achieved by attaining membership of a 'higher' group, or increasing the standing of the present group.

c) The testing and establishment of social reality. Groups develop beliefs about the way the organization operates. These may be, in some cases, incorrect. They will, nevertheless, influence the way group members behave. For example, beliefs that increasing output will lead to a reduction in the piece rate will influence production levels.

d) Groups offer a feeling of security and mutual support. By doing so they reduce uncertainty and anxiety.

e) The group may act as a problem solver for its members.

Which informal groups will develop will be determined, to a large extent, by the physical layouts required for work. Distance, in particular, has a powerful influence on who will interact with who. In general, the more frequent the interactions, the more likely informal groups are to form. Because informal groups satisfy important psychological needs, they have a considerable influence upon group members. The norms that groups develop may be either functional or dysfunctional for the organization. Where group norms are in tune with those of the organization, it would do well to capitalize on this. There is obviously a problem where they are contrary to those of the organization. In such circumstances, the organization will usually try to break up the group, often by removing key members.

The implication so far has been that formal and informal groups are entirely separate. This is not the case. Groupings that started off formal often develop powerful informal relations. As well as being a department, it may be a department of friends. The armed forces deliberately encourage this, as do some Japanese organizations. Once again, social and economic exchanges are intermixed. It is also the case that informal groupings (such as friendships outside work), provide useful channels of communication for the organization. The 'grapevine' is the everyday term for such channels.

In this chapter we will consider in more detail what happens when people work together in groups. In identifying what happens we will be, hopefully, in a better position to capitalize on the benefits of working in groups while avoiding some of the pitfalls we have mentioned above. In particular, we will be concentrating on various aspects of decision making in groups.

GROUP DECISION MAKING

Technical quality. When groups have to solve problems and make decisions the only way they can do so is to call on the expertise of those within the group. Individuals will often have their own ideas of what the 'right' decision should be. All of these individual decisions are bound to have an influence on the final decision that the group reaches. In addition, the work done by the group as a whole will have an influence on the decision. Once a decision has been reached, its technical quality does of course need to be assessed. For example, was the money invested in the best way, or did the rearranged production line work? Technical quality is, of course, essential to the well-being of the organization. This is well recognized, and a large part of our education and training is geared towards making the 'right' decision. Electrical engineers are taught to design distribution systems that are safe and reliable, accountants are taught how to deal with finance, and so on. There is, we would argue, another aspect of group working in which few people have been trained. This concerns the *organizational quality* of the decision.

Organizational quality is largely concerned not with the decision itself (i.e. the task), but with the process by which the decision is reached. It is concerned with the extent to which those who are responsible for, and will be affected by, the decision are committed to it. The degree of commitment will influence the speed and effectiveness with which the decision is implemented. Those who are uncommitted, or even openly hostile, to a decision, are unlikely to apply themselves fully when it comes to putting it into action.

If this is true then it may be necessary, on occasions, to balance technical and organizational quality. It is not often that a problem will be encountered to which there is one, and only one, correct answer. More often a choice has to be made from a number of options, all of which have some merit. In these circumstances which of the following is better? A decision which you think represents the 'best' technical solution, but which is obviously not accepted by someone who will be affected by it, or, alternatively, a decision that is not quite as good, technically, as the 'best' solution (at least in your eyes), but is one to which everybody concerned is wholeheartedly committed? Ideally, of course, what is required is the 'best' decision with total commitment. But life is rarely like that. As Sir John Harvey-Jones has said: 'There are no perfect solutions, and the best is often the enemy of the good'. The best plan, he suggests, is to 'get a three-quarters right solution and belt on with it'.

It does seem that the way in which the group works will have an important influence on the organizational quality of their decision.

What determines this is not *what* was decided, but the *process* is was decided. And although this process of decision making, influences a decision's organizational quality, it does also influ e its technical quality, as will be shown.

Participation. What then, are the main influences on organizational quality? Participation is the principal one. As mentioned earlier, people are generally more committed to those decisions which they feel are, in some way, their own. How is this feeling brought about? There are two main elements in participation: the feeling that your ideas have been properly listened to and assessed, and the feeling that you have contributed to the final decision making. These may sound like easy targets to achieve, but this is not the case, as some of your own experiences in groups will probably testify.

To start with, listening is not just the opposite of talking. Too often, the silence that is accorded someone who is speaking is not used for listening to what they are saying, but rather to prepare for your own next contribution. This is usually very easy to pick up, especially by whoever has just spoken. If true listening is taking place, then the comments that follow will lead logically from what has just been said by the previous speaker. So often, however, this is not the case. The following speaker proceeds as if the previous comments had not been made. It is as if a pebble has been dropped into a pool. A few, fast diminishing ripples, but nothing else is left. For this reason, this is often referred to as a 'plop'. No doubt you can all remember such occasions, especially when you were a relatively low status group member. Even worse is when your 'plop' suggestion is reiterated later in the meeting by a high status member, and subsequently greeted with enthusiasm. In these circumstances, there is little to be gained by further contribution and apathy sets it.

Participation in decision making is not just related to the extent to which you feel that your own ideas have been given a true hearing. We may not succeed in gaining general acceptance of our own views; indeed, we may even come to realize that there are better solutions around. The fact that our ideas are not accepted does not necessarily mean that we cannot be committed. Whether we will be committed or not often depends on our perception of the *fairness* by which the decision is made. Ideally, of course, a consensus is to be desired. This is not always possible and, if a compromise that would attract a consensus is not possible, then other means may be used. A vote is the most common way of making such decisions. At first sight, a vote means that there are winners and losers, and that perhaps the losers may be uncommitted. This need not be the case. As long as the circumstances under which a vote is taken are accepted by all, the 'losers' may accept their position and devote themselves to that decision.

MONITORING THE PROCESS

Given the importance of the decision-making process to group members' commitment, it is clearly necessary to be able to assess participation within the group. In ascending order of effectiveness, the most common indications of organizational quality are:

APATHY: No one contributes to the group discussion, not because they are in agreement, but because they are totally disillusioned.

'PLOPS': A suggestion is made, but totally ignored.

DOMINANCE: One particular individual dominates the meeting. This is often accompanied by apathy from the other members.

PAIRING: This is the simplest form of groups within a group. The psychological support offered by pairing is considerable.

VOTING: Voting is some times the only way to resolve disagreements. There are some times, however, when it is appropriate and others when it is inappropriate.

FALSE CONSENSUS: If agreement cannot be reached, one way out of the impasse is to couch the decision in such broad terms that a number of interpretations are possible. A false consensus becomes apparent when the time comes for the decision to be implemented. Each side has a different understanding of what was agreed.

CONSENSUS: This is the most desirable conclusion. Genuine agreement leads to genuine commitment.

It is also necessary to decide who should be monitoring the decision-making process. Here a problem arises. Work groups are full of technical specialists, whose purpose is to provide, when required, their professional expertise. As a result of this, they are concentrating not on the process, but on the task. This means that no one may be monitoring how people are feeling about the discussions. Perhaps the person who should be taking an interest is the chairperson, who is often the group leader. Unfortunately, the chairperson is also likely to have his or her eyes firmly on the task instead of the process. For this reason, it is perhaps unfortunate that chairpersons have to be leaders. There is no reason why the most senior member of the group should be the most skilled in interpersonal processes. Someone, perhaps everyone, should be keeping an eye on the process. In extreme cases of disagreement, a neutral chairperson may be appointed, for example, by the arbitration service ACAS in the case of an industrial dispute. They will be regulating the *process* as much, if not more than, the content of any disagreements. We should not lose sight of the fact that such a role is required in any group, *albeit* informally. It need not, and should not, be solely the function of the chairperson. All group members should bear some responsibility for ensuring the effectiveness of the group.

Some of the indicators of effective and ineffective process were given above. There is one other simple way of finding out. If you feel that a particular individual is less than happy with a particular decision, check it out. Simply ask them how they *feel* about the decision. Notice that you do not ask them what they *think* about it, which would lead you back into the task, rather than towards the process. Questions about feelings will give you information about the organizational quality of the group's decision.

Although all members should take responsibility for the effective functioning of the group, individuals may have preferences for particular group roles and it is to this that we will now turn.

Team roles. The most comprehensive consideration of team roles is most probably that of Meredith Belbin (1981). His work is based on studies of groups of managers attending various management courses. A common feature of such courses is group work involving the analysis of case studies, as those who have been on them will testify. Belbin wondered what were the characteristics of groups who did well on case studies. Initially, he tried to 'create' groups who should do well. He did this by using tests to select the most intelligent participants. The top scorers were all then placed in the same group, the so-called 'Apollo' group. In the exercises that followed these groups, rather than outperforming all others, did disastrously! This led Belbin to investigate and experiment further, using personality tests and a test for preferred team roles, developed by himself. What he found was that successful teams consisted of a *mix* of individuals, each of whom performed a different role. A summary of these roles are shown in Table 4. The names of all but one of the roles match their descriptions fairly well. What characterizes the role of 'Plant' is not at all clear from its label. The reason for this is that Belbin discovered that some groups who, on the basis of his research, should have been performing well, were not. The reason, he discovered, was that there was no one in the group who was generating ideas. As soon as he 'planted' such an ideas generator in the group, it started performing – hence the name.

Each person, therefore has a preferred role or roles, and the group, to be effective, needs all these roles to be filled. This might suggest that we need to select people who are going to join groups so as to ensure that they can fill one or more of the roles which the group currently lacks. In an ideal world, this may be so, but most group membership within organizations is predetermined, usually by technical function. How then can a knowledge of Belbin's roles help?

First we must be aware of the role preferences of individuals. You do not have to test people to discover this, just watch how they behave. In doing so, it may become apparent that people differ in the strength

TABLE 4. *Belbin's team roles (adapted from Belbin, 1981)*

ROLE	OBSERVED CONTRIBUTIONS
CHAIRPERSON	1. Clarifying the goals and objectives of the group. 2. Selecting the problems on which decisions have to be made, and establishing their priorities. 3. Helping establish roles, responsibilities and work boundaries within the group. 4. Summing up the feelings and achievements of the group, and articulating group verdicts.
SHAPER	1. Shaping roles, boundaries, responsibilities, tasks and objectives. 2. Finding or seeking to find pattern in group discussion. 3. Pushing the group towards agreement on policy and action and towards making decisions.
PLANT	1. Advancing proposals. 2. Making criticisms that lead up to counter-suggestions. 3. Offering new insights on lines of action already agreed.
MONITOR/ EVALUATOR	1. Analysing problems and situations. 2. Interpreting complex written material and clarifying obscurities. 3. Assessing the judgements and contributions of others.
COMPANY WORKER	1. Transforming talk and ideas into practical steps. 2. Considering what is feasible. 3. Trimming suggestions to make them fit into agreed plans and established systems.
TEAM WORKER	1. Giving personal support and help to others. 2. Building on to or seconding a member's ideas and suggestions. 3. Drawing the reticent into discussion. 4. Taking steps to avert or overcome disruption of the team.
RESOURCE INVESTIGATOR	1. Introducing ideas and developments of external origin. 2. Contacting other individuals or groups of own volition. 3. Engaging in negotiation-type activities.
COMPLETER	1. Emphasizing the need for task completion, meeting targets and schedules and generally promoting a sense of urgency. 2. Looking for and spotting errors, omissions and oversights. 3. Galvanizing others into activity.

of their preferences. Some people will have very strong preferences for just one or two roles. Other people may have their preferences rather less strongly spread across four or five roles. Such individuals, being more flexible, are capable of filling a number of roles. Ideally, people should be given tasks which allow them to operate in their preferred roles. For example, the Resource Investigator should be allowed to seek out ideas and developments elsewhere which may help the group.

Second, we must realize which roles are missing, and thus contributing to possible inefficiency. For example, one of our postgraduate students conducted a study into why some Quality Circles continued to meet to solve problems concerned with work, while others ceased to meet. He found that all those groups that failed lacked someone whose stated preference was the 'completer' role. Apparently these groups were good at problem and solution generation, but never carried their ideas through.

If an important role is not being filled the obvious solution is to 'import' someone to do it. This, again, is not usually possible, although some Boards of Directors and senior executives do take this into account when selecting who should join their ranks. The other alternative is to find someone within the group who would be prepared to take on this role, or even adopt the role, if it is not too alien.

The need to deal with 'people' as well as 'task' processes has now been dealt with at some length, and you may have noticed that only one of the roles (team worker) is explicitly concerned with group relationships. Most of the roles are concerned with 'task' issues, and these will be discussed next.

MONITORING THE TASK

A particularly useful model of what happens when groups are taking decisions has been developed by J. E. Thompson and A. Tuden (1959), who suggest that decisions differ on two dimensions. The way that the decision making should proceed will depend on where the particular decision lies on these dimensions.

The first dimension they call 'preference for outcomes'. Another name for this might be 'goals', or 'where we want to get to'. The other dimension they refer to as 'beliefs about causation'. This is less easy to give an alternative name. Basically, however, it is concerned with our beliefs about what causes what – 'if I do this, the result will be that'. If 'preferences for outcomes' is concerned with where we want to go, 'beliefs about causation' is concerned with how we get there.

On both of these dimensions, Thompson and Tuden suggest that individuals can be either clear or unclear. In fact, they can have varying degrees of 'clarity', but to simplify matters only the two extremes will be considered here. The resulting diagram of four boxes is shown in

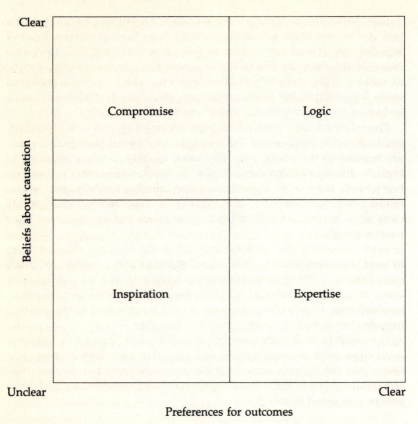

FIGURE 15. *Two dimensions of decision making (from Thompson and Tuden, 1959)*

Figure 15. The top righthand box is, perhaps, the position most people would like to find themselves in, and means that you are clear about your goals, and also clear about what you need to do to achieve them. In this situation, no decisions really need to be made. Computation is all that is required to make the decision. Contrast this with the box at the bottom left. In this situation you are unclear as to your goals and, in addition, you are unclear as to what the effects of any action you may take would be. In this situation, the model suggests 'inspiration' is required.

These are the two extremes, however. In most cases, we are fairly clear about at least one dimension. The two boxes that are most relevant therefore, are the top left and bottom righthand corners. Consider a situation in which you are clear about your goal, but unclear as to what you need to do to achieve it – the situation at the bottom righthand corner. For example, you know where you want to go on holiday, but you don't know how to get there. What you lack in this situation is *knowledge*. And this is the reason organizations set up R&D and market research departments, and why the governments have 'think tanks'. All of these are designed to give expert advice as to what the effects of various strategies will be. What is required are expert, knowledge-based judgements.

Contrast this with the situation at the upper lefthand corner. In this situation you are aware of how to achieve all the possible goals, but are unclear as to which goal you wish to pursue. This situation is entirely different from the one above, in that it concerns not knowledge but *personal preferences*. Again consider the example of where to go on holiday. You are trying to decide between two resorts. You are perfectly clear as to how to get to both, but how do you decide between your partner's preference for the beach and yours for sightseeing? No amount of extra knowledge will help you decide. In this situation, the only way to decide is by what Thompson and Tuden call 'compromise'. Their use of the word is slightly wider than normal. There are a number of ways in which a compromise can be reached. First, if an impasse is reached, then the 'compromise' may be to accept the wishes of the majority, often by means of a vote. An alternative, and possibly better, compromise is to find a superordinate goal, in other words, a goal that encompasses all the alternative goals. Thus, if you can find a holiday resort that has both scenery and beaches, the problem is solved. The last way is to appeal to a higher authority. In organizations this is often senior management who are brought in as arbitrators.

It is important to recognize which of these boxes you are currently in. If techniques of problem resolution are not appropriate, there will be, at the very least, confusion. To give an example from a continuing and controversial public debate, the question of whether, and when, abortion should be allowed raises considerable feelings. In an attempt to decide the latest date at which it should be allowed, medical experts are often produced on both sides. This is appropriate, if the question is 'when is independent life outside the womb viable?'. It is not appropriate if the question is 'when does life start?'. This latter is a philosophical and theological question. No amount of medical knowledge can provide the answer.

From the explanations above, it appears that, according to Thompson and Tuden, all our decision making takes place in just one box of their model. This is not the case. The object is, in most cases, to move from the bottom lefthand box to the top righthand box, from confusion to certainty. There are two alternative routes by which this may be achieved. One way to do this is to decide first on your goal, then decide how to get there. The other alternative is to look at all the practical alternatives, then decide which goal to adopt. Which of these is likely to be more effective? You may have difficulty answering. The probable reason is that the most common method is not one or the other, but a combination of the two. The desirability of various goals are assessed, but so are some of the associated practicalities. This is where the implications for chairpersons in particular become apparent.

The chairperson's role should be two-fold. First, it should ensure that all members of the group are working on the same dimension. (Identifying which dimension the group is working on is easier than it sounds. Just sit back and listen to the discussion in your next meeting for a few minutes.) If one subgroup is working on one dimension and one on the other, there will effectively be two meetings rather than one. The chairperson should also ensure that there is adequate discussion on the current dimension, before switching to the other. At the least, tentative ideas should be crystalized before switching to the other dimension. The effects of premature switching are often recognized by those who wish to divert a meeting away from a conclusion they do not personally like. Realizing which dimension the group is currently working on, they change the discussion to the other dimension. After an inconclusive discussion on that dimension they then initiate a switch back.

To summarize, for a group to work effectively, ensure that everyone is working on the same dimension, and that enough time is given to discussion on each to ensure that tentative, interim conclusions are reached.

The problem that Thompson and Tuden do not consider is whether the 'beliefs about causation' are correct or not. How effective, therefore, are groups at problem analysis and decision making? There are a number of characteristics of groups of which one needs to be aware.

FACTORS IN GROUP DECISION MAKING

There are both advantages and pitfalls to solving problems in groups. One of the potential advantages is that of increased motivation. If the group is cohesive and all members are committed to a course of action, then the effects are likely to be beneficial. But does a group do any better than the average of the individuals who comprise it? Does the technical quality of the decision improve at all?

Obviously, there are some situations where it is not appropriate to use a group to make a decision, as when one individual is clearly recognized as the expert in the field. However, in circumstances in which it is appropriate to use a group to make decisions, the rule appears to apply that the group will make a decision that is better than the average of all the members' individual decisions, but not as good as that of the best individual. The problem is, of course, that the 'best' individual solution can only be identified in retrospect.

There are a number of reasons for this. Groups do not appear to be better than individuals at generating ideas. Brainstorming carried out by individuals yields more ideas than when carried out by a group. Where groups gain their advantage is in the pooling and analysis of the ideas. In particular, they are good at detecting errors. This general rule of the greater efficiency of the group is just that, a general rule. There are a number of other factors that influence the effectiveness of the group.

Size and communication will be dealt with under the same heading, as they are, to a large extent, interdependent. The larger the group, the greater the problems of communication.

Parkinson's law concerning 'work expanding so as to fill the time available for its completion' has already been mentioned. He also commented on the effect of group size on group effectiveness, saying that ineffectiveness increases with size until total ineffectiveness is reached at a group size of 21. Other commentators have suggested that the optimum size is between eight and twelve. In a fairly light-hearted vein, a mathematician has calculated that, if Parkinson is correct and that each additional person adds a 'disturbance factor', then the optimum group size is, in fact, twelve.

As already suggested, the effects of size result mainly from communication problems, as more and more people wish to contribute to the group discussion. In small groups therefore, the chairperson's role (as discussed on page 94) may be fairly informal. Indeed, a small group of mature adults should be able to control themselves. When groups get larger, however, more formal management may be required. To address all remarks through the Chair in a meeting of six people is perhaps being over-formal. To do so in a meeting of 30 may be a necessity. 'Can we have one meeting please' is the common cry of chairpersons of large groups.

The channels of communication will influence both the effectiveness of the group, and group members' satisfaction. The main distinction that is made is between centralized and de-centralized groups. Let us consider some examples. For simplicity's sake we will consider a group of four people, but the same points apply to both larger and smaller groups. The different communication patterns are shown in Figure 16.

Each dot represents a group member who is allowed to communicate only along the lines. Thus, in the first case the person at the centre of the Wheel can communicate with all the other members. They, on the other hand, can only communicate with him or her. If they wish to communicate to other members they can only do so through the same central person. The degree of 'centrality' is highest in the Wheel and decreases through the Chain and Circle. The All Channel, where every

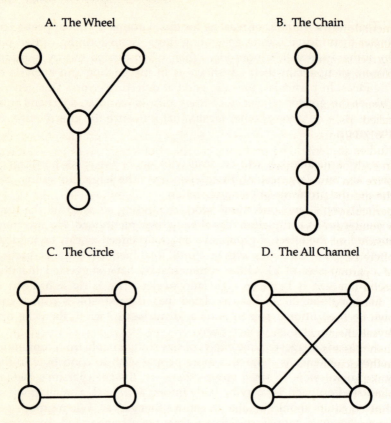

A. The Wheel

B. The Chain

C. The Circle

D. The All Channel

FIGURE 16. *Leavitt's patterns of communication (from Leavitt, 1951)*

member can communicate directly with every other member is totally decentralized.

There are two clear effects of centralization. In general, those in the central positions feel satisfied, while those in peripheral positions feel dissatisfied. The other effect is that those placed in central positions, which give control and power over information flow, begin to behave directively. In other words, they become 'leaders', irrespective of their personalities.

The degree of centralization also affects the group's efficiency, but this also depends upon the complexity of the task. Once again, for simplicity's sake we will divide the tasks into two categories, simple and complex. In general, when the task is simple, centralized groups like the Wheel are faster, and make fewer errors. When the task is complex, the picture is reversed; decentralized groups are faster, and make fewer mistakes. These generalizations are from studies on experimental groups. Unlike managerial problems, all the problems had correct answers. When a range of alternatives is available, rather than one correct solution, additional patterns emerge. These are known as *group polarization* (sometimes called 'risky shift'), and *groupthink*.

Group polarization. The first systematic demonstration of what was then called 'risky shift' was by a postgraduate student in Boston (Stoner, 1961). His dissertation looked at decision making in groups of business studies students. The problems consisted of a number of case studies. In each of these, there was an element of risk (a stake), plus a possible prize – in other words a choice dilemma. On the basis of the case study, the group had to decide what advice they would give to a person in particular circumstances. For example, what advice would you give to a young electrical engineer? At present she has a good, pensionable, steady, but rather boring, job with a large organization. She has been offered a job in a newly established computer firm, with the possibility of a partnership if all goes well. The risks are, of course, also high. The sector is very volatile, with a lot of companies failing each year.

In considering the advice to be given, each individual first makes their own decision. There then follows a group meeting in which everyone reveals their own decision, followed by a group discussion. Each individual then reassesses their own decision, in the light of the group discussion. In these circumstances, it was found that a high percentage of individuals make a more risky decision following the group discussion, hence the name 'risky shift'. At first it was thought that the reason for this risky shift could be the particular group on whom the experiments were conducted. Those in business might be expected to be predisposed towards riskier decisions. This is not the case. The experiments have been repeated across many different groups, in many different countries. The results are remarkably similar. After a group discussion people take more risky decisions. This is not to say that every individual, or every group shifts to a riskier position. Rather the effect is an average one, across a number of groups and a number of individuals.

Some years after the original work, it was realized that there was a small number of case studies that did not produce a risky shift. In fact, they consistently produced a 'cautious' shift. All the cases that produce such a cautious shift have one characteristic in common. The 'stake' involved is large. To take the earlier example of the electrical engineer, in the case study she is in her early career and the stake is therefore low. What if she were in her late career, and leaving the company meant forfeiting all pension rights?

Although most people's individual decisions err on the side of caution in such cases, a shift does still occur. It is, however, one towards even more caution. It appears that the effect of comparing and discussing decisions has the effect of polarizing the initial decision. Risky decisions become more risky, cautious ones more cautious.

The final point to be made about polarization is that the amount of shift is not uniform. In general, the more extreme the initial judgement (whether it be risky or cautious), the greater the size of the shift.

Just why does group polarization occur? The first explanation, as mentioned earlier, was in terms of 'special' groups (such as American managers). Another suggestion was that people conform to a group 'norm' so that their scores converge towards the group average. Neither of these are correct. Another suggestion was that the group leader was having a large influence. This was disproved when it was found that the risky shift occurred, even when the leader was advocating caution.

There appear to be two reasons for the shifts. The rather more obvious one is that of persuasive arguments. Each individual will have made their decision on the basis of risky items outweighing cautious items (or vice versa). The items that each person has taken into consideration will be different. When all these items are shared, there is evidence for an even riskier decision.

The other reason is based in social comparison theory. In general, we all like to see ourselves as 'above average' on desirable qualities. For example, 80 per cent of drivers rate themselves above average. This is of course logically impossible. Consider now the case of the engineer. Most people rate themselves as above average on risk taking. Not so high as to be considered foolhardy, just 'above average'. Accordingly, their decision is based on what they think is above average risk taking. But what is average? At this point they do not know. When they get in the group and share their decisions, however, they find that everyone else has similar levels of risk taking. This then is the 'average'. When they take their second decision, they now know what 'average' is so they then have to increase their level of risk in order to put themselves where they thought they were in the first place, just 'above average'! Each of these explanations, it appears, has about equal weight. Half the shift can be attributed to persuasive argument, half to social comparison.

Polarization has to be recognised as a potential influence on group decision making. If a group of normally cautious managers discusses an issue, their final decision is likely to be even more cautious. Likewise, a group of risktaking managers will make even riskier decisions. However, perhaps a potentially greater danger is that of 'groupthink'.

Groupthink. The term was coined by I. L. Janis (1972) following his study into a number of real-life, and disastrous, decisions within the American presidency. He examined the circumstances surrounding a number of important decisions which turned out to be wrong. In each case warnings sounded about the dangers were ignored. The decisions he investigated included the invasion of North Korea, which brought the Chinese into the Korean war, and the 'Bay of Pigs' fiasco in Cuba. In the latter case, President Kennedy authorized the CIA to help Cuban exiles mount an 'invasion' of Cuba. It got no further than the beach at the Bays of Pigs!

Analysing what happened, Janis suggested that, under certain conditions, commitment to the group began to override the ability to assess situations realistically. This occurs when a number of factors combine: first, the group faces a situation where a very important decision has to be made, often under severe constraints of time; second, the group is already fairly cohesive; third, the group has a tendency to isolate itself from outsiders, finally, the leader has a preferred solution which he or she actively pursues and recommends to the group. Under these circumstances the ability for rational assessment of alternatives may be seriously impaired.

There are a number of symptoms by which groupthink may be detected. These are:

▶ a feeling of invulnerability
▶ the rationalizing away of non-preferred solutions
▶ an appeal to morality
▶ the stereotyping of opponents in negative terms
▶ pressure on doubters within the group to conform
▶ self-censorship
▶ unanimity
▶ the appointment of 'mindguards' to censor undesirable information and opinions.

Fortunately for our future survival, Kennedy learnt the lessons from the Bay of Pigs in time for the Cuban missile crisis. His decision-making process was, by then, far more open to external, and dissenting, opinions. Managers need to realize that a group, especially one that is close-knit, may become liable to groupthink. The best defence against this is the introduction of new members with different ideas.

Groupthink, then, is the danger inherent in what might be considered to be a desirable quality of a group – cohesiveness.

Cohesiveness. All things being equal, cohesive groups will be more effective than less cohesive ones. In general, groups that are together a lot are more cohesive than those with outlying members. Often managers will try to encourage such cohesiveness as it brings benefits of high levels of motivation. But the dangers should also be recognized. As well as groupthink, there are potential problems when the group has to deal with other groups. This will be dealt with further in the next chapter when the damaging effects on groups of inappropriate competition and intergroup rivalry are considered.

To sum up, groups have potential benefits. They can, when used properly, increase commitment and motivation, as well as making better quality decisions. They have their dangers, however, notably polarization and groupthink. But when is it appropriate for the group, rather than just one individual, to make decisions?

WHEN SHOULD GROUPS MAKE DECISIONS?

Before going further, consider the following case, which happened to one of the authors some 20 years ago. At the time he was one of five engineers in a particular department of a firm which manufactured heavy current electrical switchgear. One member of the department was required to go to South Wales to oversee the overhaul of some switchgear in a steelworks. Such working away was required every so often. For various reasons, however, none of the five wanted to go. How should the decision be made as to who should go?

One alternative is for the manager to decide who shall go, purely on the information he or she already has. At the other end of the scale, the group itself could be allowed to take the decision. When this situation is used as a case study, the pattern is fairly predictable. In most cases people suggest that the department manager should take the decision, possibly after further consultation with the five engineers. (In real life this was the way the decision was made. The author was the one chosen. He left the firm shortly after.) Some people suggest that the group should be given the opportunity to take the decision, but with the manager reserving 'tell' (see page 87) as a fall-back. But why should the group not be able to take the decision unaided, even if they decided to draw straws?

There are three major factors we have to consider. Do they have the technical competence to make the decision? Can they cope with the emotional aspects that may go with making a decision? Finally, could they be expected to reach a conclusion? Let us take them one at a time.

1) The decision itself does not require any specific technical expertise.

2) Why assume that mature people are unable to cope with the process of reaching a decision? In other parts of their life, they will be doing this all the time.

3) Why should they not be able to come to a decision?

The last one is the reason, after the other two have been discussed, why many managers tend to maintain that *they* have to make the decision. Thinking back to the model of dependency discussed on page 75, you may realize that this is a classic sign of dependency. 'We can't make a decision, you make it for us'. It is an expectation built on experiences of Theory X management. The children of one of the author's exhibit this when trying to decide who should have the car. There is a tendency for one, or both, to turn to parents to settle the argument. Why should we? Cannot two adults negotiate an arrangement? If they are made aware that a decision *has* to be reached, then they should be capable of reaching one.

A more sophisticated and prescriptive approach has been suggested by Vic Vroom and P. W. Yetton (1973). They propose a 'decision tree' approach to how problems should be solved. Their theory is often described as a leadership theory, but we prefer to use it in the context of deciding when to use groups to make decisions as it specifically addresses the issue of *who* should make decisions. According to Vroom and Yetton, whichever approach is taken will depend upon three factors:

   i) the nature of the task i.e. technical quality;
  ii) whether group commitment is required i.e. organizational quality;
 iii) whether the problem overlaps with the job areas of others.

They suggest that the following questions are answered sequentially by the manger concerned, moving along the 'tree':

    i) Does the problem possess a quality requirement?
   ii) Do I have enough information to make a high-quality decision?
  iii) Is the problem structured, i.e. are all the causal relationships clear?
  iv) Is acceptance of the decision by subordinates important for effective implementation?
   v) If I were to make the decision by myself is it reasonably certain that it would be accepted by my subordinates?
  vi) Do subordinates share the organizational goals to be attained by solving this problem?
 vii) Is conflict among subordinates likely in preferred solution?

Following the decision tree gives an answer as to which decision-making approach should be adopted, ranging from decision making by the manager alone to total group involvement. (The full model may be found in the recommended book by Alan Bryman (1986).)

In our experience this model is rather complex for everyday usage, but the issues it highlights are extensions of the three considerations listed above. Can the group cope with the technical aspects, the emotional aspects and the responsibility of coming to a decision? These are answers that require information, not assumptions.

In summary, to produce an effective and committed group the manager must attend to both the task and the process. So far as the task is concerned, all the group members should be working on the same dimension of decision making at the same time. If half are considering goals whilst the others are considering practicalities the result will be a fragmented meeting.

The manager also needs to guard against possible distortions produced by polarization and groupthink. The effects of both can be minimized by the inclusion of new members with new perspectives. The inclusion of new members with possibly dissenting views carries the potential for disruption. It is here that attention to group processes is particularly important. Discussion should be kept very much in Adult terms (see Chapter 1). In addition, if high commitment is needed it will take time to develop as it often depends upon the group members feeling that they have been listened to and have had a genuine influence on the final decision. One final word of warning however. Some managers, realizing the benefits of high commitment, may try to manipulate the group. The group is led to believe that it can reach a decision when, in fact, the decision has already been taken elsewhere. This form of false participation is a very high-risk strategy. If the group at any time realize what is taking place, the effects are likely to be not only disastrous but counterproductive.

As we have seen, the bonds that tie groups together can have their disadvantages. Conflict between groups is another potential disadvantage and it is this that will now be considered.

5

Intergroup Conflict

This chapter deals with an issue fundamental to the working of any complex organization, whether it be a company or a nation: how to establish and maintain effective working relationships between groups which, for whatever reason, have to work together. As we will see, there are strong pressures, both economic and psychological, within organizations for intergroup conflict to arise.

A number of questions immediately arise when considering such intergroup conflict:

- Is such conflict desirable nor not?
- What are the causes and consequences of conflict?
- How can the consequences of conflict be reduced in those situations where it is considered undesirable?

As we will see, one of the main causes of conflict is competition. However, most managers would agree that some intergroup competition is inevitable and, indeed, desirable. If there was no competition, the likelihood is that the organization would become stagnant, with few pressures to induce positive change, the result being that its efficiency would suffer. The other extreme, of very high levels of competition and conflict, is also likely to be undesirable. Extreme conflict is likely to lead to levels of anxiety and tension in the work force that are counterproductive.

As shown in Chapter 4, there are advantages to be gained from working in groups. They fulfil some of our own needs and give a sense of identity. In return, they require a degree of conformity to group norms. These norms, together with a feeling of belonging, can have powerful influences on the way people behave. These become heightened when one group is in competition with another. This is, of course, well known to managers. Competitions arranged by management between different departments or branches of an organization are not unusual. Often, the effect is to increase effort, and hopefully, improve performance. Such competitions are not, however, without their dangers.

There are circumstances in which they may damage the normal co-operative relationship. For example, in many of the armed services, intercompany football matches and other competitive events are used to heighten feelings of group solidarity. Studies of the US forces in Vietnam revealed, however, that these feelings of intergroup rivalry transferred to the battlefield. Even in the face of the enemy, these groups found difficulty co-operating – sometimes with disastrous results.

It is essential, therefore, to be able to determine what level of inter-group competition and conflict is maximally efficient in any particular situation. As will be shown, this decision is one of balancing benefits against costs. It does seem, however, that the pressures that push groups towards conflict are stronger than those pulling them away from it. We will concentrate, therefore, on the pressures that push groups into conflict at levels that are undesirable, and then look at ways in which such levels can be lowered.

CAUSES AND CONSEQUENCES OF CONFLICT

To turn to the causes and consequences of conflict, Chapter 1 showed that behaviour may have a number of causes. It may be determined by an individual's 'personality'. It may also be determined by the situation. Most probably, it is determined by a combination of both. Arguments continue about the relative influence of each. To what extent, therefore, is conflict between groups caused by the personalities of particular individuals?

There is no doubt that some aspects of a group's interactions will be influenced by the personalities of those involved. However the effects described below are apparently independent of personality. They happen to everyone. Such phenomena as racial prejudice, chauvinism, and football hooliganism are all within their scope.

One explanation given for why groups compete is that people are competitive. Unfortunately, this is a circular agreement – people are competitive because people are competitive. But people do not compete with everybody. If we are to determine the causes of conflict we need to know the conditions which are necessary for it to occur. The late Henri Tajfel (1972) and his colleagues set out to answer just this question by exploring the factors that make one group discriminate against another.

DISCRIMINATION

As a European Jew during the Second World War, Tajfel had strong personal reasons for seeking to uncover the source of intergroup discrimination. One obvious reason for discrimination is that one group obtains an objective economic advantage by discriminating against another. Tajfel therefore arranged experimental situations in which there was no tangible economic advantage to be gained by discrimination. Even in these circumstances discrimination was evident.

What other factors might be causing this continuing discrimination? Although all economic advantages were removed, the group members might assume, wrongly, that they still existed. Yet another reason might be that, although there is no advantage to be gained in this particular instance, a history of hostilities exists between the groups. If these potential sources of conflict are also removed, then there should be no further reason for intergroup discrimination. But all the evidence shows that this is not the case! Groups who are not currently, nor ever have been in competition, still discriminate against each other. This discrimination goes even further. Let us take another example, again based upon one of Tajfel's experiments.

You have been asked, in an experiment, to distribute money to individuals. The individuals concerned have been allocated, at random, to one of two groups, but these groups will never meet. Your job is to distribute money to all the individuals in the experiment (£1 being the smallest unit allowed). Each allocation is done in pairs consisting of one individual from group 1 and another from group 2. The only thing you know about them is which group they belong to. On each allocation you have to distribute a total of £15. You could, for example, give £14 to one individual and £1 to the other. You could also give £8 to one and £7 to the other. How would you allocate the money? Most people say that they would operate 'fairly'. Thus, on the first allocation they would give £8 to the individual in group 1 and £7 to the individual in group 2. On the next allocation they would reverse the process. In this way they would, at the end, have given the same amount of money to group 1 as to group 2. There is no reason to behave otherwise. You can have no preferences for any of the individuals involved. You do not know who they are, and you never will.

Let us now change the situation very slightly. Exactly the same conditions apply but you have been told that *you* have been allocated to one of the two groups. Again, the groups will never meet and you have nothing to gain by discriminating for or against either group. Again there appears to be no rational reason for behaving other than 'fairly'. This does not happen! Even random allocation to a group with which you will never have interactions leads to discrimination in favour of 'your own' group!

What Tajfel, and M. Sherif (1966) before him show is that simply categorizing an individual as a member of a particular group has effects. The in-group is then favoured against out-groups. The potential for conflict is present, even where no economic pressures exist – there is tension, even before competition. Think, for example, of public feelings when a fellow national does something particularly praiseworthy or blameworthy. There is no logical reason why Australians should feel pride when an Australian researcher wins a Nobel prize, or the British shame when a group of British football hooligans do something deplorable in a foreign country. We have contributed to neither and therefore share no responsibility.

Another of Tajfel's experiments created a situation in which it was apparent that the two groups could, by co-operating, both increase their incomes. It would still be the case, however, that one group would end up with a higher income than the other. In these circumstances, the groups do not take up this higher profit option. They each appear more intent on beating the other, rather than maximizing their income.

If the implications of these findings are not immediately apparent, let us spell them out. When people are allocated to a group they discriminate, at first unconsciously, in favour of that group and against others. This is the case even when they know that they have been randomly allocated to the group, and that they will never meet the other members. Think then of the potential for discrimination when the group is meeting regularly, and particularly where members can choose the group to which they wish to belong. Why this should happen is not entirely clear. Again, the most likely explanation is that given by Tajfel, and explains the apparent desire of the groups to beat each other, rather than co-operate to beat the 'system'.

The basic assumption is that we all attempt to increase or maintain our own *positive self-image*. One way of doing this is by belonging to particular groups. These groups can be a source for maintaining or enhancing our self-image. By helping the group improve its standing and prestige, we improve our own self-image. For example, groups of professionals may often resist the erosion of pay differentials. They may do so by objecting to pay rises planned for those groups they consider subordinate to their own. (Remember equity theory and the concept of investments discussed on pages 46–49.) The group becomes, therefore, a potential vehicle for defending or improving *our* self-image. Indeed, in large, complex societies our membership of groups (e.g. professions, clubs), is most probably the major source of self-image. If the success and prestige of the group increases, so does our own. The way this is achieved is by improving the group's standing compared with other groups – hence discrimination.

COMPETITION

The distinction between groups that co-operate and those that compete is not a strict dichotomy. Every group within an organization will come into at least partial conflict with every other group with which it interacts. Discrimination may be universal, but it will only come to the surface when the groups are pushed into competition by 'economic' factors (in a broad sense of the word).

Economic factors. Each group will have its own goals. The extent to which other groups hinder the achievement of these goals will influence the level of conflict. There are a number of reasons why such hindering occurs. First, groups may be in competition for *scarce resources*. These resources may be financial, but they may also be non-financial, for example manpower. Specialist employees are often in short supply, and hence may be shared between several groups. There is obvious potential here for conflict.

As well as competition for scarce resources, there may be *differences in the actual goals* for different groups, or in the timescale over which such goals are to be achieved. For example, the goal of the service department may be to provide a particular level of service within a particular response time. This may require a certain level of stock to be maintained, so that spare parts are always available. The stock controllers, on the other hand, may have as their goal the reduction of capital tied up in stock. These two goals, both desirable, are potentially incompatible.

Finally, the degree to which groups are *objectively dependent* upon each other for achieving their goals will have an influence. There are three types of such dependence. In *pooled* dependence, individual groups merely contribute their own results to a central pool. Independent branches or subsidiary companies are of this nature. None is dependent upon any other for what they do. The potential for conflict here is very low and competition between the branches may be a highly appropriate way of improving performance. Such 'pure' pooled dependence is, however, rare. Branches are often partially dependent upon each other, and may be in competition for scarce resources supplied from the centre.

Sequential dependence is best characterized by production lines. Each stage is dependent upon the one that precedes it, but not the one that follows. Here the potential for conflict is higher, but only one way, that is, only with the group preceding yours. Again pure cases are rare.

Perhaps most common is *reciprocal* dependence. Here there is a continual flow between groups, each dependent upon the other. Planning and executing all complex activities involve such dependence. The potential for conflict to occur is at its highest. Looking at the major groups with which your own group interacts, it is normally fairly easy to determine which of these potentials for conflict are applicable.

These 'economic' factors build on the psychological predisposition for out-group discrimination and push groups into competition. The consequences of such competition will be considered next.

Psychological factors. Competition between groups has effects that are perceptual, emotional, and behavioural.

Perceptions involving both the in-group and the out-group are affected, distorting and sharpening distinctions between the groups. This does not apply to every characteristic, but only to those characteristics that are considered important for winning the competition, or that have an emotional significance for the group. Whatever the reasons, on those dimensions considered important the in-group enhances its view of itself by denying its weaknesses and exaggerating its strengths, and degrades its views of the out-group. (Notice the potential for groupthink as discussed on page 104.) These sharpened distinctions result in stereotypes, both of in-group and out-group, which, like all other stereotypes, have two main characteristics. They distort and sharpen intergroup differences and, in addition, are very stable and resistant to change.

At the emotional level, almost all emotions concerning the other group are negative. The other group is seen as 'hostile' or 'aggressive'. As a result it becomes an enemy – 'them' against 'us'. This emotional reaction also affects perceptions, not only of the abilities of the other group, but also of their motives.

These perceptual and emotional factors inevitably have a result on behaviour toward the other group. Interactions between the groups become strained. As a result, such interactions decline. When such interactions have, of necessity, to take place, group members spend more time attending to their own spokeperson's performance than to what the other group has to say.

WINNERS AND LOSERS

All these effects take place before and during competition. But what are the consequences on the group that wins and the group that loses? As you might expect, they are different for each group. Edgar Schein (1980) suggests that these effects can be summarized as follows:

WINNERS:
- Cohesion is retained, and even increases.
- There is a release of tension that built up during competition.
- There is a switch to person orientation.
- There is a 'fat and happy' feel to the group.
- The stereotypes of both in-group and out-group are confirmed.

LOSERS:
- If the result is ambiguous, then it is denied or distorted.
- If the result is unambiguous, then a scapegoat is found, either within or outside the group, e.g. the referee.
- There is continued emphasis on task orientation.
- Re-grouping for the next stage takes precedence over other activities.
- The group becomes tense and 'lean and hungry'.
- Because the stereotypes have been disproved, there is a high potential for learning.

One other way in which losers deal with their defeat is to reinterpret it. The most common way for this to occur is to claim the 'moral' victory. Although the other group may have won the 'official' contest, the in-group is credited, for example, with being the most virtuous. The effects, on both winners and losers, are to increase rather than decrease inter-group rivalry.

Competition between groups, therefore, brings both advantages and disadvantages. While the competition is under way, there is a high level of group cohesiveness and motivation. What has to be remem-bered, however, is that these very advantages will adversely affect inter-group relations. If the groups are dependent on each other to any extent, the effect may be to decrease the overall effectiveness of the organization. Given that working in groups is inevitable, how can such intergroup conflict be minimized?

MANAGING CONFLICT

WHEN IS COMPETITION APPROPRIATE?

Before looking at how conflict can be resolved, we will first look at when competition is perceived to be appropriate. As we have seen, competition can arise from two sources – economic factors and psychological factors. There is a concept developed from *games theory*, which is particularly useful when considering the economic factors. The concept concerns whether a 'game' (which is defined very broadly in this context) is *zero sum* or *non-zero sum*. A zero sum game is where, at the end of the game, the total of wins equals the total of losses. Hence, they sum to zero. To give an example, any form of gambling for money is a zero sum game. What you lose, others gain, and vice versa. A non-zero sum game is different. As well as there being winners and losers, there is the possibility that both parties can end up winning, or both can end up losing.

In general, especially within organizations, there are far fewer zero sum games than people imagine. Let us take the example of pay negoti-ations, or any such labour dispute. This surely is a zero sum game: what the employees win in the form of an increase in pay, the organi-zation loses in equivalent profits. But this is not necessarily the case. Most such situations are potentially non-zero sum, that is, both parties can gain or both can lose. Higher pay may be related to, for example, more flexible working arrangements.

Each of these types of game requires a different approach. If the game is zero sum, then competition is most appropriate. If it is non-zero sum, then both parties have the potential to gain from co-operating. The problem arises, of course, when one side is co-operating but the other is competing. This is dealt with shortly.

While by far the majority of 'games' within an organization are non-zero sum, this is not usually the case between organizations who are in the same market. Even here, however, organizations realize that it is, from their point of view, potentially a non-zero sum game. Unfortunately for them, such co-operation (for example price fixing, contract sharing, etc.) is illegal. A true market economy requires competition as a *sine qua non*. The market can cope with some organizations failing in a competitive environment. But can an organization allow a particular department or branch to fail? Most probably not, especially if there is sequential or reciprocal dependence.

Defining a situation as potentially non-zero sum does not, of course, instantly resolve all the problems. There remain the problems of how to establish co-operation, and how to resolve those differences that are bound to occur. One moves here into psychological rather than the economic considerations.

TRUST

We have already said that one difficulty is that of cheating. While one group is dealing in the spirit of co-operation, the other side is dealing competitively. The danger is, of course, that the co-operative group will get 'taken to the cleaners'. This highlights the crucial element in any co-operative venture – trust. Trust takes a long time to establish, but only one instance of 'betrayal' can destroy it. Trust is intimately linked with the degree of openness between the groups. As trust declines, so does the extent to which each group is prepared to be honest and open with the other. Such openness and honesty carries the risk of cheating. As a result, a downward spiral of decreasing trust and openness sets in.

A good example of a non-zero sum game where, until recently, there had been little evidence of trust and openness, is the superpower arms race. The problem is now to replace the downward trust/openness spiral with an upward spiral. The only way in which this can be done is by increased openness. This is often done on a tentative, step-by-step basis. If the other side does not reciprocate, the losses are limited.

COMMUNICATION

To say that openness, by itself, is the answer is inaccurate. In the 1960s it was thought that open communications between groups would, by itself, lead to conflict resolution. To translate the old French saying, 'to know all is to forgive all'. It soon became clear that improving communications was not the answer. On occasions, rather than reduce the potential for conflict, it actually increased it. The other group found out *exactly* what you wanted, and found it even more unacceptable than what they *thought* you wanted! Conflicts may sometimes be resolved by better communication, but this is not always the case.

DOMINATION

Another method of dealing with conflict is to use power to resolve issues. The group with more power imposes its wishes on the other. Dealing with conflict by domination is, we suspect, a common occurrence in organizations. It has the advantage of being quick. But it also has its own problems. Dominance relies upon one group having more power than the other. It is rare, however, for all the power to reside in one of the groups. Everyone has some power. For example, it might be thought that the armed forces, together with prisons, represent those situations where power distribution is at its most extreme. Those in authority in both organizations will freely admit, however, that smooth running is dependent, to a large extent, on at least the tacit acceptance of their authority by those who are being controlled. Even the inmates of prisons have some power. If they refuse to accept the authority of the prison officers to control, the power balance is considerably altered. Examples from some prisoners of war, or prisoners of conscience, who have been tortured are interesting. Some report that, at a particular point in their torture, they decide that they are likely to die. After this, the torturers' power over them disappears. They may kill them, but they can no longer threaten them. (The film *The Hill*, starring Sean Connery, which is set in an army prison, illustrates some of these situations.)

Using power also carries with it the problem of counter dependence (see Chapter 3). Outright rebellion may not emerge, but the potential for groups to wage 'organizational guerrilla war' may be considerable.

NEGOTIATION

Dealing with conflict by resolution (that is, seeing and understanding the other groups' needs), is not enough by itself. Nor is domination. What is required is negotiation. This negotiation will, of necessity, include elements of both resolution and dominance. To return to resolution, what is required is not 'naive openness' but 'openness in negotiation'.

To see how negotiations can proceed let us now consider a particular model which incorporates the concept of co-operation, but also adds a second dimension – that of *assertion*. (The model is a general one and hence can be applied to individual negotiating style, as well as group interactions.) One of the easiest ways to introduce the concept of assertion is to contrast it with that of aggression. Aggression does not take into account the needs of the other party, other than as an opponent. Assertion, on the other hand, is concerned with the legitimate needs of both sides. To be aggressive is to ignore the other's needs and wishes. To be assertive is to recognize that both parties have needs that have to be taken into account, if a negotiated settlement is to be achieved.

Combining these two dimensions produces a grid as shown in Figure 17. Both dimensions are, of course, continuous but, for simplicity's sake, we will consider only high and low on each. This produces four categories, together with a fifth at the point where the four meet.

Avoiding, or withdrawing, is characterized by low levels of both co-operation and assertion. The problems are therefore ignored. This may be the position of both groups, or just one of them. If both are in this position, nothing will be done to resolve the differences. If only one is taking this position, then the other's position is likely to be that of competing, or forcing. The other alternatives are ruled out as, by definition, it takes two to co-operate.

Accommodating is characterized by co-operation, but little assertion. 'Don't make waves' might be the motto of such a group. If both groups take this line it is likely that some agreement will be reached. This will not, however, be a satisfactory or lasting agreement. In order to achieve

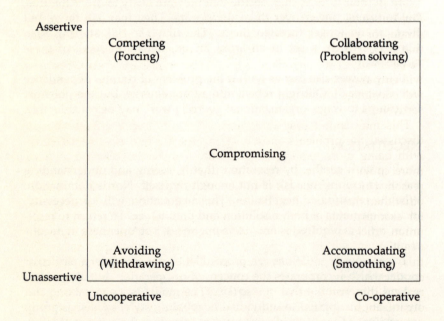

FIGURE 17. *Dimensions of conflict resolution (from Thomas, 1975)*

it, both sides will have avoided openly stating their real needs. A false consensus is the likely outcome. If only one group adopts this line, the other has two responses. The first is to ignore the co-operation and trade on the other's weakness in failing to present its needs, in other words, to force the issue to a conclusion beneficial to itself. The other alternative is perhaps more common. The norms of reciprocity, discussed in Chapter 2, often mean that co-operation is returned. The other group may, therefore, try to go for a problem-solving approach. In doing this, its members may also believe that the others are also asserting their needs. The fact that they are not reveals itself in two ways. The feeling that all is not being disclosed often produces the question 'are you sure that's OK with you?', or variations on that theme. The other effect may only reveal itself much later, when the false consensus emerges, often producing the comment 'why didn't you say this when we discussed it?'

Competing, or forcing, allows only two responses: avoidance, which allows the other group to dominate, or competition. If both groups are assertively uncooperative, the contest will eventually be determined by whichever group can bring most power to bear in that particular situation. (You may have noticed that the squares of conflict resolution model are also interpretable in terms of the OK Corral – see page 29.)

Problem solving. Except in those situations where competition is appropriate, for example in a zero-sum game, it is most probably apparent that *problem solving* is the best form of achieving a negotiated settlement. To be effective such negotiations need to be explicit and open. Openness will encourage trust and hence co-operation. Being precise and explicit will encourage movement on the other dimension, towards greater assertiveness.

This may sound easy to achieve, but it is not. We have already discussed the problems of establishing trust. There are also problems with being more explicit. People within organizations tend to have more contact with each other than they do with outsiders. For this reason it may be thought that they could be more explicit with each other than these outsiders. This may not be the case. Evidence suggests, for example, that such interactions as wage negotiations with trade union officials are likely to be far more explicit about needs than are negotiations within the organization. To understand the reasons for this, we need to return to social exchange theory (see page 46). The contract between the wage negotiators is primarily economic. Each party realizes this, and is hence prepared to express their needs. Within the organization, however, social as well as economic exchanges are involved. Once again, social and economic factors become confused.

TECHNIQUES FOR REDUCING CONFLICT

How then can conflict be either avoided or, if it already exists, defused? It will be recalled that there are two sources for intergroup conflict, economic and psychological. The economic causes should be avoided by ensuring that win/lose situations are avoided. This may not be as difficult to achieve as it appears. The majority of situations are potentially non-zero sum, despite appearances to the contrary.

So far as the psychological aspects are concerned, there are a number of ways of reducing their impact. A simple way of reducing conflict is to direct it towards a goal that both groups find acceptable. This is known as a superordinate goal, as it encompasses both of the two subordinate goals. In organizational terms, it may mean substituting conflicting group goals with those that emphasize total organizational effectiveness. The service department and the stores should be given the joint goal of achieving an agreed level of customer service, while keeping stock levels to a minimum. A variation of this is for the groups to identify a common 'enemy', against which they can join forces. The war-time spirit which this engenders leads to the competing groups forgetting their differences, at least for the duration of hostilities.

Other techniques are perhaps more practical. They include ways of breaking down people's stereotypes of other groups. Some techniques involve direct intervention, such as one based on confrontation, in which groups confront each other with their perceptions and feelings. This is obviously a 'high risk' method. The pay-offs are potentially high, but so are the risks. For this reason it is usually done with the help of outside facilitators. Each group is invited to share its perception, both of itself and of the other group. These perceptions are then openly voiced, but without any comments being allowed. The groups then separate to consider the discrepancies and the possible reasons for them. These too are then shared in a joint meeting. This method can produce beneficial results very quickly but requires expert handling.

A less risky procedure involves the forced interaction of members of the different groups. This may take place at a number of levels. Often, in order to establish credibility, the leaders have to be the first to meet. (It is interesting how President Reagan's 'evil empire' perception of the Soviet Union changed following the Reagan/Gorbachev summit meetings.) Once credibility has been achieved, it can be further developed and maintained by frequent communication and the 'swapping' of group members. It is not surprising that cultural and educational exchanges are common between countries who are trying to improve their relations. After the first inspection visit by three Russian Colonels, a British officer remarked that he had realized, with some surprise, that they were 'normal, nice, blokes'. In fact, within Nato, the armed forces also ensure that officers at all levels spend some time in other countries' units. This is also now becoming more common within organizations, especially when one organization takes over another. In this situation, however, there is a high potential for conflict from boardroom to shop floor, especially if the take-over was resisted.

To summarize, conflict between groups in organizations is almost inevitable. Indeed some competition is desirable. The inefficiency that it produces is, however, often ignored by organizations. Hard-pressed managers tend to work on short time scales, and the short-term benefits of competition outweigh the longer-term disadvantages. Managers need to take time to look at the wider perspective and to achieve a realistic balance between the benefits and dangers of intergroup rivalry in their own particular circumstances. If necessary, they should then take steps to eliminate undesirable conflict.

6

Identifying
Organizational Problems

As an exercise for this section, we would like you to try to answer the following questions about an organization with which you are familiar. This might be your present employer, but you can do it for any organization which you know well.

1. If you were asked for one piece of advice, for a new member, on how to survive and prosper in the organization, what would it be? (Examples might be 'keep a low profile', 'make yourself visible' etc.)

2. What slogan or motto would best sum up the organization? (For example, 'biggest and best', 'always second' etc.)

3. What animal would you choose to be the organization's mascot? It can be any animal, including birds, fish and reptiles, but should represent the organization as it actually is. You should then choose another animal that would represent the organization as you would ideally like it to be. (Examples given by managers have included dinosaurs, whales, moles etc.)

We will return to your advice, slogan, and animals later in the chapter.

Before attempting to describe and analyse different types of organization and their problems we need to define what we mean by an organization. Because organizations are all around us we tend to take them for granted. With the exception of the apparatus of the state and the church, most organizations are of fairly modern origin. It was the changes in production in the Industrial Revolution that led to the creation of the complex industrial and commercial organizations with which we are all familiar. Like elephants, they are easy to recognize but hard to define. Perhaps, the easiest way is to list what they have in common:

☐ They consist of individuals, organized into groups and subgroups.

☐ These individuals come together to achieve certain goals and objectives. There will usually be varying degrees of clarity and agreement concerning these goals and objectives.

☐ These individuals perform specific and specialist functions. This means they often have different skills, abilities, and responsibilities.

☐ Because of the differentiation of people into specialist functions, there is a problem of co-ordinating and controlling the various functions.

One other thing that they have in common is that they persist over time. As we will see, organizations have to adapt and, in adapting, they will change. What will remain constant, however, are the characteristics listed above.

The problems that organizations face involve two dimensions: dealing with the external environment, and managing their internal environment. It is with the latter problem, of managing and controlling the internal environment, that we will deal first. Perhaps the classic analysis of how large-scale collective activities should be organized is that of Max Weber (1970). Weber was chiefly concerned with the way that the state apparatus, or civil service, should be run. He was concerned with the concept of authority, and the mechanisms by which legitimate authority could exert its control. It was Weber who coined the much-maligned term 'bureaucracy'. Nowadays, it is synonymous with red tape and inertia but, in Weber's terms, bureaucracy is a way of exerting control effectively and impartially. It is characterized by the following:

▶ Individuals have specialized tasks, for which they are specifically qualified.

▶ Tasks are performed within the guidelines of established rules and procedures.

▶ Each individual can be accountable to only one boss. This boss holds his or her post on the basis of his or her technical competence, and exerts power that is delegated from above.

▶ Relationships, both with clients and colleagues, are based on formally established rules and procedures. Personal likings and preferences are not allowed to influence interactions.

▶ Employment, as well as being based on technical competence, is protected against arbitrary dismissal.

Mechanistic organizations. Weber's analysis, as mentioned above, concerns the apparatus of the state, perhaps the original organization. Many present-day organizations are based around such concepts of hierarchy, and delegated authority and responsibility. The army and church are prime, and historic, examples. The analogy that is often used of such systems is that they are like machines. Each cog in the machine has a particular, highly specialized function to fulfil. As long as all the cogs operate as they should, than the machine performs effectively. Like the machine, such a system is a considerable improvement over individual workers, toiling away in isolation. Just as the machine achieves this improvement by the complex interrelationship of simple components, so does the organization. The first systematic application of such mechanistic approaches to industrial organizations was by Henri Fayol (1967). His experiences of the organization of French coal mines led him, in the 1920s, to publish his views on the way in which such organizations should be structured.

According to Fayol, to be effective, organizations should be organized according to the following principles:

☐ Tasks should be specialized. This means that there should be division of labour.

☐ There should be unity of direction, in other words, those with the same sorts of expertise should be grouped together, for example all those involved in accounting should be in the same department.

☐ The manager has broader responsibilities than his or her subordinates, and is for this reason given more authority. The higher a manager is in the hierarchy, the more responsibility, and, consequently, the more authority he or she possesses.

☐ Authority should be on a 'chain' principle. Each person should answer to one, and only one, boss.

The implications for the command structure and the flow of information are clear: a strict hierarchy, along military lines, with commands being transmitted downwards. The only time the information flow is reversed is when situations are encountered that are not covered by standard procedures. The increasing levels of responsibility and authority, together with the high degree of specialization, leads to a highly centralized and highly formalized system. As you may recall from the section on communication patterns in groups (see page 101), such a highly centralized system has advantages and disadvantages. On the plus side, it is a system that is highly efficient at dealing with simple and routine tasks, for example, processing and dispatching orders for standard stock items. On the negative side of the balance sheet, however, is the effect on the workers. Such a system is demoralizing and offers little opportunity for gaining job satisfaction. While for some purposes this may not matter, for others the lack of motivation may be important.

Organic organizations. If an organization is dependent on harnessing the full potential of its workers, then it will have to adopt a structure that enables those individuals to contribute to, as well as take orders from, the system. Rensis Likert (1961) described such an organization as 'organic' rather than 'mechanistic'. The emphasis in such an organization is that communication, information processing and decision making take place at all levels. Likert argues that such a system will have the additional advantage of being flexible and adaptable. It will be able to respond to changes, either in the external environment, or in the internal environment as, for example, the organization grows. The organization is seen as a living, growing, developing organism, rather than as a fixed, unchanging, inflexible machine. The growth in communications that an organic structure implies can also produce problems. Likert suggests some ways of dealing with these, which will be considered later.

The proponents of mechanistic and organic theories suggest that their ideas are correct and desirable. They sometimes overlook the fact that *both* may be effective, but under differing circumstances. We have suggested that mechanistic structures may be appropriate for firms engaged in routine work. An organic structure may be more appropriate for highly complex operations in a rapidly changing environment.

Paul Lawrence and Jay Lorsch of Harvard Business School, in their study of firms in the plastics industry (1969), went further and suggested that, even within the same firm, different departments may have different structures. These different structures arise primarily, they suggest, as the result of pressures from different external environments. Where the environment is stable and unlikely to change, such as in basic production processes, then a mechanistic structure is appropriate. Such a differentiation of functions is linked, according to Lawrence and Lorsch, with other characteristics of production departments, in which, for example, there is an emphasis on 'task' rather than 'people', together with relatively short time horizons. For the R & D department, on the other hand, the environment may be extremely volatile and uncertain, requiring a more organic solution. This is likely to involve a more person-oriented approach, together with relatively long time horizons. The problem is, of course, that all these departments have to work together. As you may recall from Chapter 5 on intergroup conflict, differing time scales and goals may induce conflict. The organic and mechanistic structures are likely to produce such differences. These then, according to Lawrence and Lorsch, require integrating together. The problem remains as to how this integration should be achieved. It could be done mechanistically, by the use of formal rules and procedures, or organically by the opening of communication channels. The method chosen will reflect the underlying and predominant philosophy of the organization, and its stage of development.

ORGANIZATIONAL GROWTH

The concepts of 'differentiation' and 'integration' are also used by B.C.J. Lievegoed (1973) in his theory of organizational growth. Organizations do not remain static, rather they grow and develop. The way in which they develop is not, however, random. According to Lievegoed, organizations tend to develop through three well-defined phases. These phases he calls *pioneer, differentiation,* and *integration.* Each is characterized by its own style of management, organizational culture, and its own particular way of relating to the customer. In addition, however, each has its own problems, peculiar to that phase. As the organization develops, the problems become more acute. It is these emerging problems that are the driving force that push the organization into the next phase of development. Each of the phases will now be examined, together with their associated problems.

THE PIONEER PHASE

As its name suggests, this phase is typical of new small entrepreneurial companies. The most common way in which such an organization starts is that an individual, or small group of individuals, identifies an opportunity. They may do this in a number of ways, by, for instance, inventing a new product, developing a new service, or identifying a new, as yet untapped, market. In order to exploit the new opportunity, a company is established, either formally or informally. It may be as small as a sole trader. If any production is required, it is initially contracted out. The firm is too small, at this stage, to invest in or control elaborate production facilities.

The fact that the firm is small, controlled by either one individual or small group, means that communication channels are short and few in number. This offers a number of advantages. Information, for example about changes in the market, or about problems of supply, is quickly transmitted and decisions reached, enabling the organization to respond flexibly and quickly to any such changes.

As the firm grows, employees may be added but the number and length of the communication channels remain small. Most individuals will still report direct to the owner. The structure of the organization, and the channels of communication represent the Wheel shown in Figure 16 (page 102). As a result, control tends to be directive and highly centralized. It may even be seen as autocratic. Motivation is none the less high because employees can see a direct relationship between their work and the product and goals of the organization. (You may recall the concepts as task identity, task significance, etc. from Chapter 2.)

Organizational culture and style of service. The type of organizational culture and style of service is not directly addressed by Lievegoed, but is from the work of Roger Harrison (1987), who identifies four such types. The overlap between the two theories is not, of course, complete but we feel that each adds meaning to the other.)

The pioneer phase seems to be very much what Harrison calls a *power* culture, characterized by a power-oriented service style.

The power culture is authoritarian and hierarchical, usually dominated by a strong leader or group of leaders. They run the organization on the basis that 'they know best'. This may even extend to the needs of their employees. As long as they are right, they are seen as visionary as far as the needs of the organization are concerned, and benevolent autocrats by the employees.

Within such an organization the way to get on is to develop close relationships with those in power, or close to those in power. Status and influence is likely to flow from such relationships. (Here you may like to refer back to your motto and advice to a newcomer to your organization.)

The power orientation tends to be associated with a style of service based upon prestige and status. An example of such a service style is often found in exclusive restaurants or shops. Indeed, restaurants are often a popular business for the entrepreneur. Many are very tightly controlled by the owner, who is often also the chef. This particular type of restaurant often appeals to clients, on the basis of the prestige of the establishment. Advertising comes through write-ups in prestigious newspapers and magazines, and there are elaborate mechanisms for keeping out 'undesirable' clientele.

Other organizations also give different levels of service based upon certain criteria, such as wealth or status, for example first or second class travel. The difference is that the power-oriented service culture sharply demarcates the top level from the others, and concentrates its service on the former.

Problems of the pioneer phase. The problems associated with each phase are related to a number of themes. These can be to do with service style, communications, and the culture itself.

The power/pioneer service style is very much dependent upon the organization's products or service remaining exclusive. Such exclusivity is often ephemeral. In the absence of a sufficiently large clientele, the organization may have to seek other markets. In both cases it is likely to come into competition with other organizations. In the face of this competition it will need specialist advice, either from within the company, or from outside consultants. What often happens in such situations is that consultants are engaged to diagnose and provide solutions to the organization's problems. Their solutions often revolve around the creation of specialist functions within the organization, for example debtor control, marketing, etc.

The growth that leads to the establishment of specialist departments also poses problems of management style and communication channels. As the number of employees grows, the ability of the founders to maintain communication with each and every employee becomes limited. Methods have to be found by which each employee knows their function, without continual reference to the centre. In addition, the autocratic style that was accepted when the organization was small is no longer appropriate. For example, Walt Disney's company was very much a pioneer organization in its early days. When it had grown to about 1,000 employees there was a bitter strike. It is reported that Disney never understood the 'ingratitude' and 'disloyalty' which led to the strike. There is a tendency, in such situations, to look for 'troublemakers'. In reality, it is the situation that has changed, not the people. The organization has become too large for its original management style and communication systems.

One other important issue that faces organizations with autocratic leaders is that of *succession*. There are many examples of the difficulties of those attempting to take over the founder's role. This is especially the case with father–son succession. The Getty family is a good example, as is the Littlewoods company. In the latter case the founder of the football pools and mail order empire continues to exercise highly centralized control over the business empire, in the style of a benevolent autocrat. When his son tried to introduce management practices that he thought were needed to develop the firm, he met so much resistance that he quickly resigned. All these pressures, therefore, push the organization towards the next phase – that of differentiation.

THE DIFFERENTIATION PHASE

The move towards differentiation is an attempt to solve the problems of communication and control, created by the growth of the organization and the associated employment of specialists. It is strongly influenced by the thinking of traditional writers on organizations, such as Fayol. It is perhaps the most common structure within large organizations, and is characterized by specialization and separation on a number of dimensions. For example:

▶ *By function* – there are separate departments for production, sales, personnel etc.

▶ *By product* – there are separate divisions for each product or product family.

▶ *By location* – because of the size of the organization there are often different divisions, based on geographic considerations.

▶ *By hierarchy* – level in the hierarchy becomes important.

With increasing numbers of employees, communication needs to be controlled in some way. One way is to create standardized rules and procedures that will eliminate the need for personal guidance on routine matters. Often, there is a specialist department whose sole function is to keep the rule book and systems up to date. This, as we have seen, may have the effect of reducing the levels of employee involvement. This effect may by mitigated by the use of plans and goal setting, which allow discretion within the established goals of the organization. In general, however, fairly mechanistic systems for managing people are in operation. Jobs are carefully specified and filled by systematic selection procedures. The same is true of disciplinary procedures. The hierarchy is clearly specified and there are formal lines through which people report. The organizational structure is the traditional 'tree', with the chief executive at the top, delegating control through successive levels of management.

Organisational culture and service style. The differentiated phase is generally characterized by what Harrison refers to as a 'role culture'. Power is not exercised according to personal whim, but by reference to formal systems and procedures.

The advice normally given to a new entrant to the organization is 'follow the rules'. The high degree of formalization means that the individual is protected against arbitrary power, as long as they stay within the system.

An extreme example of such a culture is provided by one very large multinational in which one of the authors worked as a consultant. Every individual within the management structure had a reference number, except those at the top of the tree who were described by a letter. Thus, the Personnel Director was PN. The second in command was PN1. If another individual reported directly to PN, they were PN2. His or her deputy was likewise designated as PN21, and so on. In large departments, such as production (headed by P), there were quite long reference numbers. At the level of first line supervision, numbers such as P21343 were in use. The real significance of the system lay in the strict rule that memos should not be addressed to individuals by name, but by reference number. Typists and secretaries had instructions that, if a memo was addressed by name, they were to replace it with the appropriate code. Not surprisingly, there was a large manual, which had to be updated regularly, containing all the reference numbers. The rationale behind the system was that it was the role that was important – individuals come and go. (In that company, at that time, quite frequently!)

It can be imagined how depersonalizing this approach was, and it is only fair to add that the system has since been changed.

The service style of the role culture is the one most commonly found in practice. The central concept around which service revolves is the *transaction*. The customer is also seen as a role, and the system is geared toward making the transactions with that role as efficient as possible. The provision of goods is normally on a large scale with the emphasis on prices, costs, and profit margins. Because of the large scale, the emphasis is upon the typical customer who is 'managed' by the system, much as are the organization's employees. The customer is a statistic, rather than a person. Examples are to be found everywhere. Fast food outlets, airlines, railways, and large stores, for example.

Problems of the differentiation phase. Formal lines of communication in the highly differentiated organization become quickly overloaded. In order to counter this, the organization develops rules and procedures so that trivial information is standardized. As we have seen, this may have the undesirable effect of demoralizing the employees, in which case other methods are developed so that discretion is increased, but within limits specified by the organization. Communication between individuals in different sections or departments is a particular problem. Theoretically, all such communication has to go up the hierarchical 'tree' from its origin, until it reaches a point at which a particular individual has responsibility for both the departments concerned, and then down the tree to the recipient. This is both slow and cumbersome, and adds to the overload on the communication channels.

Because of this difficulty in handling information, the organization becomes slow to adapt to environmental changes. It has been said that the nervous system of the dinosaur was so ineffective that a primitive hunter could cut off its tail and be a mile away before the animal noticed. So it is with some large organizations. One way of adaptation is similar to that adopted by individuals when faced with overload (see section on job design in Chapter 2).

In an attempt to make the organization more adaptive, there is often a move to create self-contained tasks. This is sometimes called decentralization, and includes concepts such as cost centres which are most often divided by product or by location. Each branch is given the specialists required to operate as a totally independent company. It is responsible for its own costs and profits. This 'pure' form of decentralization is, however, relatively uncommon. Most are hybrids, in which some functions are devolved but others are not. Those departments that are centrally maintained tend to be those where economies of scale are possible, or where the work load does not justify the employment of local experts. An example of the first might be Purchasing, and of the latter, Personnel. It is not uncommon to find that organizations in this stage, 'cycle' between centralization and decentralization, as they gradually realize that both have their strengths and weaknesses.

Another major problem that the differentiated structure engenders is that it encourages intergroup rivalry and conflict that is likely to be dysfunctional. As we have seen, the lack of communication is an important factor in the generation of such hostility.

Especially in the early, rules and procedures, part of the differentiated phase, people feel undervalued. This applies to both employees and customers. They often have information that could be of value to the organization, but there is no apparent way to get it into the system. For example, in one of our local supermarkets there is a device on sale to stop kettles furring up with lime scale. It is on sale in one of the 'impulse-buying' positions. Unfortunately, the whole of the region has very soft water – so soft, in fact, that it can be used in car batteries in place of distilled water. It is quite likely that the person whose job it was to put these on display is fully aware of this, but the system isn't. Furthermore, the fact that they have been on display for some time suggests that there is no easy way to get the information into the system. The way that organizations attempt to overcome these feelings of being undervalued is by giving the employees more autonomy and making customers feel that they are important. 'Quality Circles', 'Customer First' and other such schemes are examples of such attempts, and can be seen as ways of starting to change the culture.

In summary, therefore, there are two main pressures on the differentiated organization. The channels of communication are based not on actual need, but on *position* within the hierarchy, which means the organization is slow to adapt. Secondly people in the organization feel and, in fact, are, underutilized. These problems stem from the separation and specialization of functions within the organization. Specialists are required, but they need to be integrated rather than separated.

THE INTEGRATION PHASE

It is much harder to give characteristics of the integration stage of organizational development, mainly because so few integrated organizations exist. Those that do are mainly smaller ones, such as consultancy firms and advertising agencies. However, within large organizations it is not unusual to find some of the characteristics of integration. Indeed, there may be some sections and departments that are fully integrated. There are a range of methods by which an organization may achieve such integration. The particular method chosen will often be specific to that organization, but there are certain common characteristics. These include more adaptable styles of leadership, along the lines of those suggested by Hersey and Blanchard, together with a greater emphasis upon teamwork and the performance of the team, rather than on that of individuals. Decision making becomes more decentralized with the use of more participative techniques. All of these operate from an organic, rather than mechanistic, set of assumptions. The organization is not seen as static, rather growth and change are seen as inevitable and natural.

There are two systems which perhaps typify the integrated organization. These are the concepts of *link pin* and *matrix*. Link pin was originally suggested by Rensis Likert (1961). On the surface, it involves only a small change to the way that the organizational chart is drawn (see Figure 18). However, it represents a considerable difference in relationships within the organization. The replacement of lines of authority, by interlinking triangles, indicates that each group has the responsibility for setting and achieving objectives at its own level. It is also responsible for signalling to the rest of the system if there are problems in achieving these objectives. This will allow the rest of the system time to adjust to the change in circumstances.

The other difference between link-pin and the traditional hierarchy, which gives the system its name, is that many managers are members of two or more groups. They become the 'link pins'. As such each manager has the responsibility to ensure that there is compatibility between these groups. This dual membership extends in two directions. Traditionally, links are 'upwards', but they can also be 'sideways'. Thus,

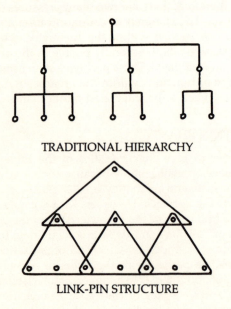

TRADITIONAL HIERARCHY

LINK-PIN STRUCTURE

FIGURE 18. *Traditional and link-pin organizational structures (adapted from Likert, 1961)*

a member of one function (for example production), may also be a member of the personnel group. If the system works well, this can solve the problem suffered by traditional organizations of communication and compatibility between functions. Traditionally, any requests for information would have to go up the tree and then down again, with the reply following the same path. The link-pin system allows for quicker and more accurate sideways transfer of information.

In differentiated organizations, such channels are not encouraged. They may develop informally, but if something goes wrong, the 'culprits' are usually instructed to 'follow the correct procedure in future'. The reason for this is that such organizations are built on the premise that authority and responsibility are delegated down the hierarchy. The link-pin system, however, is based upon personal responsibility for the setting and achieving of objectives which are to be co-ordinated with the rest of the organization. As such, it is very compatible with management by objectives (see page 50), as long as the objectives are drawn wide enough to allow personal responsibility and discretion, and, ideally, are set by individuals themselves, in consultation with the levels above and below them. In passing, it is the authors' belief that the reason for the failure of some MBO schemes is that it is introduced into strong role cultures, which traditionally do not allow such discretion.

Matrix organization, as its name suggests, is built on the fact that many organizations have two dimensions that have to be managed – products and people. This produces a 'matrix' as shown in Figure 19. It is perhaps

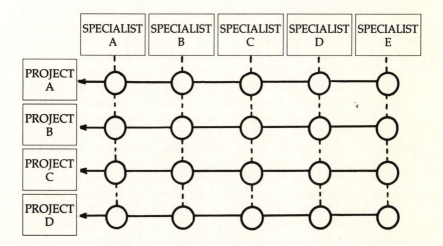

FIGURE 19. *The matrix organization (from Tse, 1985)*

best introduced by way of examples. We will use two, one from our own direct experience and, lest it be thought that it only applies to 'ivory towers', one from the retailing sector.

The Manchester School of Management has a number of 'product lines'. These are the courses that we run. The largest is the undergraduate degree, but there are also various masters and doctoral programmes, and tailor-made courses for business and industry. All these products are multidisciplinary. The undergraduate course, for example, covers psychology, accountancy/finance, production, industrial relations, and many other specialist subjects. Because of this they require the services of specialist staff from all these areas. The specialist staff are organized into sections (for example psychologists, economists, accountants), each headed by a professor. Each of the lecturers will teach on most, if not all, of the product lines (i.e. courses).

However sections and products do need to be integrated. There are already section heads in charge of each speciality. What is also required is for each product to have a 'product leader'. In the case of our products these are course directors. They may be from any of the sections and are rarely, if ever, section heads. The 'managers' for each of the dimensions are now established – section leaders and product leaders. All that is required is for each of the circles on the matrix to be filled by a particular specialist, for example an economist to teach on the masters degree. The specialist may be any member of that section, including the section head.

The thought that immediately occurs to some people is that each specialist ends up with at least two bosses: the section leader and the product leader. This is true, but does it cause problems? Jesus said that 'no man can serve two masters', but in a true matrix organization, the 'bosses' are not masters but *co-ordinators*. Since all section heads teach, and none of them are product leaders, they are all both 'bosses' and 'subordinates'. Indeed, the situation often arises where a section head is 'subordinate' to one of his or her own section members. In industry and commerce, the same principles apply. Individuals working in specialist functions need to be integrated into the production function. As an example of this consider the matrix structure shown in Figure 20. This is the matrix structure reportedly used in the engineering department of one of the UK's most successful retailers, Marks and Spencer.

In matrix, as well as link-pin systems, traditional ideas of authority and responsibility disappear. No one need be permanently 'in charge', but the system can cope with both day-to-day management and emergencies. It would be unwise to claim that such a system has no problems. The matrix structure requires a very high degree of inter-dependence (see page 76). As such it is demanding, but also highly effective. It would also be unwise to claim that there is only one type of

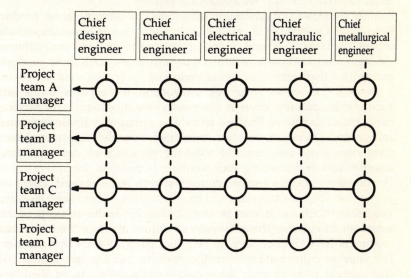

FIGURE 20. *The matrix structure of Marks and Spencer's engineering department (from Tse, 1985)*

matrix possible, or that it is appropriate to every situation. Because matrix structures are organic rather than mechanistic, each organization will develop its own variation. In addition, there may be some situations (such as production lines), where the tasks are so simple that mechanistic structures are more appropriate.

Culture and service style. There are two cultures and styles that appear to be relevant to integrated organizations. These are *achievement* and *support*. The achievement culture is oriented to making a difference in the world, by achieving a goal or ideal in which it has faith. In this respect its quest is missionary. The members of the organization are also committed to the goal, and are able to use their talents and skills in ways which they find personally rewarding.

The service style derives from the strong internal values and beliefs of the organization. The organization produces what it considers its customers *ought* to want. The customer becomes the target and 'good' customers accept, without question, the organization's expertise. Such a culture is quite compatible with a power culture (see page 127). Indeed, many small organizations show elements of both. Again, examples may be found in restaurants. Many are particularly power oriented, but show achievement orientation in that they strive for perfection in the food they provide. Often their belief that they are providing such high standards does not allow for contradiction. We know of at least one well-known establishment that throws out customers who have the temerity to ask for any form of extra seasoning. As far as the restaurant is concerned, the food is served 'correctly' seasoned. In manufacturing industries, such cultures are often found in smaller high-tech organizations, such as Apple computers, or Clive Sinclair's original company.

There are, however, some larger organizations, such as 3M, which appear to be moving towards both matrix structure and achievement, rather than role culture. Staff are actively encouraged to develop schemes and products to which they are committed. Provided they can make a good case, they are provided with the resources to develop them. Another way of describing such a culture is that it is 'intrapreneurial'. The members act like entrepreneurs, but within the organization.

The support culture, at least in terms of service, is the opposite of the achievement culture. The achievement culture involves the belief that customers have, if necessary, to be educated as to what they require. The support culture starts from the premise that the function of the organization is to provide what customers require. Again there are restaurants that operate on this philosophy. Whatever the eccentric tastes of the customer may be, the restaurant is there to cater to their needs, and to provide a welcoming and supportive environment. Like the achievement culture, however, the rewards and motivators within the organization are largely intrinsic. In the support culture, these are usually associated with the personal bonds that develop between individuals in the organization, and between the organization and individuals. Employees trust the organization to be responsive to their needs and they, in turn, are responsive to the organization's needs.

In terms of structure of achievement and support cultures, it may well be that matrix is best suited to achievement and link pin to support. For reasons we have already stated, this is not a hard and fast rule; each organization will find its own solution.

Problems of the integration phase. The problems associated with the two styles of culture and service are fairly clear. The danger with the achievement culture is that it may produce what no one wants. The classic example is perhaps the Sinclair C5. Alternatively, the organization may produce a better and more advanced device, which is incompatible with previous models. Customers may be happily using these old models when spare parts become unobtainable. This appears to happen frequently in the computer industry. The danger for the support culture, on the other hand, is that customers become more and more demanding. In addition, the organization may spend a disproportionate, and unprofitable, amount of its resources catering for small minorities.

The organizational problems associated with the integration phase are less easy to describe. Throughout the development, from pioneer, through differentiated, to integrated, solving the problems of each stage produces different problems. It is not yet clear what problems are produced by integration. Possibly, just the never-ending one of the need to get people to work together effectively.

This section has related the stage theory of organizational development with that of culture and service style. This is because of the considerable degree of overlap that exists between them. There are, however, some other alternatives which complete the picture. Figure 21 shows all the possible combinations of cultures with different development stages, together with an indication of the likelihood of each one.

The differentiated organization that has a power culture is an interesting combination. It occurs because, despite the founder's desire to hold on to day-to-day control, the organization becomes so large that this proves impossible. The only alternative is to differentiate, with power very clearly seen as devolved from above.

The pioneer company may also be either achievement or service oriented. Which of these occur, if either, will depend upon the beliefs and orientation of the founder. They depend upon the organization remaining small. The problems arise for such an organization when it either grows or is taken over. In growing, it may be that it can 'skip' the differentiated phase and move to full integration. If it is taken over, this will usually be by a much larger organization, which is often differentiated. The subsequent clash of cultures can lead to many problems, and often leads to the departure of many of the original staff.

This would be a good place to review your answers to the questions at the beginning of this chapter. The purpose is to see what they tell you about the culture and phase of development of your organization. The advice to a new member can be very revealing. Does your advice, for instance, suggest that it is necessary to be wary of authority or to follow the rules? This would suggest a role culture. If the advice is to watch out for political manoeuvring, this could imply a power culture. Similar comments apply to the organization's slogan or motto. Whatever your advice or motto, see how it relates to the four cultures. In the same way, what does your animal mascot tell you about your perception of the organization? Animals like dinosaurs or elephants suggest a role culture. More social and co-operative animals (for example bees or wolves) might suggest a support culture, although in the latter case one with predatory overtones.

CULTURE

PHASE	PIONEER	DIFFERENTIATED	INTEGRATED
POWER	Classic small entrepreneurial company owned by powerful boss who keeps tight control	Privately owned company too large for owner(s) to control everything; some specialization	Unlikely to occur contrary to the philosophy of integration
ROLE	Unlikely to occur, small, tightly knit, company does not need role differentiation	Classic large companies	Impossible combination
ACHIEVEMENT	Quite common. Culture defined by pioneer who specifies the mission	Can occur in small pockets within role cultures e.g. research depts.	Classic 'matrix' commitment to jointly defined mission
SUPPORT	Can occur if pioneer believes in supportive approach	Can occur in small pockets within role cultures e.g. training depts.	Classic 'link pin'

FIGURE 21. Relationship between an organization's phase of development and its organizational culture

PROBLEM SOLVING

(Before reading further you should turn to Appendix 6.)

As has been seen, there are a number of problems associated with each phase of an organization's development. In addition to this, each organization will have issues which are specific to itself. These may be concerned with improving co-operation between certain individuals or departments, improving the communication systems, or even changing the basic culture. It is the job of the manager to deal with these problems. This involves 'influencing' within the organization. To do this it is necessary to develop an *influence strategy*, by identifying who needs to be influenced and the best way to do this.

INFLUENCE STRATEGIES

From an examination of the literature on management, John Beck and Charles Cox (1984) suggest that there are four ways of exerting an influence in organizations. These four approaches have considerable pedigrees, having been discussed by Machiavelli as well as contemporary writers. Interestingly, those writers who mention all four approaches are in a minority. The four influence styles are outlined below. Although the overlap is not perfect, there is a strong relationship between these styles and the four organization cultures (role; power; support and achievement) described in the previous section.

Political style relies heavily on informal influence, which is exerted in two characteristic ways. The first of these is the formation of alliances within the organization. These are networks of individuals who have compatible interests, and who hence support each other's causes. This type of network has always been particularly strong in British organizations and, indeed, in British society generally. The second method of political influence is by the strategic use of information. By withholding information and then releasing it at the right time, and in the right direction, and desired actions can be encouraged. This selective use of information is often accompanied by persuasion and 'selling'.

The individual who uses the political style extensively will tend to see the organization as a 'jungle', where quick thinking and good contacts are essential. As a result they will be careful to maintain a network of contacts and friendships. A useful indicator of a person's preferred style is the way that he or she approaches conflict situations. Because conflict disrupts the smooth working of informal networks, the political individual will try to keep conflict to a minimum, often by smoothing over problems.

The political style is a very common one, particularly in organizations with power and role cultures. The main reason for this is that it is the only way of challenging control. In the power culture, this control is exerted directly from the centre, while in the role culture it is delegated downwards from the top.

There is often a very strong feeling that politics in organizations is, by definition, a bad thing. This is partly because much political activity is seen as game playing, with the object of advancing personal, rather than organizational goals. Also politics can have negative consequences, such as low levels of trust and the wasting of time in manoeuvring for position. However, it is now becoming accepted that some types of political activity can be positive. In addition, because it is often the only effective way of coping with authority, it is widespread within organizations. Managers therefore need to know about it if they are to be effective.

The various types of political activity and their consequences have been neatly classified by Simon Baddely and Kim James (1987). They suggest that there are two independent dimensions to politics. The first is 'politically aware' versus 'politically unaware'. To this one can add 'politically skilled' versus 'politically unskilled'. Baddely and James's other dimension is concerned with whether people are acting with integrity and in the organization's interests, or whether they are playing games and seeking to advance their own interests at the expense of others. The combination of these two dimensions produces four 'types', as shown in Figure 22. Each type has its own animal mascot. BOX 1 represents the clever individual who is playing games, but is politically aware and skilled. The mascot of this position is the *fox*. This is the style that has given rise to the traditionally negative view of an organizational politician, and is not recommended. BOX 2 is the individual who is playing games, but is politically unaware and unskilled. The mascot here is the *donkey*. This individual is politically inept and blunders around trying to pull off political coups. They are, however, easily outmanoeuvred by more skilful politicians. BOX 3 is the individual who is acting with integrity but is politically unaware. The mascot is a *sheep*. this individual is easily taken advantage of (and led to the slaughter) by more politically aware and skilful members of the organization, especially foxes. As a result these individuals are often left wondering 'what happened?', in various meetings and other situations where they have been outmanoeuvred. BOX 4 is the wise individual, who is politically aware and acting with integrity. The mascot is the *owl*. This is the style of the competent manager who will only use the political style in appropriate situations.

Formal/Authoritarian style relies predominently upon the authority conferred on the individual by the organization, and is therefore usually dependent upon the individual's position within the hierarchy. The way in which this authority is used will be determined by the formal

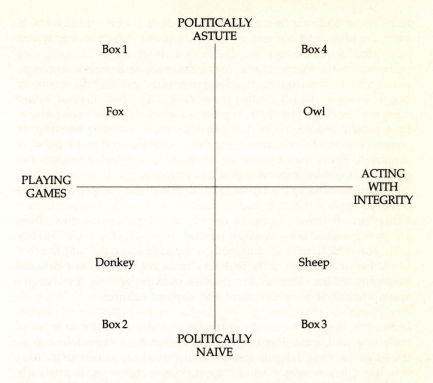

FIGURE 22. *Four types of organizational politician (from Baddely and James, 1987)*

rules of the organization. Individuals who use this influence style predominantly view the ideal organization as a well-ordered system – 'a place for everything, and everything in its place'. They tend to view the organization in rather feudal terms. Membership means that benefits are accepted but also, as a result, duties are owed. Employees, therefore, owe loyalty to the organization, upon which the formal/authoritarian manager will call. Such an individual, as well as exerting authority, will also respect the authority of those above him or her. In extreme cases the same individual may behave like a tyrant with subordinates, but meekly follows orders from superiors. The method of resolving conflict is, of course, by reference to higher authority. This higher authority will arbitrate and 'hand down' a decision. The formal/authoritarian style is well suited to, and hence very common in, differentiated organizations and role cultures.

Open style relies on generating trust and commitment through openness and honesty. The basic assumption underlying this approach is that a consensus can be reached within the organization about what needs to to be done, and that this is achieved by dealing openly and honestly with the ideas and feelings involved. It is the style that was widely advocated by social scientists in the 1960s and early 1970s. The individual who predominantly uses this style is most probably democratic in orientation, and believes in individual responsibility and joint decision making. The way in which conflict is resolved is by open discussion, and even confrontation, between the parties involved. This may prove to be a painful process, as it makes explicit the differences between the people concerned, both concerning the values involved and the actions proposed. These then have to be resolved. Like interdependence (see page 76), it can be uncomfortable, but effective.

A large number of managers say that this is their preferred style. In our experience it is not so widely used in practice. Once again there is a difference between 'espoused theory' and 'theory in practice'. There are, perhaps, good reasons why it is not widespread. Open confrontation with powerful figures is dangerous, especially in power and role cultures. Because of this, it is probably most commonly used between colleagues on the same level or in close working groups. It is a highly appropriate style in achievement and support cultures.

Laissez-faire style. The essence of the laissez-faire style is that if things are going well, leave them alone. The laissez-faire approach is to set things going, or to delegate responsibility, and only intervene if things look like going wrong. If used inappropriately, however, the potential for disaster is obvious. For this reason, it is, for managers, perhaps the least popular of the four styles. The manager who does use this style most probably values independence and believes that organizations should be 'self-organizing systems'. Accordingly, conflict is something that should not exist and is to be avoided.

This style is probably most appropriate in achievement cultures, where individuals are highly committed to their tasks. The present authors are members of such a culture, where laissez-faire management is highly appropriate. (You may recall that an achievement culture generates products that it believes the customer ought to want. This book is such a product!)

It should be emphasized that all these influence strategies are appropriate in the right context. In pure cultures, one style might predominate, but most organizations are a blend of cultures. It is essential, then, to be aware of the culture within each section or department of the organization, and adjust your influence style accordingly. Flexibility of style is the route to greatest efficiency in influencing organizations. Sometimes selecting the appropriate style is intuitive, but, more often, an analysis of the situation is required. Useful insights may be obtained by identifying individuals who seem highly successful in this respect, and comparing their strategies with those who are unsuccessful.

Your choice of strategy in Appendix 6 may give you some indication of your own preferred style. Because it is simplified it should, of course, be treated with some caution. The four paragraphs are meant to represent the four main styles, in the following order: political; formal; open and laissez-faire.

Some guidelines can, however, be given on the selection of an appropriate influence style. This will depend on a number of factors, but particularly on the type of goal, the people involved, and the organizational culture. A summary of these, which also integrates some concepts from previous chapters, is given in Figure 23. From the figure it will be seen that the formal style is likely to work best in a role culture in situations where the goals are clear, simple and relatively short term and you are not concerned to develop other people's commitment to them. If the others involved are dependent and have low motivation, this will make a formal style a necessity. The open style is most appropriate in support cultures in situations where the goals are complex and long term and you are working with people who are highly motivated and interdependent. The open style will also be important where it is necessary to generate high commitment to goals. The political style is probably effective in a range of situations between the extremes outlined above. As already noted, it is common in power cultures, but may also be the only way for more junior members in role cultures to cope with authoritarian senior managers. The laissez-faire style is appropriate in dealing with individuals who are highly motivated and committed to their goals and who are able to work independently. This situation will often be found in achievement cultures.

In our experience there is a danger that managers overuse one favoured approach. Since flexibility is important, this means that, by definition, they are at times using that style inappropriately, and inevitably get a reputation as some kind of organizational bastard. The overuser of political style becomes a 'scheming bastard', of formal an 'autocratic bastard', of open an 'awkward bastard', and of laissez-faire a 'lazy bastard'. An important question for the reader is, what possible reputation do you have?

GOAL CLARITY

In order to solve problems successfully in organizations it is important to be clear, not only about the different possible influence strategies, but also about the goals you are pursuing. A common classification of goals or objectives within organizations suggests that there are three basic levels: personal, team and organizational. As explained below, these all subdivide into task, development and status goals.

Personal goals satisfy the needs of the individual. There are three levels of such needs. Most obvious are the *task* goals. These are the actual

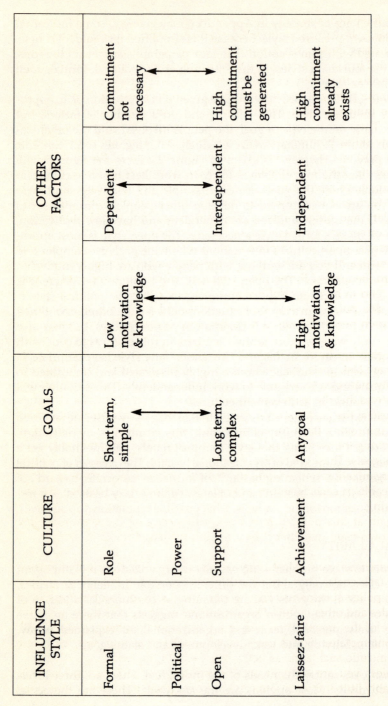

INFLUENCE STYLE	CULTURE	GOALS		OTHER FACTORS		
Formal	Role	Short term, simple	Low motivation & knowledge	Dependent	Commitment not necessary
Political	Power				
Open	Support	Long term, complex		Interdependent	High commitment must be generated
			High motivation & knowledge		
Laissez-faire	Achievement	Any goal		Independent	High commitment already exists

FIGURE 23. *Factors determining managers' choice of influence style*

work for which the individual is responsible. These may be clear or unclear, self-defined, defined by the supervisor, or jointly defined. In many cases these goals are relatively clear and may even be formally recorded in a job description. Often, however, even where a job description exists, the clarity of these goals may be less than perfect. In such cases, the potential exists for ambiguity about roles.

The individual also needs to be clear about his or her *development* goals. These are concerned with personal growth and the development of new skills, both professional and personal. They are not limited to work, and so may also include goals that are part of the individual's private life. They are linked to a third group of personal goals that Beck and Cox have referred to as *status* goals. These are concerned with both short-term and long-term career plans. In the short term, issues such as salary and other forms of recognition are involved. In the longer term, career advancement issues are important.

Personal goals are important because they draw attention to, and legitimatize, the fact that people work for organizations for personal reward. Because of the emphasis in organizations on tasks, goals at that level tend to be better defined than the other two.

At this point it would be useful to spend a few minutes defining your own personal goals at task, developmental, and status levels.

Team goals are those of the work group, section, or department. Again there are task goals and developmental goals, and again the former are usually more clearly defined than the latter. Task goals concern the work objectives that the team is required to achieve, and are similar in nature to those at the personal level. Developmental goals are often concerned with improving team functioning and may, for example, be aimed at improving the way individuals work together. The team may also have status goals. These are often concerned with the team's standing within the organization or the world as a whole. Goals of this nature are often noticeable in such functions as research, sales and marketing, and advertising.

Again at this point it may be worth specifying the team goals for your own team, whether it be a section or department.

Organizational goals. Most organizations have very clear statements of their task goals. They are normally enshrined in corporate plans and other policy statements. They define the nature of the business, and set sales and other targets. Developmental goals are concerned with the future of the organization and any programme of changes that might be contemplated. Status goals are often far less clear at this level, but may include such aims as being the 'best' in the field.

Unless you are on your organization's Board of Directors, there is probably little influence you can have over goals at this level. This does not mean that it is a pointless exercise to consider them. In fact, for effective goal management it is important to know what they are.

Goal clarity is arguably one of the most important factors in the success of an organization. The organization needs to be clear as to where it is going, and what type of organization it is. Where such goals exist they are usually heavily value laden. Warren Bennis (1983), in his study of chief executive officers in US organizations, identifies five essential 'competencies'. The most important of these he defines as follows:

> Vision: The capacity to create and communicate a compelling vision of a desired state of affairs – to impart clarity to this vision and induce commitment to it.

In the UK, Walter Goldsmith and David Clutterbuck (1984), writing of managers as leaders, say that they should 'provide a clear mission, which they believe in passionately themselves and incite others to subscribe to'. Leadership thrives, they suggest, when people have clear objectives. Again in the UK, Charles Cox and Cary Cooper (1988), in their book on high flyers, quote one managing director as saying that an essential skill for the job is 'to be visionary: this is needed to cope with a changing world and to exploit the future'.

In Chapter 2 the importance of setting clear goals for individuals was considered. Such clarity is also required at the organizational level. However, once goals have been specified at each of the levels, it will often be the case that they will be in conflict with each other. This will itself require management. Sometimes it will involve compromise or, better still, finding a superordinate goal. The techniques discussed in Chapter 4 on group dynamics will need to be used.

This chapter has examined how the structure and culture of organizations change as they cope with problems, in particular those associated with growth. If managers are to be effective they will need to be aware of the predominant culture of the organization, or part of the organization, that they are trying to influence. The nature of the culture, as we have seen, will determine which style of influencing is likely to be most effective. We have argued that managers tend to have their own preferred style but, because the appropriate style will vary from situation to situation, managers need to develop more flexibility. Finally, we suggest that there is no point in trying to influence the organization to change in particular ways if you are not clear as to the goals you are trying to achieve. Individuals, teams, and organizations all need to be clear as to their goals. The next chapter considers the methods available to organizations for planning and undertaking systematic change.

7

Organizational Change

This chapter is concerned with the way in which organizations change in order to cope with changing conditions. The generic name for the study of such changes is organizational development (OD). These changes may be in the external environment, for example markets and competitors, or they may be internal, for example through growth. Internal pressures push the organization into different structures, as discussed in the previous chapter. Whatever the source of the change, they will inevitably have an effect on the people working in the organization. It is with the effects of such changes, and how they can be managed, that we will be concerned.

Change in organizations is difficult because of two, built-in, forms of resistance. First, organizations, particularly those in the differentiation phase (discussed on pages 128–131), are not *meant* to change. They are specifically designed to be stable. It is expected that they will continue, irrespective of the comings and goings of individual members. Second, the individuals themselves may be unaware of the changes that are taking place in the rest of the organization, and hence of the need for themselves to change.

Both these factors mean that there is often considerable inertia in the system. If you refer back to the animal mascot you chose for your own organization (in the previous chapter), you may find that resistance, or slowness, in reacting to change is a characteristic of the animal. (It may even go as far as the dodo which, of course, became extinct.) This issue of resistance to change, and how to overcome it, will be considered later in this chapter. First, we will deal with the concept of the *change agent*.

CHANGE AGENTS

It is a well-accepted principle within OD that it is impossible to carry out major changes within an organization without the assistance of an independent consultant. These consultants may be internal or external. In some organizations, usually very large ones, individuals may be employed full time to act as change consultants. It is important, however, that they are seen as independent and not associated with any particular power group within the organization. This is often very dificult to do and, hence, there are strong arguments for employing people who are genuinely external and independent.

The reason why an independent, external view is needed is very simple. It is usually impossible for the individuals involved to get a clear and unbiased view of their ways of working and interacting. A good analogy is that of the marriage guidance counsellor. The role of the counsellor is to act as an independent and unbiased observer, who works with both parties to help them understand their situation and plan for ways to improve it. The OD consultant fulfils a similar role for the members of an organization, whether they are working at a team-building level, or on wider, organizational, change. Unlike marriage guidance counsellors, they work with more than just two people.

The use of external consultants in organizations is not new, but there are a number of important differences between traditional 'expert' consultants and OD consultants. The term 'change agent' has come to be used as an alternative for the latter, as a way of making these differences explicit. Traditional expert consultants are hired to go into the organization, diagnose what is wrong, and propose an expert solution. They may be experts in accounting, marketing etc., depending upon the problem. The change agent, on the other hand, works with the members of the organization, helping them to identify the problems for themselves and helping them develop their own solutions. They do not work at the 'task' level like the expert, but at the 'process' level.

The expert consultant is sometimes described as working with a medical model approach because he or she behaves rather like a general practitioner. Symptoms are presented, a preliminary diagnosis is made which is checked by looking for additional confirming symptoms. A cure is then prescribed and is often actually implemented by the expert. The client organization is relatively passive in this process and takes little responsibility for improving the situation, just as the patient tends to be regarded very much as an object to be repaired. (To be fair, this is the traditional view of medicine, which is also beginning to move towards greater patient involvement.)

The change agent works not on a medical, but on a therapeutic model. In this role, it is not possible to prescribe a 'cure', because there is no agreed concept of what constitutes good health in interpersonal relationships, just as there is no definition of a perfect marriage. All the change agent can do is to work with the clients to help them find a solution which they find satisfactory, or, at least, better than the current situation.

INDIVIDUAL CHANGE

Organizational change can take place at three levels – individual, group or team, and organizational. Individual change is really the basis for all change. Unless individuals change in some way, nothing changes. At management level, management development programmes are the major method by which such change is encouraged. Their focus is often on developing the skills individuals need to cope with their present jobs, but it may also include the development of skills for the future. If any wider programme of organizational change is planned, it will need to include plans for individual change.

How a training programme or any other individual change programme is set up will depend on the assumptions that the organizer holds about how people learn. These same assumptions are also fundamental to the strategy taken for any other level of change, so they are worth examining in relation to their implications for the design of change interventions. There are three broad sets of assumption about learning on which social scientists tend to work.

Assumptions about learning. First, there is the *behaviourist* approach, based on the work of Skinner. This was discussed in some detail in Chapter 2, so we do not need to say much about the basic theory here. A change agent working on these assumptions would look for those reinforcements which are producing the current behaviour. Having precisely specified the new behaviour, the object would be to set up a schedule of reinforcement, to encourage the necessary change. Behaviour modification can be carried out in this apparently manipulative way, but it does not have to be. It is quite possible to discuss the desired change with participants and to help them set up their own specification of new behaviour and schedules of reinforcement, so that control is very much in their own hands. In fact, in our view this is usually the best way to proceed.

Another set of approaches to training is based on *cognitive* assumptions. The behaviourist approach assumes that change is best brought about by considering external factors. The cognitive approach, on the other hand, is based on a belief that behaviour is controlled by internal factors, such as the individual's beliefs, assumptions, and theories about the situation. To change his or her behaviour, therefore, you have to change these internal theories. There are a number of assumptions about how this is done. One view, known as the *structuralist* approach, considers the mind as rather like a computer, and training is a matter of 'reprogramming' it. This is done through well-designed courses that feed in appropriate new information. Such courses will only be effective if the individual is prepared to take on board the new ideas supplied, which is by no means always the case. In recognition of this, an alternative assumption, known as the *functionalist* approach, is based on the belief that people will learn once they realize that they have a practical need for the information offered. This will occur when they are given the opportunity to experiment and learn things for themselves. Training involves a range of activities, from courses designed around case studies and practical exercises, to quite long-term real life projects.

The third set of assumptions which has had considerable influence on change processes derives from the *humanist* school. One of the most influential members of this group was Abraham Maslow (see pages 34–35). Humanists believe that, given the right conditions, human beings are naturally committed to growth and development, the potential for which is unlimited. The role of the trainer or change agent then becomes that of providing the right conditions. Some insights on how this is done are provided by Carl Rogers (1967). Originally a psychotherapist, his ideas have been widely accepted and used in education and training. In his view, it is impossible to 'teach' anything of value to another person. As he puts it,

> It seems to me that anything that can be taught to another is relatively inconsequential, and has little or no significant influence on behaviour. . . . I have come to feel that the only learning which significantly influences behaviour is self-discovered, self-appropriated learning.

This may seem a little extreme, but it does draw attention to the fact that it is impossible to 'teach' someone who does not want to learn. People will only learn (and change), if they want to. The role of the trainer/change agent is to try to bring about conditions where they will want to change.

Thinking along humanist lines has brought about an approach to training known as *self-development*. In this approach, individuals become responsible for directing their own development. They define their own learning objectives, decide for themselves which is the best way to achieve them, and evaluate their own progress. The training department staff become consultants, helping and supporting people while they do this. Much of the development under this system comes from 'real life', for example by taking on more challenging work to gain new experience and skills. People may still attend courses, but only when they, themselves, decide that this fulfils the needs they have identified. The use of this approach stems from the fundamental belief that people are responsible and will organize their development in a way that is compatible with the needs of the organization, and will be committed to achieving organizational goals. This is, in itself, a humanist assumption.

The values of the humanist movement have had a very strong influence on current practice in training and organizational development generally. They are equally compatible with support and achievement cultures in organizations. Self-development consequently requires a high degree of interdependence between the individuals involved. In the more traditional training systems, either cognitivist or behaviourist, there is more likely to be mutual dependence or straight authority/dependence. In general, trainees involved in these systems are relatively passive and learn (or fail to learn) what is presented to them within the framework provided.

In order to make clear the assumptions underlying each of the above approaches, we have tended to concentrate on the differences between them. It is, however, important to note that they are all quite compatible with each other. People learn as the result of reinforcement. They also have internal maps and theories about how the world works, and changing these will change their behaviour. Their internal maps will, in fact, change as a result of changes in reinforcement patterns. There is also overwhelming evidence that learning is, in general, more effective if people are in charge of it themselves. The wise change agent will, therefore, use all the approaches as appropriate – the contingency approach again!

TEAM BUILDING

Group or team building is the second most frequent form of change intervention. Indeed, a review by J.I. Porras and P.O. Berg in 1978 estimated that 40 per cent of OD interventions involved team building. As already mentioned, teams are an essential part of organizations. They exist wherever several people need to co-operate to complete a task. The emphasis in team building is usually on the manager and his or her immediate group of subordinates and focuses upon improving the way that actual teams operate together. It may also be used at a more casual level, for example with people who work together occasionally, but are not part of a formal team.

The origins of team building go back to the work of Elton Mayo, who built upon the Hawthorne studies (discussed on pages 33–34) to demonstrate the importance of social relationships at work. Other influences are the work of Kurt Lewin at the National Training Laboratories, and the development of the 'T-group' movement. In order to improve a team's effectiveness it is common, in practice, to concentrate on one or more of a number of themes, for example:

▶ *Increasing mutual trust* among team members.

▶ *Increasing awareness* of both your own and other people's behaviour.

▶ *Developing interpersonal skills*, such as listening, giving feedback, bringing others into the discussion.

Deciding which themes are to be developed will depend upon a number of factors, in particular the theoretical orientation of the consultant working with the team, together with the consultant's diagnosis of weaknesses in the team. Ideally this diagnosis should be made in co-operation with the team members.

STRATEGIES FOR TEAM BUILDING

There are a variety of approaches used in team building. These derive largely from different assumptions about how people best learn (i.e. change), and assumptions about the best sort of environment for effective teamwork.

Sensitivity training is based on the assumptions underlying *T-groups* and *encounter groups*. These terms are very broad and hence difficult to define precisely. T-groups (the 'T' simply stands for training) involve a wide range of activities, many of which are very similar to those used in other approaches, such as encounter groups. In general, the group consists of some eight to ten people, and the aim is for them to learn from their own behaviour and interactions. Emphasis is placed on developing a climate of trust and openness, thus fostering a high level of interpersonal feedback and the acceptance of feelings. The trainer or 'facilitator' is there to help the group achieve these objectives, not as a formal expert teacher; he or she operates very non-directively. The focus of the group can be at the level of personal learning and growth, or the understanding of group activity, or learning at the organizational level, or any combination of the three.

T-groups are very clearly and firmly rooted in the values of the 1960s and early 1970s. These include a strong belief in the importance of openness and trust, if people are going to work together well. Much emphasis is placed upon 'authenticity' – being open and expressing inner feelings. Unfortunately, these values are often in conflict with the norms of most organizations. Chris Argyris (1962) has pointed out that the norm in most organizations is to value rationality as effective, and suppress feelings as ineffective. This is based on the belief that as individuals start expressing feelings they become more emotional, less rational, and therefore less effective. But individuals' natural reaction to this norm is to suppress the expression of their feelings, even those that are perfectly reasonable. This becomes so automatic that they may not even realize that they are being suppressed. Since these emotions are not recognized or expressed, they gradually build up until they burst out, often as anger. The trigger that sets off the outburst may often be a very minor event. Because they are now so emotional that they are out of control, they may be ineffective. This can confirm the organization's assumption that feelings and emotions are bad. The individual therefore makes a resolution not to give vent to their feelings in future, and the whole cycle starts again. According to Argyris, people need to recognize their feelings as they develop, and deal with them in some way. In classic T-groups, this would be by openly expressing them.

Mainly because of the difference between the values of T-groups and those of most organizations, this approach was never widely accepted and has now fallen into disuse. Such a clash of values led to poor transfer from the training situation to the 'real world' of the organization. There was even some evidence that people were less effective after such training, although a minority did show positive change. This was most probably because open and supportive behaviour were inappropriate in political and formal organizational cultures. Other problems concerned the unpredictable nature of T-groups themselves – because of the open structure, anything could happen (or sometimes not happen). There were also ethical problems. Because T-groups are both powerful and personal, there is a strong case for participation being voluntary. There are, however, strong group and organizational pressures on the individual in such a 'voluntary' situation. In addition, if some members did not choose to attend, the effectiveness might of necessity be reduced.

Most OD practioners in the late 1960s and 70s saw T-group values as the way organizations *ought* to be. That is to say, that an ideal organization would have a climate of high openness and trust. However, despite plugging this approach for some 20 years, nothing has changed in the real world of organizations. They have not become more trusting and open. Most practitioners have, therefore, abandoned these values and espoused the contingency model of 'horses for courses'. The valuable and valid legacy of sensitivity training in current thinking is to have emphasized that humans are both rational and feeling beings.

Role negotiation is, in a way, at the opposite end of the scale to sensitivity training. It was developed by Roger Harrison (1972), in order to take account of the issue of power in organizations.

In preparation for the negotiations implied in the technique's name, each team member considers each of the other members and prepares a list of items under the following three headings:

It would help me increase my effectiveness if you would:

Do more of, or do better, the following:

Do less of, or stop doing, the following:

Keep on doing (i.e. maintain unchanged) the following:

Members then meet in pairs to negotiate the changes that they would like to see, and those they are themselves willing to make. The negotiations are 'genuine' ones, in the form of 'I will agree to do X if you stop doing Y' or, 'I will do A if you will do B'. Negotiations continue until both parties are happy and agreement has been reached. They are then written down and signed by both parties. It is part of the agreement that if one of the parties does not keep to the bargain, the other can use the sanction of withdrawing their half. The intention is that the negotiations should be done in such a way that there is an incentive to keep to the agreement, so as to gain the benefits promised by the other. Harrison makes the point that it is not legitimate, or necessary, to probe into individual feelings. What is required, however, is honesty. Threats and pressures, on the other hand, may be used, but it should be remembered that their use may lead to defensiveness. The role of the consultant is to help the negotiators understand and keep to the guidelines, and to help them clarify the requirements for change. It is, of course, important that the consultant does not actually influence the items, but simply helps the individuals clarify their own ideas.

Structured approach. This is based upon cognitivist assumptions that change is best brought about by providing information so as to understand about the processes within groups. The core of this approach is a team building 'workshop' or training course. This comprises a series of exercises, each designed to focus on some aspect of team working. The exercises are usually of a type known as 'substitute task exercises'. These are tasks that are not related in any way to the normal work of the group, but are designed to highlight some aspect of group process, such as competitiveness, goal clarity, or decision making. The fact that the task is unrelated to normal work makes it easier for the group to focus on the process, and avoids undue attention being focused on the particular task being undertaken. It is common to use short questionnaires and other measures to bring out key aspects of team processes. These activities, assisted by interventions from the consultant, help the group and individuals to gain a better understanding of how their present methods of working could be improved.

Packages provide a virtually ready-made team-building programme, which can be taken and 'plugged in' as needed. They are usually fairly highly structured and based on a particular theoretical framework. Often they are aimed more at developing the skills of the team leader, than at total team development. A good example is the use of Blake and Mouton's Managerial Grid (see page 67). The approach can be used to enable the manager or team leader to clarify his or her current style in terms of 'concern for task' or 'concern for people'. Exercises are then available to enable the individual to develop towards the optimal style, which is high on both concerns. The package can also be used to explore team members' preferences for different styles.

Another widely used package is provided by John Adair (1968). This, also, is mainly directed at the team leader. Adair argues that there are three sets of need which must be met if a team is to work effectively. These are:

TASK NEEDS – practical things to do with getting the work done.

GROUP NEEDS – concerned with keeping a cohesive team.

INDIVIDUAL NEEDS – the personal goals which each individual hopes to achieve through membership of the team.

It is important that attention is paid to all three of these. For a fully effective team, all must be fulfilled. It is possible to take the view that ensuring these needs are met is the leader's responsibility, in which case training concentrates on team leadership. Alternatively, if the view is taken that responsibility is shared by all team members, the concepts are used as a framework for reviewing how effectively the group is functioning. Exercises are used to highlight the importance of each set of needs, and how well they are being fulfilled.

Interaction process analysis is an approach that enables participants to analyse what type of contribution each person is making to the group, and what the implications are for group effectiveness. It is based on the work of Robert Bales (1951), who designed a rather complex classification of the types of interaction which take place between individuals in groups. The original classification is too complex to master and use quickly, so various simpler versions, such as the one shown in Figure 24, have been devised.

One way in which this is used is for team members to take it in turns to observe the group either when it is working normally or in special training sessions, and classify and count the types of contribution made by each team member. Alternatively, the consultant can undertake this task. The results are fed back to the group, who consider their implications, both for individuals and the group as a whole. It is not uncommon to find that certain individuals' contributions tend to be predominantly of one or two types. They are often surprised to discover this. Sometimes this is true for the group as a whole. There may, for example, be a great deal of *giving* of opinions and suggestions, but no *asking*. Sometimes categories such as *gives support* are noticeably lacking. If this is the case, it is necessary for group members to widen the range of contributions they are making.

Team roles. There are a number of theories which suggest that, for a group or team to operate effectively, there must be a number of specific

In developing appropriate categories of interactions between group members it is almost impossible to give absolute definitions of what should be included in each. Nevertheless, listed below are definitions and examples which should be of assistance for a trainer developing his or her observational and analytical skills.

GIVES SUPPORT
Raises others' esteem	*'Great idea!'*
Gives reward	*'You're looking fine'*
Shows solidarity	*'I'm with you on this one'*
Gives help	*'What was your point, Dave?'*
Builds on suggestions	*'. . . and then we could . . .'*
Agrees	*'Yes, let's do that then'*
Shows acceptance	*'Okay then'*
Understands	*'I see what you're getting at'*
Complies	*'If that's what you want'*
Gives non-verbal signs of encouragement	*'Mm'* ; nod

GIVES SUGGESTION
Makes proposals	*'It could be in the by-pass value'*
Suggests direction	*'Let's begin with looking at the sales figures'*
Offers autonomy for others	*'What do you think about it, Geoff?'*

GIVES OPINION
Evaluates	*'That's not very helpful'*
Analyses	*'The way I see it, the problem is . . .'*
Expresses feelings	*'I'm annoyed by it'*
Expresses wishes	*'I hope to get through it all this morning'*
Interprets	*'It seems to me that the situation is . . .'*
Imposes	*'Look, let me tell you'*

GIVES INFORMATION
Informs	*'It's 4.30'*
	'I was amazed'
Repeats	*'What I said was . . .'*
Clarifies	*'I meant the same thing'*
	'That's what I'm saying'
Confirms	*'Yes, that's right'*

ASKS FOR INFORMATION
Seeks facts	*'Where are the figures?'*
Seeks information	*'How did you do that?'*
Asks for repetition	*'What was that?'*

ASKS FOR OPINION
Seeks feelings	*'How do you feel about that?'*
Seeks wishes	*'What do you want to do?'*
Seeks interpretations	*'How do you see it?'*
Seeks evaluations	*'Do you think that's a good idea?'*

ASKS FOR SUGGESTIONS
Seeks direction and ways of taking action	*'How can we go about this?'* *'Anybody got any ideas?'*

SHOWS DISAGREEMENT
Shows resistance, rejection	*'No, I'm not too sure about that'*
Withholds help	*Silence, non-verbals*
Defends and asserts	*'Not at all!'*
Antagonizes others	*'You really believe that!'*
Attacks others	*'You're wasting my time!'*

FIGURE 24. *Example of categories for interaction process analysis (adapted from Bales, 1950)*

roles represented. One of the best known is that of Meredith Belbin, whose theory was discused in Chapter 4 (see page 95).

The question arises, of course, as to which of these different approaches to use. This will depend upon a number of factors – namely the situation, the skills and preferences of the consultant, and the assumptions about how change takes place. One of the most important situational determinants will be the organizational culture. In a power culture, role negotiation may be appropriate. In a role culture, a structured aproach might work better. In relation to the skills and preferences of the consultant, although there is evidence to suggest that all the techniques described above can be effective, people do, obviously, tend to do best that at which they are most skilled. This is a legitimate factor to take into account when choosing a technique. The assumptions about change and the way people learn have been discussed above; there are also assumptions about strategies for change which will be discussed later in the chapter.

There is, of course, no harm in taking an eclectic approach, and mixing assumptions and approaches as appropriate. Here, as in other contexts, it is important for consultants to be flexible in their behaviour and to be able to use a variety of methods. If managers should be flexible in their influence styles so, surely, should consultants.

ORGANIZATIONAL DEVELOPMENT

The term 'organizational development' is used as a generic title for any aspect of change in organizations, but is perhaps best reserved for contexts concerned with changing the total organization. In this context it has been defined in number of ways. For example, Richard Beckhard (1969) suggests that an OD intervention has five characteristics. It is:

1. Planned
2. Organisation-wide
3. Managed from the top, to
4. Increase organisation effectiveness and health, through
5. Planned interventions in the organisation's 'processes' using behavioural science knowledge.

The emphasis in OD is, therefore, on the human processes and interactions within the organization. It is not concerned with such aspects as the technology or the production process, although changes in these may be the trigger that makes an OD programme necessary. This link is made clear in another definition of OD, by Warren Bennis (1969):

OD is a response to change, a complex educational strategy intended to change beliefs, attitudes, values and the structure of organisations so that they can better adapt to new technologies, markets and challenges, and the dizzying rate of change itself.

Although these two definitions tell us what OD is, they do not describe how it is done. This is, however, much more difficult, as there is a bewildering array of approaches and techniques in use. Indeed, R. Kahn (1974) has suggested that OD 'is a label for a conglomerate of things an increasing number of consultants do, and write about.' Following his lead we will outline some of the typical types of OD activities. Wendell French and Cecil Bell (1984) have provided a list of what they call the 'major families of OD interventions'. As they point out, no OD programme will contain anywhere near all the possible types of intervention, but the list shows the wide range of possibilities which is available. Any particular programme may concentrate on one, or a limited range of interventions.

INTERVENTIONS

The list below starts by mentioning briefly interventions that have already been considered in this book.

1. *Intergroup activities*
Organizations need different teams and groups to interact with each other effectively. As we have seen in Chapter 5, this does not always happen. Interventions to improve these intergroup relations were also described in Chapter 5.

2. *Diagnostic activities*
Before future goals and strategies for change can be considered, there is a need to know the organization's present situation. Methods for undertaking such a diagnosis vary. Traditional methods include organizational surveys and questionnaires. Projective techniques, such as choosing an animal to represent the organization, can also be informative.

3. *Techno-structural or structural activities*
These interventions involve changing the organization's structure. Examples of this were given in the previous chapter, when the link-pin and matrix types of structure were discussed.

4. *Process consultation activities*
These are designed to help the client understand the processes that are taking place in the organization, and to develop strategies to improve how people work together. There is a wide range of such activities which may be aimed at group, intergroup or organizational level.

5. *Activities based on 'packages'*
As with team building, ready-made packages are also available for total organizational development. Perhaps the best known example of this category is, again, that of Blake and Moutons' Managerial Grid.

6. *Third-party peace-making activities*
This is another method of resolving conflicts, or at the very least a lack of co-operation, between different groups in the organization. The consultant is the third party, whose role is to resolve such conflicts.

7. *Coaching and counselling activities*
Such activities involve working with individual members of the organization to help them resolve problems. These problems may be work related, or may be of a personal nature. It has now been largely accepted that employees cannot leave their personal problems totally behind them when they go to work. Personal problems inevitably affect work performance. Many organizations are following the lead of companies in the USA and providing counselling sevices for their employees. These may be either 'in house' (usually attached to the medical department) or 'out house' consultants. Such services have generally been shown to be cost effective, as in the Post Office.

8. *Planning and goal-setting activities*
We have already discussed the area of goal management. Often OD consultants can be useful in helping define goals, both at individual, group, and organizational level.

9. *Strategic planning activities*
These are designed to help top management define the organization's 'mission', together with the long-term strategies for achieving it.

THE PROCESS OF CHANGE

OVERCOMING INERTIA

Whatever type of intervention is being used, change takes energy, since there is always inertia in the system that has to be overcome. Kurt Lewin (1974) has suggested that change is a three-stage process, whether it be at an individual, group, or organizational level. These three stages he refers to as *unfreezing, change* and *re-freezing*. He describes them as follows:

Unfreezing. Before any change can take place, the established methods and patterns of behaviour have to be broken down. People may be unaware of these established procedures until their attention is directed to them. Only when they are drawn to attention may their effectiveness be challenged. This demonstration of current ineffectiveness is essential for change to take place. People will only willingly become involved in a change process once they have accepted the need for change. The early activities of an OD programme are usually designed to bring about this unfreezing.

Change. Once current behaviours are unfrozen, it is possible to work on the change process. This can be done using any of the OD interventions described above.

Re-freezing. For people to operate effectively, their behaviour must be reasonably stable. An individual or organization in a state of constant change would achieve nothing. This means that the new behaviour must be allowed to stablilize. Usually people are very good at doing this for themselves. All that is needed is for time for re-freezing to occur naturally. Sometimes activities are included towards the end of a change programme that are designed to enable participants to look forward and review the effects of the planned changes. If these are perceived as beneficial, this review will aid the change process.

An important point to note is that change does not happen by itself. There must be some source that initiates the change. This source must have sufficient power to be able to influence others in the direction of the desired change. In OD programmes, the source is usually located somewhere in the management hierarchy. There is, in fact, a view that any OD will only be successful if it is initiated by top management. This, it is suggested, is the only group with sufficient power to make the OD programme happen. This is usually referred to as the 'start at the top and work down' approach. In the experience of the present authors, this is not the only possible approach. We have known successful OD projects that have started at the bottom and worked up. It is, of course, true that change is a lot easier with the support of top management and, in some cases, impossible without it. However, power exists at all levels of organizations. An understanding of the different sources of power is, therefore, essential to an understanding of the process of change.

SOURCES OF POWER

A useful classification of the sources of power has been provided by Charles Handy (1985). He has done so by modifying the original classification developed by John French and Bertram Raven (1959). There are, Handy suggests, essentially five sources of power.

Physical power is derived from the possession of superior physical force. For obvious reasons, it is rarely found in industrial or commercial organizations. It remains, however, the ultimate source of power in society through state control of the police, prisons, and the armed forces. It was also, at one time, widely used in schools, but this has changed. It is still to be found in industrial disputes, often on the picket line. As Handy points out, however, physical power does not have to be used for it to be effective. The fact that it is there, is often enough to endow considerable influence. This influence is expressed through straight-forward *coercion*.

Resource power, as its name suggests, derives from control of resources, which can be physical (e.g. money and materials), or psychological (e.g. the ability to confer status through such things as promotion). These categories are not, of course, mutually exclusive and may overlap. The form of influence derived from resource power is *exchange*. The desired behaviour is produced, in exchange for the resources controlled by the power source. It is, in essence, a form of bargaining or negotiation.

Position power is sometimes referred to by the French and Raven title of 'legitimate' power. Position power derives from the position or role occupied by the individual. Managers, by virtue of the position they hold, have the 'right' to control their department. Such rights are often most explicitly expressed in relationships with trade unions as 'manage-ment's right to manage'. Position power ultimately relies on being backed up by resource or physical power. The method of influence is primarily through the *rules and procedures* of the organization. To be effective, it depends upon everyone accepting the rules. If these are challenged, then the back-up source of power is called into play.

Expert power derives from one individual having greater knowledge or expertise than others. The possession of information which is not avail-able to others is a potential source of considerable power. Influence is wielded by the process of *persuasion*. This can range from the logical presentation of data to support a desired course of action, to the more emotional appeals of advertising and propaganda.

Personal power is derived from sheer force of personality – often referred to as *charisma*. Religious leaders and some political leaders, especially the successful ones, are good exponents of this type of power. High personal power, coupled with high expert power (real or assumed) will give the individual the status of a 'guru'. Influence is by *inspiration*. People do things because they are inspired by a charismatic leader.

Traditionally, that is to say from the 1950s to the 1970s, the prevailing values in OD led to the use of expert power as the influence for change. Many consultants, particularly those of the 'guru' type, also exercised considerable personal power, and some still do. There was a tendency to believe that many of the ills of organizations were the result of using resource or position power. The job of OD, it was argued, was to remove or reduce the use of such forms of power. Physical power was, of course, completely beyond the pale. The ideal, and therefore effective, organization was seen as one where people worked together in an atmosphere of openness and trust, setting goals by consensus, to which there would be a high degree of commitment. This was effectively a blend of the support and achievement cultures discussed in the previous chapter. As previously mentioned before, these 'openness and trust' assumptions have had little effect and, towards the end of the century, a new spirit of realism is evident. This accepts organizations 'as they are', and plans change within the confines of that reality. It is known, therefore, as the contingency approach.

STRATEGIES FOR CHANGE

While openness and trust remain the ideal of many OD consultants, there is a recognition that most organizations do not operate on these principles. As a result of this acceptance, it follows that change strategies have to be adapted to suit the prevailing circumstances. This has, in reality, always been implicitly accepted. Robert Chin and Kenneth Benne (1976), for example, have defined what they call 'general strategies for effecting change in human systems'. They suggest there are three of these that provide a good framework for defining change strategies, both in organizations and, more widely, in society as a whole.

Empirical-rational strategies. This approach assumes that people are basically rational. Change can be effected, therefore, by showing that it is in the individual's own interest to change. This is sometimes referred to as 'enlightened self-interest'. Change is achieved by the use of data and rational persuasion. The assumptions underlying this strategy lie deep in traditional education, and include a belief in the benefit of research and the general dissemination of knowledge. The source for such a change is primarily expert power.

Normative-re-educative strategies. This group of strategies does not deny the rationality of human beings. It places more emphasis, however, on the belief that behaviour is largely determined by the social and cultural norms of the group or society to which people belong. Individuals have a strong commitment to conforming to, and maintaining, these norms. Successful change is therefore accomplished by changing these norms. This is achieved by a mixture of education and persuasion. Both expert and personal power may be involved in such change strategies.

Power-coercive strategies involve the use of physical, resource, or position power to coerce individuals into changing. The use of physical power is widely used by governments when adopting this strategy. At the organizational level, resource or position power is the more usual source. Chin and Benne point out that passive resistance, along the lines used by Gandi, is also an example of power-coercive approach. It is effectively a battle of wills between two sources of power.

An interesting example of the use of these strategies is provided by the attempts of the British government to get both drivers and front-seat passengers to wear the seatbelts provided in cars. A considerable amount of time and money was spent using empirical-rational strategies. These involved advertising campaigns giving information on safety factors – 'you know it makes sense'. All this had little effect. The government then switched to a power-coercive strategy. Not wearing a seatbelt became an offence, punishable by fines. The result was that seat-belt usage leapt overnight to in excess of 90 per cent. The maintenance of this high level of seat-belt wearing is now most probably due to normative-re-educative influences. Wearing seatbelts has become the norm. While the threat of fines is still in the background, we suspect that most people would, even without this, continue with the new behaviour. In Kurt Lewin's terms, power-coercive strategies were necessary for the unfreezing and change processes. Normative-re-educative strategies produced the re-freezing.

INDIVIDUAL ADAPTATION

So far change strategies have been considered from the point of view of someone trying to change others. To complete the picture we need to consider how change takes place within the individual. Herbert Kelman (1958) has provided a framework for this. He suggests that there are three mechanisms for change. These can be seen as responses to the attempted influence of others.

Compliance. Individuals change simply because they are unable to resist the pressure being placed upon them. This is a common response to physical, resource, or position power. In some cases, if there are rewards, or at least no costs, for the individual, the change may become internalized and hence relatively permanent. Often, however, this is not a good way to create change, since the response is, at best, relatively passive. When the pressure is removed, the original behaviour is likely to recur. At worst, it results in counterdependence, and individuals may expend considerable energy and ingenuity in finding ways to avoid changing.

Identification is a frequent response to personal power. The person being influenced changes because of their desire to resemble the source of power. This may be because of admiration of the individual concerned or because they are inspired by them. Religious conversions are often of this nature, but it can also occur in educational and therapeutic situations. The lifetime of change by identification may be long, with the change becoming internalized. It may equally be quite short lived, particularly if less admirable aspects of the source of influence suddenly become apparent.

Internalization is the most effective form of change, since the individual accepts the change and adopts it as part of their own self-image. Inevitably, this form of change is likely to take longer than the previous two, hence time must be allowed for it to occur. It is likely to be slowed even further if there are strong pressures for change. The individual must be allowed to develop commitment in their own time. However, once this commitment has developed, the change is relatively permanent. The best approach to influence such a change is by expert power.

RESISTANCE TO CHANGE

Finally, we need to look at resistance to change, particularly as there are two popular myths concerning it.

The first myth is that people universally dislike change, and will attempt to avoid it. While it is certainly true that change programmes occasionally provoke resistance, this is by no means a universal reaction. Indeed, on many occasions people enjoy change and look forward to it. If this were not so, the rapid rate of change in the world, which has been previously noted, would not have taken place. The reality is that the majority of the population of the developed world has happily adapted to enormous changes, both in technology and their way of life, over the last few decades. It may be, however, that people differ in their readiness to accept change. E. Rogers and F. Shoemaker (1971) have suggested that people fall into five different types: innovators, early adoptors, majority (early), majority (late), and laggards.

Innovators are quick to adopt new ideas and to change accordingly. They are also risk takers as some of the new ideas may prove to be mistaken. *Early adaptors* follow close behind the innovators but are rather more respectable and in conformity with societal norms. They are not seen by the rest of society to be as non-conformist as the innovators. The *early majority* take on change once it has started to become accepted, while the more conservative *late majority* wait to see all the effects before adopting change. Finally, the *laggards* are very suspicious of change and are slow to adapt.

Rogers and Shoemaker suggest that the largest number of people fall into the two 'majority' classifications, with far fewer occupying the extreme 'innovator' and 'laggard' positions. It might also be the case that individuals vary according to the nature of the change. One of the authors is almost certainly in the 'laggard' classification when it comes to using computers, but is, in other areas, much more adaptive.

The other myth is that resistance to change is necessarily a 'bad' thing. Sometimes such resistance may be healthy. Both people and organizations need periods of stability to re-freeze and absorb the changes that have already taken place. Also, the existence of resistance may be an indicator that, for some reason, a particular change is not considered desirable. In such cases a closer look is needed at the causes for the resistance.

Where beneficial change is resisted it may be for a number of reasons. Sometimes people believe that the change is likely to be to their disadvantage. On occasions this may indeed be true. It can hardly be a surprise if a person's job is at risk that they will resist related changes. The fear of change is often enhanced by the secretive manner in which change programmes are planned and implemented. This is often done, of course, because management fear that people will find ways of blocking the changes if they are aware of them in advance. Paradoxically, the secrecy itself makes people suspicious and often leads to the very blocking behaviour the management had hoped to avoid. Secrecy becomes a self-fulfilling prophecy.

Change will always involve some effort, as new ways of doing things have to be learnt. For some people the fear of the unknown will be a major factor, especially if there are high levels of insecurity and dependency.

Other sources of resistance may lie in the social system. The existing norms of the group or organization will usually be very powerful. These are necessary, of course, as they provide the rules within which people relate to each other and work together. Change may require that these norms are changed in some way. Problems may also arise if change programmes are instituted in only one part of an organization. This may cause imbalances elsewhere, which will be resisted as a means of restoring the balance. Other resistances of a social nature may be due to the change agent threatening vested interests or 'sacred cows'. In OD programmes carried out by outside consultants there may also be an element of suspicion of outsiders.

OVERCOMING RESISTANCE TO CHANGE

There is overwhelming evidence that the best way to reduce resistance to change is to involve those whom it is going to affect in the decision-making process. Individuals who have been involved in the diagnosis, planning, and implementation of change are far more likely to feel positively about it. It is best of all if all the necessary information is freely available and if decisions are then taken by consensus. There will, however, be occasions when it is not possible to be totally open (for example if some of the information is commercially sensitive). The general rule should be that good communication and feedback channels should be established between the source of change and those who are to be affected. Even where there are short-term costs, such as need for retraining, it is necessary to show that there will be long-term benefits, such as better pay or more security. Obviously, it will be easier to affect change if there is a general climate of *trust* in the organization, where people feel that their fears will be listened to, and their problems recognized and dealt with in a sympathetic manner. Ideally, the programme itself should be open to change in the light of such feedback.

8

Managing
your Boss

Before we describe some of the ways in which you can influence your boss two points need to be made.

First, in order to make sense of this chapter you will need to have read the rest of the book, as it draws upon theories presented in other chapters. Second, we want to reiterate the caveat at the beginning of the book – do not expect a 'in one bound Jack was free' solution. Dealing with other people, and in particular *bosses*, is not only complex, but also highly risky to your career development. The large number of variables that influence interactions means that no two cases will be the same. What we can do, however, is to highlight the important factors involved, and suggest ways in which they can be used. We will also describe some examples of common 'types' of manager, and consider how they might be influenced.

It is a general rule about all interactions that the only person over whose behaviour you can have *direct* influence is yourself. The only way, therefore, in which you can hope to change your boss's behaviour is by changing your own. In deciding what you should be doing there are three factors that you will need to take into account: your own needs, behaviour and personality; your boss's needs, behaviour and personality; and the situation in which the interaction takes place. (One particular aspect of the situation is organizational culture, which has a strong influence on which management styles and sanctions are acceptable.)

YOUR NEEDS, BEHAVIOUR AND PERSONALITY

As pointed out in Chapter 6, it is essential for you to be clear about what precisely it is that you want to achieve. If you recall, it was suggested that there are three types of personal goal: task, status and developmental. These differ both in their nature and their timescale. Often people are fairly clear about task goals but rather less so about developmental ones. One way of highlighting long-term developmental goals is to pose yourself the question 'would I be happy doing my present job for the rest of my working life?' If the answer is *no*, then ask yourself 'is there another job within the organization that I would like?' If the answer to this is also *no*, then start considering other alternatives.

In dealings with your current manager, it is more likely that there will be disagreement about task and status goals. Problems about task goals often revolve around lack of clarity about tasks and responsibilities. Problems concerning status goals, on the other hand, may often be related to feelings of inequity, arising from perceived underreward. As we saw in Chapter 2, a common cause of inequity is that the two parties have different perceptions about what are to be taken into account as 'investments'. There are two possible approaches to this situation. The most obvious is to convince the boss to accept that your efforts do count as 'investments'. However, there is often a difference between what an organization *says* it rewards, and what it *actually* rewards! Once again espoused theory and theory in practice differ. The other alternative, therefore, is to 'play the game' – identify what it is the organization really rewards and concentrate on this. The easiest way to do this is to look at people who have recently been successful and, for instance, been promoted.

Your goals will also be influenced by the balance of the needs for achievement, power and affiliation identified by David McClelland and discussed in Chapter 2. Identifying the balance of these needs may give you some insight into the realism of your goals. Someone who is high in the need for affiliative assurance, for example, is unlikely to make a successful task-oriented manager.

Behaviour only continues if it is reinforced (see Chapter 2). In interactions there is a continual feedback loop between the behaviour of both parties. Each will influence how the other behaves. The question that you have to answer is 'which of my boss's am I encouraging or discouraging?'. Another question concerns the compatibility, or otherwise, of your style of working with that of your boss. Are you an Adaptor or an Innovator? Is your behaviour pattern more type A or type B?

YOUR BOSS'S NEEDS, BEHAVIOUR AND PERSONALITY

As previously pointed out, the possible combinations of needs, behaviours and personalities is very large. We will, therefore, describe some of the more common managerial 'types' that we have encountered, and use them as case studies. Before doing so we will consider two possible types of approach to understanding people's needs and behaviour, drawing upon theories considered in previous chapters.

The causes of people's behaviour can be considered as either determined by *internal* factors or *external* factors. Transactional analysis (TA) and McClelland's 'needs' for achievement, power and affiliation are both explanations based on internal factors. Behaviour modification (BMod) and management 'style' theories, on the other hand, do not concern themselves with internal explanations, but look solely at the behaviour and the way that external consequences encourage or discourage the behaviour.

Both these approaches have their uses and are most powerful when used together. Those based on external consequences are most probably safest to use when considering other people's behaviour, as there is no need for interpretations about their personality or motives that may prove to be wildly inaccurate.

AN INTERNAL EXPLANATION: TA

One of the most useful theories for gaining insight into interpersonal behaviour is that of TA. It is particularly useful when looking at boss –subordinate interactions, as it can take into account the imbalance of power in the situation. In order to understand more fully these interactions we need to introduce one more concept of TA theory – that of *stroking*. A stroke is defined as a unit of recognition, and stroking is concerned with the feelings aspect of transactions. Recognition, as we saw earlier, is a powerful need for most people, and in interacting with someone, we of course implicitly recognize their existence. The way in which we do this can vary, and this will have an effect upon the feelings of those involved. First, strokes can vary in their intensity. An example of a mild stroke would be when you nod and say 'good morning' to a colleague. If you have been away on business for a week, then you would usually get more powerful strokes from your family on your return. Strokes can also be either positive or negative. Positive strokes are intended to make the recipient feel comfortable and good about themselves, for example compliments. Negative strokes, on the other hand, are intended to make the recipient feel uncomfortable and bad about themselves, for example 'tickings off' and 'put-downs'. Finally, strokes can be either conditional or unconditional. A conditional stroke is, as the name suggests, conditional on you doing something, for instance praise for a good piece of work. An unconditional stroke is not dependent upon a specific behaviour, it is given merely for 'being there'. (One of the reasons why dogs make such good pets is that they give many such unconditional strokes and, as a result receive them!) In general, unconditional strokes are more powerful. This is important, as the convention in most organizations is that recognition is conditional. It contrasts with the situation in families, where more unconditional stroking takes place.

The assertion that non-contingent stroking is more powerful than contingent stroking may appear to contradict the advice given in Chapter

2 which explained that rewards should be contingent upon the occurrence of desired behaviour. The apparent contradiction occurs if stroking and rewards are interpreted as being one and the same. This is not the case. The essential feature of stroking is that it entails the recognition of another individual as a person to be valued because they are a person, not because of what they do. Rewards, on the other hand, should be specifically related to the person's behaviour. For example, to greet another person and perhaps enquire after their well-being for no other reason than that they are a person is non-contingent stroking. To praise someone for a specific piece of good work is a contingent reward. The two do not operate in opposite directions; in fact it is probably most effective to use them together.

Stroking is closely linked to existential position, which was examined at the end of Chapter 1. The strokes that we give, and hence those that are returned, will depend on our position at the time. These will, in turn, influence the position we then take up. Strokes from the I'm OK, You're OK position will nearly always be positive. Even if we are giving the other person adverse feedback about one of their actions or pieces of work, because we feel positively about the *person*, the stroke will still be positive. Receiving such strokes helps to promote or maintain a position of I'm OK, You're OK in ourselves. From other positions, we will tend to give negative strokes, and receiving negative strokes will tend to push us towards the favourite Not OK position (commonly in managers I'm OK, You're Not OK). What often happens is that we get into cycles of stroking, either positive cycles or negative cycles.

We have assumed that most people prefer positive strokes. There are some people, however, who actually prefer negative strokes. This occurs, according to the theory, from the stroke patterns established in early life between such people and their parents, or other significant adults. In any large organization you are likely to come across a small number of such individuals. They tend to be unhappy much of the time, and appear 'deliberately' to do things which will generate negative responses from others. They also operate much of the time from one of the Not OK positions. In extreme cases, it will be almost impossible to give them positive strokes. Those that are given will either be ignored or interpreted negatively in some way – 'he's only being nice because he's been told to'. In BMod terms, what is for most people punishment is, for these individuals, a reinforcer.

The inclusion of the concept of stroking makes the analysis of the transactions between you and your boss more complicated, but it is important, as it determines how you feel and, to some extent, your existential position. An ideal relationship would be one in which both you and your boss work from I'm OK, You're OK, in which all ego states of Parent, Adult and Child are freely available and where there is plenty of positive stroking. In our experience this is comparatively rare in British industry. However, once you know about strokes, you can learn to ignore negative strokes that tend to push you towards an ineffective Not OK position. This does not mean that you should ignore any negative feedback concerning your behaviour or performance. This information is, of course, necessary if you are going to adapt future behaviour effectively.

In reviewing the interactions between yourself and your boss it is useful to consider the ego states from which he or she usually operates. It may be that all three are used, but often there is a predominant use of either one or two. Most likely this will be Parent and/or Adult. It is important to consider what effect this has on you – which of your ego states does it 'hook'? As we saw in Chapter 1, heavy Parent will tend to hook your Child, either compliant or rebellious. Once you have analysed the interaction, you may then decide to 'cross' the transaction, perhaps to Adult, again as described in Chapter 1. At first you will almost certainly find it difficult to cross transactions, as it often goes against old and well-established habits. However, with continued practice you will find it becoming easier. Another factor to be aware of is that, when dealing with a Parental boss, he or she usually has a more powerful Parent than you, since they have the backing of the power provided by their position in the organization. This is another good reason for avoiding responding from the Not OK Parent position.

We have been suggesting that Adult–Adult (problem-solving) transactions are preferable to Parental ones, but there are occasions where you may wish to cross one of these transactions. For example, if your boss operates from a predominantly Adult state, then it may be appropriate on occasions to inject some creative Free Child into the transaction.

AN EXTERNAL EXPLANATION: BMod

Whilst TA is an 'internal' approach, BMod is an external approach. It views behaviour as being largely determined by its consequences. For successful implementation of BMod techniques, attention has to be directed towards *specific* behaviours. Because of this it is difficult to give examples of applications to generic problems. Where we feel that certain specific behaviours are likely to be common to a particular managerial 'type', we will comment upon them.

We will now apply some cases, but at this point it should be pointed out that much of what follows is based upon our personal experiences, and those of managers on programmes we have run. There is very little experimental work in this area and therefore generalizations should be treated with caution. In analysing these cases we will take into account the following factors (as discussed at the beginning on this chapter):

ORGANIZATIONAL CULTURE: The culture of the organization within which you work will constrain the type of power that the boss can bring to bear. Most readers, we suspect, will be within role cultures. This means that the only legitimate forms of power that can be used are those of 'legitimate', 'information' and 'position' power. Occasionally, particular managers may have some 'personal' power.

POSSIBLE NEEDS: The needs identified by McClelland are useful, in that they indicate what is likely to be reinforcing to a particular manager. What is the balance between your boss's needs for achievement, power and affiliation? As we have said before, you will not be able to change your boss's style but, if you wish to change specific behaviours you will need to establish what reinforcers are encouraging them. Analysing his or her needs will help to identify relevant reinforcers.

PERSONALITY: The interaction between type As and type Bs, and between Adaptors and Innovators was dealt with in Chapter 1. In TA terms you need to identify which particular ego states your boss prefers to use, and respond accordingly. In particular, you need to identify what he or she does that tends to push you into the Not OK Parent or Child position. Once you have identified this, you can then learn to ignore it.

MANAGEMENT STYLE AND SANCTIONS: At this point, as well as considering the sanctions that the boss has at his or her disposal, it is worth identifying your own sources of power. The chapter on motivation showed just how important praise and feedback can be as reinforcers. This does not only apply to subordinates; bosses also react to social reinforcers. In terms of power, the main ones that subordinates have at their disposal are those of expert power and information power. Almost everyone has some power through their control of information. This can have a somewhat negative source. Almost any employee has the power to disrupt the organization's smooth running by sins of omission as well as commission.

SOME MANAGERIAL 'TYPES'

THE BUREAUCRAT

The bureaucrat is generally pleasant and mild mannered, but is often slow and cautious in making decisions. When faced with a problem or suggestion his or her usual response is to suggest that you check to see if the idea is in accordance with established 'custom and practice'. If the problem or the suggested solution is novel, his or her response is to send memos to all those who are likely to be affected, asking for their reactions. In addition, a committee or working party might be formed to advise or decide on the issue. If you, as a subordinate, do anything in a way that is not sanctioned by the organizational rules and procedures, then you are likely to receive a reprimanding memo. This memo will be in addition to any possible verbal reprimand, and will be concerned with the way you went about the task, rather than about the outcome. Thus, you may actually be praised for what you accomplished, but admonished for breaking the rules to get the task done. These responses tend to have a demotivating effect upon subordinates, who tend not to bother taking any initiatives. If you want a quiet life, you learn how to work to the rules.

ANALYSIS

ORGANIZATIONAL CULTURE: The bureaucrat is mainly found in role cultures.

POSSIBLE NEEDS: Like most managers, the bureaucrat is likely to have a high need for power. The main expression of this is in a need to control others, which can be achieved in a number of ways. According to McClelland, these range from sheer domination to subtle influencing techniques. Bureaucrats exercise control through strict administration of the rules. In this way, a high degree of certainty and predictability can be achieved. When their needs are blocked by higher authority, they tend to operate new instructions to the letter, waiting for a collapse so that they can say 'I told you so!'.

PERSONALITY: Almost by definition, the bureaucrat is likely to be an Adaptor rather than an Innovator, and type B rather than type A. For those Innovative type As who have to deal with them, the interactions may be somewhat frustrating. In TA terms, the bureaucrat is highly Parental. However, unlike some other types of manager, the Parent in this case is the internalized 'Organizational Parent'. As with any Parent, the intention is to hook the Child of subordinates. If all is going well, then responses will be from the Compliant Child, but subordinates and others may sometimes rebel. One of the reasons for such revolts may be that the strict bureaucrat allows his Parent to be in control, when the Adult should be realizing that the situation has changed and, therefore, overriding the Parent. Such a bureaucrat would not stop World War III if it meant breaking the rules. Such extremes are, fortunately, rare. Finally, bureaucrats are often low on Free Child, unable or unwilling to 'let themselves go'. They are, however, high on Adapted Child and readily comply with the demands of the system.

MANAGEMENT STYLE AND SANCTIONS: Bureaucrats will tend to be authoritarian, but will stay within the rules and their own limits of authority. They will tend to use the powers provided by the organization when dealing with subordinates. These are generally those of *position power*, based on their position within the organization, and *resource power*, based on their control of rewards. When dealing with superiors they will generally be compliant but, if they believe that rules are being broken, they may use their control of information as a source of power. This may be used either positively, for example, by the 'leaking' of information damaging to a superior, or negatively by holding back information that would allow the system to take corrective action.

HOW TO COPE

Given that the bureaucrat is usually a type B Adaptor, any innovations should be presented, if possible, as adaptations of present systems. In addition, do not expect a quick response. In our experience the best approach is to become fully familiar with the rules and regulations of your organization, so that you can present proposals in such a way that they are seen to be consistent with the system. If this is not possible, then avoid pushing your preferred, and possibly innovative, solution. Rather, present the problem, together with your own 'tentative thoughts' on the matter, as a request for help. Under these circumstances bureaucrats often show considerable ingenuity in redrafting your 'thoughts' so that they fit the current systems, or in finding alternative interpretations of the rules.

There will be occasions when you find yourself being pushed by the bureaucrat's Parent into a Not OK position, either Parent or Child. You should recognize this and stay in I'm OK, You're OK Adult. Both Child and Parent responses will be counterproductive. The Not OK Parent is particularly dangerous as, in most cases, the boss's Parent carries more 'clout' than yours.

The advice that BMod would offer in coping with such a boss is to examine each specific behaviour that the boss does that you wish to change, and identify the reinforcers that are maintaining it. Then remove the reinforcers and institute a process of change. In looking for the reinforcers, some clues may be gained from considering the balance of needs. The bureaucrat, as we have seen, has a high need for control and order. It is also likely that he or she has a low need for affiliation. Unfortunately, it is often the case that subordinates have little that they can use as reinforcers with their boss. The exception to this is their control over their own behaviour. You should analyse specific situations to see if there are any ways in which your behaviour is actually reinforcing behaviour in your boss that you wish to discourage.

THE AUTOCRAT

Autocrats have very strong views on what ought to be done in any situation. These are derived from their own personal convictions concerning what should be done, rather than the organization's rules. They do not listen very well to their subordinates and issue instructions which are expected to be carried out without question, except on matters where clarification is required. Such managers are intolerant of those who make mistakes and people who 'do not understand'. They will get quite angry in these situations, but in a cold, withdrawn manner. Sometimes they appear inconsistent, since while they are autocratic with their subordinates, they are often helpful to their peers, and even 'fawning' in relations with someone higher up the organization. In the eyes of their subordinates, they can be either 'tyrants' or 'benevolent autocrats', depending upon how they are treated.

ANALYSIS

CULTURE: The autocrat is probably most common in power or role cultures.

POSSIBLE NEEDS: Like the bureaucrat, the autocrat has a high need for power, but their source of power is their personal convictions, not the rules of the organization. There is research evidence to suggest that those with a high need for power are sensitive to power differentials. Their behaviour may vary, however, depending on whether the difference is in their favour or not. This would explain the apparent contradictions in their behaviour to different groups in the organization. If the balance is in their favour, as it is with subordinates, then direct power can be used. Faced with those who have greater power, they gain power by ingratiating themselves. This can be done by doing favours or flattering the more powerful individual. There is evidence to show that those managers with a high need for power do, in fact, respond positively to such ingratiation from their subordinates. With their peers, the autocratic manager can gain some temporary increase in their power by giving help when asked, especially if the other manager then feels in some way obligated.

PERSONALITY: It is likely that autocrats can be either type As or type Bs. Likewise, they may be either Adaptors or Innovators. In TA terms, they are almost certainly highly Parental and low on Child. They are also likely to have a well-functioning Adult.

MANAGEMENT STYLE AND SANCTIONS: Like the bureaucrat, the autocrat will use those sanctions that his or her position in the organization provides. These are position power and resource power. If the organization accepts they may also use coercive power. The benevolent autocrat is likely to use resource power quite effectively, giving infrequent, unpredictable, but large rewards (variable ratio reinforcement).

HOW TO COPE

As with the bureaucrat, the only way to deal with the autocrat is to stay OK and Adult. Any confrontation should be on the basis of data. Because of their need for power, the technique of ingratiation is often effective, although to some distasteful. Again, because of their high need for power, they are sensitive to power from other sources. If the subordinate has more 'expert' power, and is prepared to stand up to the autocrat, this may be respected. In general, if you have a source of power that is unavailable to your manager (normally expert or informational), then he or she will often cultivate the relationship. This is, however, a high risk strategy, and should be tried with care. The information or expertise you have may only be of temporary value.

In extreme cases, autocrats are often brought down by a grouping of their subordinates . Realizing that their individual powers are not strong enough to confront the autocrat, political alliances are made between the subordinates, so as to increase their power base. An act by the autocrat that clearly and seriously breaks the organization's rules often acts as a trigger for concerted action by the subordinates. The autocrat is either removed or his or her powers strictly defined and limited, often by devolving powers to a committee.

In BMod terms, this type of boss may gain reinforcement from being able to control other people. It is likely, therefore, that he or she will get reinforcement from those situations in which they win a 'fight'. For this reason confrontation should be avoided unless you are certain of victory.

THE WHEELER-DEALER

Wheeler-dealers are often very senior managers who spend much of their time negotiating with other departments over the allocation of resources and such matters as purchasing and sales. They clearly enjoy this type of activity and, as a result, spend a lot of time doing it, leaving their own department very much to run itself. They are not always successful in the negotiations, possibly because they are impatient and do not 'suffer fools gladly'. When they are in their own department, they will make 'sorties' around the staff, asking how they are getting on, checking on the progress of various projects and generally giving encouragement. Staff are not given much guidance and are often left to sink or swim, but initiatives by staff are usually well supported. Non-performers tend to be ignored. There is a general feeling of dynamism in the department, but also a certain amount of chaos. Type A Innovators are likely to find this exciting, but type B Adaptors are likely to feel uncomfortable.

ANALYSIS

CULTURE: The wheeler-dealer is most at home in power, achievement, and support cultures. They are likely to be less happy in a role culture, but may sometimes exist in small pockets of the organization that have their own culture.

PERSONALITY: The wheeler-dealer is almost certainly an Innovator; the rules are made to achieve objectives and, if achieving the objectives means that the rules have to be ignored, so be it. We suspect that most are also type A, but there is no reason why some should not be type B. They are likely to have a high need for power and achievement. Because they are aware that they need other people in order to achieve their objectives their need for power is more socialized than the autocrat or bureaucrat. Control is achieved by interpersonal influence rather than coercion. In TA terms, he or she is likely to have moderate Parent and an effective Adult. The Child is likely to be very active, demonstrating itself in enthusiasm and intervention.

MANAGEMENT STYLE AND SANCTIONS: The wheeler-dealer's style may range from the consultative, through participative to laissez-faire. He or she often delegates quite considerably but sometimes, especially at times of stress, they may show a flash of authoritarianism. Often they will regret this when things cool down, and smooth the feathers they have ruffled. They often use personal power and people will work hard for them because they admire them. Approval is withdrawn from those not performing up to the mark.

HOW TO COPE

With this type of manager, it is essential to become proactive. Wheeler-dealers expect their staff to use their own initiative and only value those who do. It is no use waiting to be told what to do – nothing will happen and you will be written off as ineffective. You should be prepared to make your own decisions about what needs to be done and then get on with them, making sure that the boss is kept informed. The boss should be informed rather than asked, the assumption being that you will go ahead unless there are objections. Keeping the boss informed also means that you maintain a high profile with him or her. Problems with this type of boss often centre on getting the more mundane jobs done. The boss does not gain reinforcement through them and, likewise does not reinforce those who do them, no matter how well. As a result people learn that doing mundane jobs does not pay off. Often they get thrust on to the most junior member of staff (either in terms of seniority or tenure). If you're in this position you need to negotiate with colleagues to ensure that boring tasks are shared out evenly. Depending on your colleagues, it may be possible to do this by open agreement or it may be a more political process. Since the boss values enthusiasm and energy (Child), find something to be enthusiastic about, hook his or her enthusiasm, then point out that mundane jobs are preventing you devoting your energies to it!

LAISSEZ-FAIRE

Laissez-faire managers have often been promoted because of their high level of technical competence. They are not, however, interested in managing. They are very energetic, enthusiastic and creative and give strong verbal support to initiatives. In some respects they are very similar to the wheeler-dealer, but their interests are on technical aspects of the job rather than managerial ones. Their interpersonal skills are good and they maintain good relations with their staff. The main problem is similar to that of the wheeler-dealer – the department is largely left to run itself. This means that there are problems about who to assign these routines jobs to and that they are not carried out satisfactorily; some team members find this frustrating.

ANALYSIS

CULTURE: Found in almost all cultures, but perhaps most appropriate in an achievement orientated organization.

POSSIBLE NEEDS: A high need for achievement which is directed towards their profession rather than the organization. They may also be relatively high on need for affiliation, especially on affiliative assurance. This means that they need to be liked by their subordinates. If they have a good working relationship with their team, they are reluctant to lose members, even if it means promotion for the person concerned.

PERSONALITY: Again like the wheeler-dealer, they are likely to be Innovators. In TA terms, they tend to be low on Parent but with a highly effective Adult, particularly in relation to their professional specialism. They are particularly high on Child, which is reflected in their creativity and their desire to be liked by others.

MANAGEMENT STYLE AND SANCTIONS: The management style is that of laissez-faire, with very little use of sanctions. The main sanction is the removal of social contact.

HOW TO COPE

Given the similarities between the laissez-faire manager and wheeler-dealer, the method of copying with them is very similar. There is an additional problem however, in that while the wheeler-dealer at least manages relationships with other departments, the laissez-faire manager does not. As a result, staff have to manage both internal and external relationships. There will be no problem, however, with the technical output of the department.

Because they have a high need for affiliation, they are susceptible to social reinforcers, especially from the group as a whole. Such social pressures may be used as threats or reinforcement, in order to encourage the manager to undertake those tasks that the group considers to be his or her responsibility.

THE RELUCTANT MANAGER

The reluctant manager, like the laissez-faire manager, will have been promoted on the grounds of technical competence. The main difference between them is their behaviour towards their subordinates. Reluctant managers generally leave their department to run itself but, unlike laissez-faire managers, they do not encourage their staff in any way. If a technical problem arises then they will offer help, if asked, and this help will be highly effective. The management of the department, both internally and externally, is ignored. In some circumstances, however, the reluctant manager may appear to be bureaucratic. Since he or she is not interested in managing, following the organization's rules provides the easy way out. When something non-routine happens, it is often very difficult to get a decision of any sort.

ANALYSIS

ORGANIZATIONAL CULTURE: Although reluctant managers may be found in any culture, like laissez-faire managers, they are more common in achievement cultures.

POSSIBLE NEEDS: They are likely to have a high need for achievement, but a low need for power and affiliation. It is the low level of need for affiliation that is perhaps most noticeable.

PERSONALITY: They are likely to be high Innovators but, because they have no interest in management, this only shows in their technical activities. They are likely to be type B. In TA terms, they are high on Adult, especially with regards to their professional expertise. They are particularly low on Child.

MANAGEMENT STYLE AND SANCTIONS: Their management style is so laissez-faire as to be almost non-existent. Sanctions are rarely used.

HOW TO COPE

The main problem with reluctant managers is getting them to engage in any interpersonal interactions at all. This, of course, has the advantage that you can get on and do what it is you like doing. Indeed, you could almost take over the running of the department yourself, if that is what you want. Because of their dislike of social interaction and management, any request for advice on managerial matters is dealt with in whichever way is quickest. This is in accordance with the Premack principle in BMod (see page 63), which suggests that we spend longer on those jobs that we like. In these circumstances, it is perhaps best to use your control of information selectively. Present a number of alternatives from which the manager can choose, with your own preferred alternative strongly supported by evidence.

If you are seeking to change any specific behaviour, then you will need to watch to see if there is anything in the work situation that reluctant managers find rewarding. In TA terms, is there anything that hooks their Free Child and gets them excited?

THE OPEN MANAGER

This manager has a very firm belief in the value of participation and getting everyone involved. He or she holds regular meetings to review progress and decide on future actions, as well as *ad hoc* gatherings of subgroups or the department as a whole to deal with issues as they arise. Most people appreciate this, but there is the feeling that, on occasions, too much time is spent ensuring that all involved are committed when this commitment is not really necessary.

ANALYSIS

CULTURE: Open managers can be found in almost any culture, but are most at home in support or achievement cultures.

POSSIBLE NEEDS: They have little need for power, high need for affiliation (supportive rather than assurance) and may have a high or low need for achievement.

PERSONALITY: They are likely to be middle of the range on Adaptor/Innovator. In TA terms the open manager is flexible and can use all three ego states.

MANAGEMENT STYLE AND SANCTIONS: Such managers are highly participative and will only use position and resource power if and when required. They may also have some personal power and are admired by their subordinates.

HOW TO COPE

There are very few problems in dealing with the open manager, except perhaps in deciding how open you are going to be in return. The danger with being too open is that the information you divulge may be used to your disadvantage, either at another time, or by other people. A related problem may be that the manager is open in situations that may not be appropriate, for example, in relations with other departments who are behaving politically. The solution to this is to talk openly with the manager about strategies regarding relations with the rest of the organization.

As the open manager engenders commitment, there is also a danger that you will become too involved and take more work on than is good for you. In these circumstances, you will need to learn to say 'no'. Fortunately, because the open manager's repertoire includes all three ego states available this can be done on an Adult–Adult basis.

Appreciation of their openness is most probably a reinforcer to these managers. Any lack of enthusiasm from their subordinates will be noticed and questioned.

These then are some of the most common managerial 'types' that we have experienced. It is, of course, rarely the case that any particular boss fits one, and only one description. Most bosses are an amalgam of two or three types. If you are to influence your own boss you need to analyse him or her along the lines we have discussed above.

STRATEGIES FOR MANAGING YOUR BOSS

Having decided what you want to do, you need to work out your strategy. As outlined in Chapter 6, there are four basic strategies which apply as much to influencing your boss as they do to influencing the organization as a whole. It is, of course, possible to combine several of them or to try one first and, if it proves to be ineffective, move to another. This, in itself, it also part of your strategy.

THE LAISSEZ-FAIRE REACTION

We suspect that some of you reading this chapter will have already experienced the laissez-faire reaction. It arises when you come to the conclusion that, having tried other approaches, there is nothing you can do to change your boss or the situation. All you can then do is to decide how best you can adapt to the situation. This adaptation may simply consist of not allowing the interactions with your boss to push you into a Not OK position, which will mean working heavily from your Adult. At the other extreme, it may mean looking for another job.

There are no set rules to suggest when the laissez-faire approach is appropriate. Factors that need to be taken into consideration include the degree of rigidity of both your boss and yourself, and the level of effort you think will be required to produce the desired change. There are times when it is quite appropriate to come to the decision that it is not worth trying to change things, because the costs of doing so outweigh the benefits. If you have come to this decision, there are three important aspects to be considered. First, are you sure that you have made a valid judgement about the difficulties and effort involved? Second, have there been any changes in circumstances since you made the decision? An extension of this is to be sensitive to any changes in the future that may alter the relative balance of costs and benefits. Finally, having made the decision, be aware that you will have no further reason to complain about the situation. You either have to accept the situation or leave it.

THE OPEN APPROACH

This is often the best one to try first, or at least consider first. Have you tried simply talking openly to your boss about the issue and how you feel? If you go for this approach, make sure you are working from I'm OK, You're OK, and think about appropriate ego states. Most probably it is best to stick to Adult.

The open style will probably work best in a support or achievement culture, where the boss uses an open style (all ego states from I'm OK, You're OK), gives a high level of strokes, and possibly has a high need for affiliation. It will be less effective in a power or role culture, and with bosses who are highly Parental and work from I'm OK, You're Not OK. It could be disastrous in a situation where others are using highly political styles.

THE FORMAL APPROACH

The formal approach makes use of formal systems within the organization. You should identify any formal appeal procedure that may be relevant. In using the formal system, it is essential to stay in Adult (that is, follow the rules) and, as always, I'm OK, You're OK.

The formal approach will work best in role cultures and with those bosses who tend to be Adult and follow the rules themselves i.e.

bureaucrats. It is unlikely to be effective in support and achievement cultures, which value spontaneity. In political cultures, it is likely to be seen as naive.

THE POLITICAL STRATEGY

If other approaches do not work, you will have to think of something more subtle. This does not mean, however, that you have to be under-hand or negative; use the political strategy with care and with con-sideration of others. The essence of this strategy is either to develop alliances, or to use information selectively. Only you will be aware of which particular alliances are possible in your situation, so we will concentrate on some other ways of political influence.

One of the best methods is to analyse your boss's behaviour using BMod concepts. What does he or she find reinforcing or punishing? In order to discover this, you need to look at how they spend their time. For example, which things or situations do they tend to avoid or escape from? These may not be easy to discover, as they occur infrequently. Indeed, they may only be revealed by accident. One of the authors discovered such a punisher in his interactions with a senior adminis-trator. It so happened that the author was, for once, in a highly frustrated and emotional state about a particular issue. When questioned about it by the administrator he exploded in what he considered to be right-eous indignation. To his surprise he found that the administrator could not cope with this emotional outburst based on frustration.

Some of the 'political' techniques used by salespeople are also instruc-tive. All these play on the other person's desire to display a consistent and socially acceptable image. The 'foot in the door' technique uses acquiescence to a small request as a building block to larger requests. There is research evidence to show that people who have complied with a small request for help on a particular matter will later agree to larger requests about the same matter. A similar technique is what the Americans call the 'low ball' approach. The sales representative negotiates a price for an article with the customer but, just before the deal is finalized, he or she suddenly 'finds' that they are prevented from concluding the deal at the original price. The common excuse is that the final price has to be sanctioned by the sales representative's boss, whose approval is withheld. Evidence suggests that the customer accepts an increase in the price that they would not have accepted at the start of negotiations. Finally, the 'door in the face' technique plays upon the potential customer's image of themselves as a reasonable person. An original request is submitted that is so extreme that it is immediately turned down – the door is metaphorically slammed in their face. The refuser realizes that this is possibly rude and, hence, is in a position where they seek to establish that they are really a polite person. In this condition, they are more likely to agree to a lower request which itself would have been refused if presented before the outright refusal.

The political approach is often appropriate in power cultures and sometimes in role cultures, where the boss uses positional power very heavily. It may also be the favoured approach where the boss is heavily Parental and controlling, whatever the culture. This is often the case when the boss has a high need for power. It is generally inappropriate in support cultures, and with bosses who are supportive and open.

Type A/Type B
Personality Questionnaire

Each of the 13 items listed below has two extremes (e.g. easy going – hard driving), one at each end of a continuous scale. Circle the number which you feel most closely represents your own behaviour.

a)	Never late	5 4 3 2 1 0 1 2 3 4 5	Casual about appointments, easy going
b)	Not competitive	5 4 3 2 1 0 1 2 3 4 5	Very competitive
c)	Anticipates what others are going to say (nods, interupts, finishes for them)	5 4 3 2 1 0 1 2 3 4 5	Good listener
d)	Always rushed	5 4 3 2 1 0 1 2 3 4 5	Never feels rushed (even under pressure)
e)	Can wait patiently	5 4 3 2 1 0 1 2 3 4 5	Impatient when waiting
f)	Goes all out	5 4 3 2 1 0 1 2 3 4 5	Casual
g)	Takes things one at a time	5 4 3 2 1 0 1 2 3 4 5	Tries to do many things at once, thinks about what he/she is about to do next
h)	Emphatic in speech, (may pound desk)	5 4 3 2 1 0 1 2 3 4 5	Slow, deliberate talker
i)	Wants good job recognized by others	5 4 3 2 1 0 1 2 3 4 5	Cares about satisfying himself/herself no matter what others may think
j)	Fast (eating walking etc.)	5 4 3 2 1 0 1 2 3 4 5	Slow doing things
k)	Easy going	5 4 3 2 1 0 1 2 3 4 5	Hard driving
l)	Hides feelings	5 4 3 2 1 0 1 2 3 4 5	Expresses feelings
m)	Many outside interests	5 4 3 2 1 0 1 2 3 4 5	Few outside interests

Now turn to page 197 to check your score. *(Adapted from Bortner, 1969)*

Case Study:
'Take a Memo'

You are John Andrews, the manager of a department in a large civil engineering firm. The function of one of the sections of your department is to examine contracts, in fine detail, to ensure that the firm receives every payment to which it is entitled, and that payments to subcontractors are justified. Mistakes can be extremely costly.

Answering to you are sixteen clerks, some of whom have been trained by the company, others who have been recruited from other, similar, companies. There is a range of experience in this group, and a small number receive extra salary in recognition of their greater experience. These individuals do not, however, have any formal seniority and are the same level as the others. Although much of the work follows a pattern, non-standard situations do occur. The rules state that any queries or problems that are encountered have to be referred upwards to you. Your department has, on rare occasions, to send someone to assist on contracts elsewhere in the country. These temporary postings are not liked by your staff. At present you are just about coping with your present number of staff.

Recently a serious mistake occurred on one of the contracts, resulting in the company being unable to recover £150,000 for work it had done. On investigation you find that a less experienced clerk, Jim Slater, had come across a problem and, rather than approach you, sought advice from one of the more experienced clerks. As it turned out the advice was incorrect. You interviewed the clerk responsible for the job who admitted going outside the official channel, even though he was fully aware of the rules. He also admitted that he had every opportunity to come and seek your advice. The only explanation he can offer is that 'He didn't want to bother you'.

On arriving at your desk this morning, you find some memos awaiting you from the following people:

Bob Jeffries: Contracts Director (Your boss's boss)
Bill Owen: Contracts Manager (Your boss)

Steve Holland: One of the managers of a department with which you have to liaise and work
Mary Gibson: Manager of the Personnel department
Jim Slater: The clerk who made the error.

MEMORANDUM

To: **J Andrews**

From: **Mr B Jeffries – Contracts Director**

It has come to my attention that, because of a mistake by your department, the company stands to lose at least £150,000 on the Lakeside contract. I hold you personally responsible.

I will not tolerate this kind of inefficiency and slackness in managers who are under my control. I demand an immediate explanation and to know what you are going to do about it.

MEMORANDUM

To: **All Departmental Managers**

From: **Mr B Jeffries – Contracts director**

It has been brought to my notice that timekeeping in my part of the company is bad.

All departmental managers will send a memo concerning this matter to every member of staff under their control.

MEMORANDUM

To: **John Andrews**

From: **Bill Owen**

I've just had a meeting concerning the payments on the Lakeside contract which you told me about yesterday. I now consider this to be 'water under the bridge' but perhaps you could let me have your suggestions as to what we can do in order to ensure it doesn't happen again.

MEMORANDUM

To: **Mr J Andrews**

From: **J Slater**

As a result of the error concerning the Lakeside contract I feel that I have no option but to offer my resignation.

Although I accept that I broke the rules concerning this matter, I followed the course of action that has become common practice in the department and believed, at the time, that I was behaving correctly.

MEMORANDUM

To: **John Andrews**

From: **Steve Holland**

John

Can you possibly help me, I'm really in a jam. One of my clerks is leaving on Friday and his replacement will not arrive for three weeks. Any chance that you can help me out by lending me one of yours until then? I'm really stuck and would appreciate it.

Cheers!

Steve

MEMORANDUM

To: **John Andrews**

From: **Bill Owen**

The Contracts Director has informed me that three of your clerks are required on the contract in the Shetland Islands for a period of four weeks, starting next Monday.

I appreciate that this will put your department under pressure for this period, and that it will not be popular for those sent, but there are very good reasons why their presence is essential.

MEMORANDUM

To: **John Andrews**

From: **Mary Gibson – Personnel**

I've heard that three of your clerks are required in the Shetlands from next week. Not a very popular posting by all accounts.

Is there anything that I can do to help in the way of making their lives a little more comfortable while they're up there?

(Handwritten note, stapled and marked confidential, from Steve Holland.)

John

Have you seen the memo over timekeeping from that sod Jeffries! Typical of him! What about meeting for a pint after work today and figuring out how we can get our own back? I'm really fed up with his attitude towards us.

Steve

Case Study:
Organizational Behaviour Modification

CHESTNUT HOSPITAL

Chestnut Private Hospital is having a problem with absenteeism among its nurses, porters, and administrative clerks. There is no simple pay rule of the 'no work, no pay' kind. In fact, as in the case of many companies, an employee benefit scheme is in operation. On the basis of the scheme, employees can be absent for 3 days, without providing a certificate. Absences of between 4 and 7 days require completion of a 'self-certificate' and thereafter a doctor's certificate is required. As a 'caring employer' the hospital makes up statutory sick pay to normal pay.

The present approach to excessive absences has involved the use of various sanctions. These have included a series of formal warnings which lead eventually to termination of employment, and secondary sanctions such as threats relating to the effect of excessive absence on promotion opportunities and wage increases. Trade union influence and activities are virtually non-existent, with only about 15 per cent of the employees being members.

Although the actual daily cost to the hospital has not been calculated, the minimum cost has been estimated at about £40 per person in terms of wages and fringe benefits paid, loss of productivity and cost of temporary staff where necessary.

There is no turnover problem and the staff at all levels are excellent, gained by paying above the NHS rates. When staff are present there is no problem relating to their work output. The problem seems to be purely related to absenteeism.

As a management consultant you have been asked to give guidelines which will lead to a cost-effective solution. What do you suggest?

(Adapted by D. S. Taylor from Stephens, T. A. and Burroughs, W. A. (1978) An application of operant conditioning to absenteeism in a hospital setting. *Journal of Applied Psychology* 63, 518–521. Copyright 1978 by the American Psychological Association. Adapted by permission.)

Career Questionnaire

Answer each question using the following key:

1: Strongly disagree   5: Slightly agree
2: Moderately disagree   6: Moderately agree
3: Slightly disagree   7: Strongly agree
4: Neither agree nor disagree

a) 'I believe that individuals have little control over their career paths.' _____

b) 'I will not push for promotion until I feel the time is right.' _____

c) 'I feel that most people exaggerate the influence they feel they have over their career paths.' _____

d) 'I sometimes feel that my career is out of my control.' _____

e) 'In this organization it tends to be who you know rather than what you do that leads to promotion.' _____

f) 'I feel the support of powerful people is more important than job performance in determining promotion in this organization.' _____

g) 'It is important to be "well-in" with the powers that be in order to get promotion.' _____

h) 'I feel that I can improve my chances of promotion only by concentrating on those aspects of the job which my superiors will notice.' _____

i) 'I think I needed a great deal of luck to get to my present position.' _____

j) 'It doesn't matter how hard you work, if luck is against you, you will not succeed in a career.' _____

k) 'There is a lot of truth in the saying that you have to be in the right place at the right time in order to get promotion.' _____

l) 'I think that you have got to have a lot of luck if you are going to get very far in your career.' _____

Now continue reading p. 59 before working out your final score (which is explained on p. 197).

Leadership Style Questionnaire

Think of some of the people with whom you have dealt in groups in the past, either at work, or in social situations. Recall the person with whom you found it most difficult to work.

Describe this person on the scales below. You should work quickly. The whole scale should take you less than two minutes. Circle the number that you feel best represents the individual concerned.

Pleasant	8	7	6	5	4	3	2	1	Unpleasant
Friendly	8	7	6	5	4	3	2	1	Unfriendly
Rejecting	1	2	3	4	5	6	7	8	Accepting
Tense	1	2	3	4	5	6	7	8	Relaxed
Distant	1	2	3	4	5	6	7	8	Close
Cold	1	2	3	4	5	6	7	8	Warm
Supportive	8	7	6	5	4	3	2	1	Hostile
Boring	1	2	3	4	5	6	7	8	Interesting
Quarrelsome	1	2	3	4	5	6	7	8	Harmonious
Gloomy	1	2	3	4	5	6	7	8	Cheerful
Open	8	7	6	5	4	3	2	1	Guarded
Backbiting	1	2	3	4	5	6	7	8	Loyal
Untrustworthy	1	2	3	4	5	6	7	8	Trustworthy
Considerate	8	7	6	5	4	3	2	1	Inconsiderate
Nasty	1	2	3	4	5	6	7	8	Nice
Agreeable	8	7	6	5	4	3	2	1	Disagreeable
Insincere	1	2	3	4	5	6	7	8	Sincere
Kind	8	7	6	5	4	3	2	1	Unkind

Now turn to page 198 to check your score.

(Adapted by Gibson et al., 1985 from Fiedler and Chemers, 1984)

Change Strategies

You have an excellent idea for an improvement to existing procedures which will result in considerable cost savings. However, implementation of the idea will require changes in the operating procedures of several departments, and in the ways in which they interact. From past experience you expect that several heads of department will resist these changes, offering a variety of reasons as to why they will not work.

As Chief Executive which of the following approaches would you be most likely to take?

1. Discreetly sound out the reactions of each head of department, partly to test the strengths and weaknesses of your idea, but also to establish their reactions, so that you can enlist the aid of the more enthusiastic managers to help you convert the others.

2. Send a memo to all heads of department outlining the plan and stating your intention to implement it. Follow this up with meetings with individual managers to brief them on the necessary changes and set a timetable for the change.

3. Call a meeting of all heads of department, outline your idea, and then explain that the purpose of the meeting is to consider all the implications, both positive and negative, and then make a decision about implementation. You are happy to abide by the outcome of this meeting.

4. Sound out the reactions of the heads of department. If they are strongly negative accept that the time is not right and leave the change until a more suitable occasion, on the basis that it is better to get it done properly at a later date, when conditions are more favourable, than go for a half-hearted attempt now. If they turn out to be enthusiastic, you would, of course, go ahead now.

If, after selecting one of the above, you wish to suggest some other alternative, please note it below.

SCORING FOR APPENDIX 1

Each item scores on an 11 point scale, but some of the scales vary.

The following scales score from 1 on the left to 11 on the right:

b, e, g, k, l m

The following score from 11 on the left to 1 on the right.

a, c, d, f, h, i, j

So, for instance, if you are only very occasionally late, and have therefore completed item a) as shown below, your score for the first scale would be 10.

a) Never late ◄ 5 ④ 3 2 1 0 1 2 3 4 5 ► Casual about
                                             appointments,
                                             easy going

Your final score is the sum total of all the scales.

SCORING FOR APPENDIX 4

Put your score for each question in the spaces provided, and carry out the calculations shown.

$$(8 \quad - \quad \underline{\quad}) + \underline{\quad} + \underline{\quad} + \underline{\quad} = \underline{\quad} \ (I)$$
$$ \text{(a)} \qquad \text{(b)} \qquad \text{(c)} \qquad \text{(d)}$$

$$\underline{\quad} + \underline{\quad} + \underline{\quad} + \underline{\quad} \qquad = \underline{\quad} \ (P)$$
$$\text{(e)} \qquad \text{(f)} \qquad \text{(g)} \qquad \text{(h)}$$

$$\underline{\quad} + \underline{\quad} + \underline{\quad} + \underline{\quad} \qquad = \underline{\quad} \ (C)$$
$$\text{(i)} \qquad \text{(j)} \qquad \text{(k)} \qquad \text{(l)}$$

The 'I' scale measures the strength of your belief that control over your career is under your own control.

The 'P' scale measures the strength of your belief that control over your career is under the control of powerful other people.

The 'C' scale measures the strength of your belief that your career is controlled by luck or chance factors.

You might like to compare your score on each of the scales with those of a sample of British managers. The first figure for each scale is the

average score. The second figures show the range within which approximately two-thirds of the managers' scores lay.

Internal	19	15–23
Powerful Others	16	11–21
Chance	14	10–18

SCORING FOR APPENDIX 5

To obtain your score, add up the numbers you have circled.

▸ If you have scored 57 or lower, you are a low LPC leader and tend
  to be task oriented.

▸ If you have scored 64 or higher, you are a high LPC leader and tend
  to be relationship oriented.

▸ A score between 58 and 63 would suggest that there is a 'mix' of the
  two approaches in your leadership style.

REFERENCES

Adair, J. (1968) *Training for Leadership*. London: Macdonald.

Anderson, C.R. (1977) Locus of control, coping behaviours, and performance in a stress setting: A longitudinal study. *Journal of Applied Psychology, 62,* 446-451.

Argyris, C. (1962) *Interpersonal Competence and Organizational Effectiveness.* Homewood, Ala.: Dorsey.

Baddely, S. and James, K. (1987) Owl, fox, donkey and sheep: Political skills for managers. *Management Education and Development. 18,* 3-19.

Bales, R.F. (1950) *Interaction Process Analysis.* Cambridge, Mass.: Addison-Wesley.

Bales, R.F. (1951) *Interaction Process Analysis: A method for the study of small groups.* Reading, Mass.: Addison-Wesley.

Bandura, A. (1977) *Social Learning Theory.* Englewood Cliffs: Prentice Hall.

Bandura, A. (1982) Self-efficacy mechanism in human agency. *American Psychologist, 37,* 122-147.

Beck, J. and Cox, C.J. (1984) Developing organizational skills. In C.J. Cox and J. Beck (Eds) *Management Development: Advances in practice and theory.* Chichester: Wiley.

Beckhard, R. (1969) *Organizational Development: Strategies and models.* Reading, Mass.: Addison-Wesley.

Belbin, R.M. (1981) *Management Teams, Why They Succeed or Fail.* London: Heinemann.

Bennis, W.G. (1969) *Organizational Development: Its nature, origins and prospects.* Reading, Mass.: Addison-Wesley.

Bennis, W.G. (1983) The artform of leadership. In S. Scrivastra and associates (Eds) *The Executive Mind.* San Francisco: Jossey-Bass.

Berne, E. (1972) *What do you say after you say hello?* London: Corgi.

Berthold, H.C. Jnr (1982) Transitional contingency contracting and the Premack principle in business. In R. O'Brien, A. Dickinson and M. Rosow (Eds) *Industrial Behavior Modification: A Management handbook.* New York: Pergamon.

Blake, R.R. and Mouton, J.S. (1964) *The Managerial Grid.* Houston: Gulf Publishing.

Bradford, L.P., Gibb, J.R. and Benne, V.D. (1964) *T-Group Theory and Laboratory Method.* New York: Wiley.

Brown, R. (1986) *Social Psychology: The second edition.* New York: Free Press.

Bortner, R.W. (1969) A short rating scale as a potential measure of pattern A behaviour. *Journal of Chronic Diseases, 22,* 87-91.

Bryman, A. (1986) *Leadership in Organisations.* London: Routledge.

Cattell, R.B. (1965) *The Scientific Analysis of Personality.* Harmondsworth: Penguin.

Cattell, R.B., Eber, H.W. and Tasnoka, M.M. (1970) *Handbook for the Sixteen Personality Factor Questionnaire (16PF).* Champaign, Ill.: Institute for Personality and Ability Testing.

Chin, R. and Benne, K.D. (1976) General strategies for effecting changes in human systems. In W.G. Bennis, K.D. Benne, R. Chin and K.E. Carey (Eds)

The Planning of Change, 3rd ed. New York: Holt, Rinehart & Winston.

Cox, C.J. and Cooper, C.L. (1988) *High Flyers*. Oxford: Basil Blackwell.

Dornstein, M. (1988) Wage reference groups and their determinants: A study of blue-collar and white-collar employees in Israel. *Journal of Occupational Psychology*, 61, 221-235.

Drucker, P. (1954) *The Practice of Management*. New York: Harper.

Ernst, F. (1971) The OK Corral: The grid for 'get-on-with'. *Transactional Analysis Journal*, 1, 4.

Eysenck, H.J. (1975) *The Equality of Man*. London: Fontana.

Eysenck, H.J. and Eysenck, S.B.G. (1977) *Psychoticism as a Dimension of Personality*. London: Hodder & Stoughton.

Fayol, H. (1967) *General and Industrial Management*. London: Pitman.

Fiedler, F.E. and Chemers, M.M. (1984) *Improving Leadership Effectiveness: The leader match concept*. New York: Wiley.

Fleishman, E.A. and Harris, E.F. (1962) Patterns of leadership behaviour related to employee grievances and turnover. *Personnel Psychology*, 15, 43-56.

French, J.R.P. and Raven, B. (1959) The bases of social power. In D. Cartwright (Ed) *Studies in Social Power*. Ann Arbor, Institute for Social Research: University of Michigan.

French, W.L. and Bell C.H. (1984) *Organizational Development*, 3rd ed. Englewood Cliffs: Prentice Hall.

Friedman, M.D. and Rosenman, R.H. (1974) *Type A Behaviour and Your Heart*. New York: Knopf.

Gibson, J.L., Ivancevich, J.M. and Donnelly, J.H. Jnr (1985) *Organizations: Behavior, structure, process*, 5th ed. Plano, Tex.: Business Publications.

Goldsmith, W. and Clutterbuck, D. (1984) *The Winning Streak*. London: Weidenfeldt & Nicholson.

Hackman, J.R. and Oldham, G.R. (1976) Motivation through the design of work: Test of a theory. *Organizational Behavior and Human Performance*, 16, 250-279.

Handy, C.B. (1985) *Understanding Organisations*. Harmondsworth: Penguin.

Harrison, R. (1972) When power conflicts trigger team spirit. *European Business*, Spring, 27-65.

Harrison, R. (1987) *Organization Culture and Quality of Service*. London: Association for Management Education and Development.

Hersey, P. and Blanchard, K.H. (1982) *Management of Organizational Behavior: Utilizing human resources*. Englewood Cliffs: Prentice Hall.

Herzberg, F. (1966) *Work and the Nature of Man*. Cleveland: World Publishing.

Janis, I.L. (1972) *Victims of Groupthink*. Boston: Houghton Mifflin.

Kahn R. (1974) Organizational Development: Some problems and proposals. *Journal of Applied Behavioral Science*, 10, 4.

Kelman, H.C. (1958) Compliance, internalization and identification: Three processes of attitude change. *Journal of Conflict Resolution*, 2, 51-60.

Kirton, M.J. (1984) Adaptors and Innovators: Why new initiatives get blocked. *Long Range Planning*, 17, (2), 137-143.

Kline, P. (1987) Factor analysis and personality theory. *European Journal of Personality*, 1, 21-36.

Lawrence, P.R. and Lorsch, J.W. (1969) *Developing Organizations: Diagnosis and action*. Reading, Mass.: Addison-Wesley.

Leavitt, H.J. (1951) Some effects of certain communication patterns on group performance. *Journal of Abnormal and Social Psychology*, 13, 151-156.

Lewin, K. (1947) Group decisions and social change. In T. Newcomb and E. Hartley (Eds) *Readings in Social Psychology*. New York: Holt, Rinehart & Winston.

Lievegoed, B.C.J. (1973) *The Developing Organization*. London: Methuen.

Likert, R. (1961) *New Patterns of Management*. New York: McGraw Hill.

Locke, E.A. and Latham, G.P. (1984) *Goal Setting: A motivational technique that works*. Englewood Cliffs: Prentice Hall.

Locke, E.A., Frederick, E. Lee, C. and Bobko, P. (1984) Effect of self-efficacy, goals, and task strategies on task performance. *Journal of Applied Psychology*, 69, 241-251.

Maslow, A.H. (1971) *The Farther Reaches of Human Nature*. New York: Viking.

Mayo, E. (1975) *The Social Problems of an Industrial Civilization*. London: Routledge & Kegan Paul.

McClelland, D.C. (1961) *The Achieving Society*. Princeton: Van Nostrand.

McGregor, D. (1960) *The Human Side of Enterprise*. New York: McGraw Hill.

Mischel, W. (1986) *Introduction to Personality*. New York: Holt, Rinehart & Winston.

O'Brien, R., Dickinson, A. and Rosow, M. (Eds) (1982) *Industrial Behavior Modification: A management handbook*. New York: Pergamon.

Porras, J.I. and Berg, P.O. (1978) The impact of organizational development. *Academy of Management Review*, 3, 249-266.

Randell, G.A. (1973) Performance appraisal, purposes, practices and conflicts. *Journal of Occupational Psychology*, 47, 221-224.

Randell, G.A., Packard, P. and Slater, J. (1984) *Staff Appraisal*, 3rd ed. London: Institute of Personnel Management.

Rogers, C.R. (1967) *On Becoming a Person*. London: Constable.

Rogers, E. and Shoemaker, F. (1971) *Communication and Innovation*. New York: Free Press.

Rotter, J.B. (1966) Generalized expectancies for internal versus external control of reinforcement. *Psychological Monographs*, 80, Whole No. 609.

Schein, E.H. (1980) *Organizational Psychology*. Englewood Cliffs: Prentice Hall.

Sherif, M. (1966) *Group Conflict and Cooperation: Their social psychology*. London: Routledge & Kegan Paul.

Stephens, T.A. and Burroughs, W.A. (1978). An application of operant conditioning to absenteeism in a hospital setting. *Journal of Applied Psychology*, 63, 518-521.

Stoner, J.A.F. (1961) *A Comparison of Individual and Group Decisions Including Risk*. Unpublished Master's thesis, School of Management, Massachusetts Institute of Technology.

Tajfel, H. (Ed) (1972) *Differentiation Between Social Groups: Studies in the social psychology of intergroup relations*. London: Academic Press.

Taylor, R.W. (1911) *Scientific Management*. New York: Harper.

Thomas, K. (1975) Conflict and conflict management. In M. Dunnette (Ed) *Handbook of Industrial and Organizational Psychology*. Chicago: Rand McNally.

Thompson, T.E. and Tuden, A. (1959) *Comparative Studies in Administration*. Pittsburgh: University of Pittsburgh Press.

Tse, K.K. (1985) *Marks and Spencer: An anatomy of Britain's most efficiently managed company*. Oxford: Pergamon.

Vroom, V.H., and Yetton, P.W. *Leadership and Decision Making*. Pittsburgh: University of Pittsburgh Press.

Warr, P. (1982) A national study of non-financial employment commitment. *Journal of Occupational Psychology*, 55, 297-312.

Weber, M. (1970) Bureaucracy. In O. Grusky and G.A. Miller (Eds) *The Sociology of Organizations*. London: Free Press.

Wright, P.L. and Taylor, D.S. (1984) *Improving Leadership Performance*. Englewood Cliffs: Prentice Hall.

SUGGESTED READING

GENERAL
For up-to-date reviews of many areas of organizational psychology, refer to the *International Review of Industrial and Organizational Psychology* edited by C.L. Cooper and I.T. Robertson and published annually by Wiley, starting from 1987.

PERSONALITY
Cooper, C.L., Cooper, R.D. and Eaker, L. (1988) *Living with Stress*. Harmondsworth: Penguin.

Cox, M. and Cox, C.J. (1977) Alienation in the workplace: A transactional analysis approach. In R.N. Ottoway (Ed) *Harmonizing the Workplace*. Beckenham: Croom Helm.

Harris, T.E. (1980) *I'm OK, You're OK*. London: Pan.

Pervin, L.A. (1980) *Personality: Theory, assessment and research*, 3rd ed. New York: Wiley.

MOTIVATION
Luthans, F. and Kreitner, R. (1975) *Organizational Behavior Modification*. Glenview, Ill.; Scott, Foresman, & Co.

Robertson, I.T. and Smith, M.J. (1985) *Motivation and Work Design: Research and practice*. London: Institute of Personnel Management.

Steers, R.M. and Porter, L.W. (1987) *Motivation and Work Behavior*, 4th ed. New York: McGraw Hill.

LEADERSHIP AND MANAGEMENT STYLE
Bryman, P. (1986) *Leadership in Organisations*. London: Routledge.

Cox, C.J. and Cooper, C.L. (1988) *High Flyers: An anatomy of management success*. Oxford: Basil Blackwell.

Randell, G.A., Packard, P. and Slater, J. (1984) *Staff Appraisal*, 3rd ed. London: Institute of Personnel Management.

Wright, P.L. and Taylor, D.S. (1984) *Improving Leadership Performance*. Englewood Cliffs: Prentice Hall.

GROUP DYNAMICS AT WORK
Luft, J. (1984) *Group Processes*, 3rd ed. Palo Alto: Mayfield.

Payne, R. and Cooper, C.L. (1981) *Groups at Work*. Chichester: Wiley.

INTERGROUP CONFLICT
Schein, E. (1980) *Organizational Psychology*. Englewood Cliffs: Prentice Hall.

IDENTIFYING ORGANIZATIONAL PROBLEMS

Beck, J. and Cox, C.J. (1984) Developing organisational skills. In J. Beck and C.J. Cox (Eds) *Management Development: Advances in practice and theory*. Chichester: Wiley.

Harrison, R. (1987) *Organisational Culture and Quality of Service*. London: Association for Management Education and Development.

Stewart, V. (1983) *Change: The challenge for management*. New York: McGraw Hill.

ORGANIZATIONAL CHANGE

Bennis, W.G., Benne, K.D., Chin, R. and Corey, K.E. (1976) *The Planning of Change*. New York: Holt, Rinehart & Winston.

Blake, R. and Mouton, J. (1969) *Building a Dynamic Organization Through Grid Organization Development*. Reading, Mass.: Addison-Wesley.

French, W.L. and Bell, C.H. (1984) *Organizational Development*, 3rd ed. Englewood Cliffs: Prentice Hall.

Huczynski, A. (1987) *Encyclopaedia of Organizational Change Methods*. Aldershot: Gower.

Patten, T.H. (1981) *Organizational Development Through Team Building*. New York: Wiley.

Acknowledgements

Figure 12   Bryman, P. (1986) *Leadership in Organisations*. Reprinted by permission of Routledge.

Figure 13   Paul Hersey/Kenneth H. Blanchard, *Management of Organizational Behavior: Utilizing human resources*, 3/e, (c) 1977, p.164. Adapted by permission of Prentice Hall, Inc., Englewood Cliffs, New Jersey.

Figure 15   Adaptation of a figure from James D. Thompson and Arthur Tuden's 'Strategies, Structures and Processes in Organizational Decision', in *Comparative Studies in Administration*, James D. Thompson *et al.* (eds). Published in 1959 by the University of Pittsburgh Press. Reprinted by permission of the publisher.

Figure 22   This figure first appeared in *Management Education & Development*, Vol. 18. We are grateful to the Editor for permission to reprint it here.

Appendix 3 Copyright 1978 by the American Psychological Association. Adapted by permission.

INDEX